# DISCIPLINE AND INDULGENCE

Critical Issues in Sport and Society

*Michael Messner and Douglas Hartmann, Series Editors*

Critical Issues in Sport and Society features scholarly books that help expand our understanding of the new and myriad ways in which sport is intertwined with social life in the contemporary world. Using the tools of various scholarly disciplines, including sociology, anthropology, history, media studies, and others, books in this series investigate the growing impact of sport and sports-related activities on various aspects of social life as well as key developments and changes in the sporting world and emerging sporting practices. Series authors produce groundbreaking research that brings empirical and applied work together with cultural critique and historical perspectives written in an engaging, accessible format.

# DISCIPLINE AND INDULGENCE

## COLLEGE FOOTBALL, MEDIA, AND THE AMERICAN WAY OF LIFE DURING THE COLD WAR

JEFFREY MONTEZ DE OCA

RUTGERS UNIVERSITY PRESS
New Brunswick, New Jersey, and London

Library of Congress Cataloging-in-Publication Data
Montez de Oca, Jeffrey
Discipline and indulgence : college football, media, and the American way of life
during the cold war / Jeffrey Montez de Oca
pages    cm. — (Critical Issues in Sport and Society)
Includes bibliographical references and index.
ISBN 978–0–8135–6127–1 (hardcover : alk. paper) — ISBN 978–0–8135–6126–4 (pbk. :
alk. paper) — ISBN 978–0–8135–6128–8 (e-book) (print)
1. Football—United States—History—20th century. 2. Football—Social aspects—
United States—History—20th century. 3. College sports—United States—
History—20th century. 4. Cold War—Social aspects—United States. 5. Cold
War—Influence. 6. Mass media and sports—United States—History—20th
century. I. Title.
GV950.M66 2013
796.332′630973—dc23          2012038506

A British Cataloging-in-Publication record for this book is available from the British
Library.

Visit our website: http://rutgerspress.rutgers.edu

Manufactured in the United States of America

For My Family

# CONTENTS

# ACKNOWLEDGMENTS

On the evening of October 17, 1998, while en route to a seminar at New York University, I entered a subway station to catch a northbound train. While hurrying across the platform to a waiting train I did not realize it was heading toward Yankee Stadium for the first game of the 1998 World Series. As I approached the train two young men popped their heads out and beckoned me to their car, and the one nearest to me then heartily pounded my back as I entered. These two men were part of an unusually boisterous group of fans clad in "official" Yankees wear that had taken over the subway car and renamed it "Yankee Train!" As weary commuters entered Yankee Train, the group repeatedly exploded in a ritual celebration that included back slaps, cheers, and high fives.

What was most striking was the way in which the men used their bravado, the train's shared civic space, and a wider sense of Yankeedom to perform a masculine identity. As the train lurched into motion, two of the members performed a special cheer: the first one shouted "O!" to which the second replied "Neill!" This call-and-response chanting increased in pitch, volume, and speed ("O"–"Neill," "O"–"Neill," "O"–"Neill") until the first participant climatically purred "O'Neill!"—a reference to the Yankees' star right fielder Paul O'Neill. A single member of the group, wearing a replica Derek Jeter jersey, performed another ritual whenever the train pulled into a station. The Derek Jeter fan would melodically chant his ego ideal's full name two or three times from the doorway before shouting the oath, "I love you Derek!" Although I was stunned, I appeared to be the only one among the otherwise reclusive New York commuters who was agog by this inversion of normative social behavior and the way in which a group of men reaffirmed their heterosexual masculinity through homoerotic rituals and oaths. To everyone else, they just seemed like "boys" having fun. It was after all Yankee Train rolling toward the World Series after a long drought, and perhaps I am too much of a Mets fan. In any case, a sport sociologist was born on that October evening.

I began this endeavor with a simple question: what is the relationship between spectator sports and individual identity? Under the guidance of Toby Miller and Anna McCarthy, I began to complicate that question and ask it in turns of U.S. history. How has sport been used to support tendencies toward territorial and economic expansionism in U.S. history? These questions took on greater urgency during the early days of the Global War on Terror. Before long, I felt the questions were outgrowing a narrow broadcast history, and the project became a cultural history of American football during the early Cold War. There just seemed to be something about the Cold War that made football meaningful and desirable to so many Americans.

As the project grew at the University of Southern California, no one played a more significant role in helping, guiding, and encouraging me than Michael Alan Messner. I owe an enormous debt of gratitude to Mike, who has been a mentor, muse, collaborator, confidant, and above all else a friend. Many other people at USC helped me along the way, including Barry Glassner, Mary Dudziak, Lynn Spigel, David James, Gaspar Rivera-Salgado, Elaine Bell-Kaplan, Jon Miller, Merrill Silverstein, Neil Gross, and Macarena Gómez-Barris. I owe thanks to Ellen Summers and Lisa Douglas, who helped me at the NCAA library. A group of close friends also helped me along the way, so thanks go to Jose Prado, James Thing, Robert Hollenbaugh, Cheryl Cooky, Melanie Heath, Rigoberto Rodriguez, and Belinda Lum.

After a few years of rest, I picked this project up again in earnest at the University of Colorado, Colorado Springs. At UCCS Katherine Mack and Stephany Spaulding have been of indescribable help; their support made this book possible. Other colleagues who have helped me along the way include Jerome Hodos, Tabatha Farney, Michael Forbes, Christina Wagner, Nancy Davis, David Newman, Jonathan Nichols-Pethick, and Christopher Bondy. Douglas Hartmann, David Andrews, and Mary McDonald have been wonderful supporters. Peter Mickulas at Rutgers University Press has invested trust and guidance in me. In addition, Yoke-Sum Wong and David Katzman have also provided invaluable feedback.

One person stands out among everyone else in caring, support, and patience. Riho Sakai made it possible for me to work long hours and take short breaks. She supported and pushed me when I wanted to quit. She also crisscrossed the country with me and gave birth to our two beautiful boys, Seneca Kento and Takaya David. I have also received material and emotional support as well as inspiration from my parents, Barbara DeOca, Clifford DeOca, Dennis Miller, and Vicky DeKay. And while Seneca and Takaya have not provided material support, they certainly provide plenty of diversions and distractions.

# DISCIPLINE AND INDULGENCE

# 1 · INTRODUCTION

ON SELECT SATURDAY mornings, our fall ritual began in the parking lot of Kentucky Fried Chicken on Shattuck Avenue in Berkeley, California. A bucket of golden fried chicken and a jug of Dr Pepper went into a bag that my father and I carried across the University of California campus to Memorial Stadium. Measuring and metering of time as we relocated ourselves in space was central to the ritual. The expedition was timed so that we arrived in the stadium just at noon to watch the boys stretch, jog, and cut crazy patterns on the grass as they warmed up for the one o'clock game. Our postgame walks down the hill gave us time to reflect upon the games and gave my father the opportunity to teach me the requisite knowledge of a competent fan. I learned the difference between a four-three and a three-four defense, when to run a draw play or a blitz, and that Jim Brown was the greatest running back ever. But the knowledge shared was more than simply technical and historical knowledge that I was later quizzed on. For instance, I learned that American Indians like us do not stand up during the national anthem, what to eat when Mom was not around, and, more generally, how to engage intellectually with mass culture. Watching football involves more than sitting with your eyes and mouth open since it is a performance situated in the fabric of social life.[1] Despite walking farther to the game than the average fan and boycotting the national anthem, my father and I participated in a larger social process that ties football fans across the nation together on Saturday afternoons. Watching football allowed us to build a shared history, language, and set of values available in good times and bad.

College football is a social institution with its own history, lore, values, norms, rituals, and traditions. In the early Cold War (1947–1964), the period under consideration, college football games were, for the most part, performed simultaneously in regions across the country on Saturday afternoons.[2] Since individuals, families, and friends have their own private traditions, experiences, and memories as they participate in the time-space of the national culture, people personalize a general process. Personalizing, or adhering to a national culture in a variety of divergent ways, allows fans to experience a broadly shared lifestyle as their own. For instance, my father's tradition of sitting during the national anthem allowed us to express agency while participating in an obligatory, overtly patriotic and militaristic moment that we disliked. This means that at the same time that we consciously stood out among the crowd in the stadium, we also integrated ourselves into an imaginary community of resistant American Indians as well as an imagined community of patriotic Americans. So although few of the thousands of people we encountered in stadiums around the country felt the need to express agency in the same way as us, they were simultaneously making their own individual investments and creatively producing their identities in a national process. Personalizing a general process allows participants of a national culture to exercise agency by producing themselves as subjects at the same time that they integrate themselves into the organization of society (Gruneau 1983/1999). *Discipline and Indulgence* explores this duality of experience—the way that the general, external, and objective is experienced uniquely, internally, and subjectively.

In the process of researching and writing *Discipline and Indulgence* I came to wonder why I chose to study college football during the early Cold War. Of course, I chose a topic that excited me, but still I asked myself, why the fascination with football? After all, it is a pretty silly game that can foster antisocial behaviors (see Burstyn 1999; Card and Dahl 2010; Curry 1991, 2000; Finley and Finley 2007; Gems 2000; Messner 2002; Messner, Dunbar, and Hunt 2000; Messner and Stevens 2002; Miller 2009; Miller et al. 2006; Sabo 2001; Sabo, Gray, and Moore 2000; Trujillo 1995). Only later did I realize that in many ways those Saturday afternoon rituals animate much of this book. In part, researching *Discipline and Indulgence* kept me in touch with a childhood and a relationship with my father long since past. But beyond the search for a lost time, sense, and feeling is an important subnarrative of my anecdote. I became a football fan so that my father and I could develop a shared sense of identity. Cheering for the Golden Bears of California in Memorial Stadium created a space of manly bonding and enabled me to develop a sense of "Americanness"—albeit as a hyphenated American. While I like to think of this as an identity handed from father to son, my father did not learn the game from his father. He became a football fan as part of an Americanization program carried out in a New York State boarding school for American Indians.[3] Football was used in boarding schools to instill an Anglo-American masculinity in Indian boys so that they could develop a desired sense of manhood and assimilate into "American civilization" (Adams 1995, 184–185; Oriard 1993, 233–235; also Powers-Beck 2001). Our Saturday ritual and its repetition of steps within a rigidly structured leisure schedule is one residual aspect of the forced assimilation program my father experienced. Refusal to recognize the imperialist state during the national anthem at the same time that we participated in it is another.

Michael Messner (2002) argues that sport should always be understood on multiple levels, as interactive, cultural, and institutional. We can see through the anecdote about my father and me that sport is *interactive* in that people produce themselves by acting upon each other and sport is *cultural* by adhering to norms, conventions, shared meanings, and collective representations in specific settings. Another aspect of sport fandom that my anecdote reveals, visible in the KFC chicken, the stadium tickets, and the games' radio and television broadcast rights, is its commercial nature. Sports fans' desire for creative, agentic expression is constantly managed and contoured by *institutional and economic* imperatives, especially the need for capital accumulation. Therefore, *Discipline and Indulgence* is interested in how culture and the production of identities intersect with the political and economic organization of society. Ultimately, *Discipline and Indulgence* attempts to illuminate how individuals form and perform a sense of self or embodied subjectivity through sport participation within the imperialist history of the United States, which is to say that while we create our histories, we do so in social, historical, and institutional contexts larger than ourselves.

## UNDERSTANDING THE PRESENT BY LOOKING TO THE PAST

*Discipline and Indulgence* owes a tremendous debt to the administrations of George W. Bush and Tony Blair. In late 2001, the United States initiated the Global War on Terror, and the U.S. corporate media widely supported the military operations, including the "apolitical" world of sport. For instance, the National Football League (NFL), always a bellwether of reactionary politics in the United States, responded to the crisis by changing the logo for Super Bowl XXXVI from an innocuous symbol of New Orleans (the site of the game) to an overtly nationalistic symbol. The logo became a calligram that featured a map of the nation overlaid with the U.S. flag. It had "Super Bowl XXXVI" written across it and was encircled by the game's location and date. The Super Bowl's broadcast featured surviving past presidents reading speeches from Abraham Lincoln, and the rock band U2 presented a halftime music extravaganza honoring people killed during the September 11, 2001, attacks on the United States. And since 2002, we have witnessed an increased collaboration among the military, the media, and sport (Butterworth and Moskal 2009; Falcous and Silk 2005; King 2008; Kusz 2007).

The increased collaboration of the military, the media, and sport within the Global War on Terror illustrates a broader process of *militarization* in the early twenty-first century. Michael Geyer defines militarization as "the contradictory and tense social process in which civil society organizes itself for the production of violence" (Geyer 1989, 79). In other words, militarization largely emerges out of civil society and produces a set of interlocking governmental and nongovernmental institutions as well as a system of thought that perceives war as a seemingly normal and logical aspect of life (Geyer 1989). As militarization develops, war becomes defined less in terms of interests than in terms of identities. Militarization turns into *militarism* when "war is not the continuation of social organization by other means, but [when] war becomes the very basis of social organization" (Geyer 1989, 80). Militarism can thus be understood as a set of values and beliefs in the efficacy of the military and the use of military force to solve issues of domestic and international policy that emerge out of a complex of political and economic institutions and that are generalized throughout a population to the point that militaristic values and beliefs become a banal aspect of everyday life.

In 1956, the eminent sociologist C. Wright Mills argued that following the Second World War the role of the military changed from being suspect in civil society to being a respected institution that directly informed political decisions. Mills found this troubling because military personnel are professionalized within a worldview that sees military force as a logical solution to nonmilitary problems. The military (like sport) claims to be outside of politics; however, military technicians were increasingly making decisions formerly made by civilian leaders. Mills saw the growing role of the military in the governance of society as reversing the historical relations of power between the two spheres of U.S. society. Furthermore, military technicians were increasingly being called upon to comment and advise on political and economic issues beyond just the military. The increasing importance and prestige accorded to the military led to what Mills called "military metaphysics," or an understanding of the world, reality, and human existence through a framework of militarism (Mills 1956, 202–276). Indeed, when standing for the national anthem and color guard becomes obligatory and when fighter planes flying over stadiums are celebrated, militarism has become a mundane aspect of national culture.

Militarism conceptually and materially links separate and distinct spheres of life to the military, war, and "national interest." For instance, recent scholarship demonstrates how the sport-media complex fosters cultural and institutional linkages between the NFL and the U.S. government's War on Terror as in the heroic-scandal-filled coverage of citizen-soldier-athlete Pat Tillman (King 2008; Kusz 2007).[4] So although football games are empirically distinct physical events from military battles, the militarization of U.S. society allows them to articulate together as interdependent elements in a larger institution of war (Jansen and Sabo 1994). They become emotionally linked in the popular imagination and in a larger imperialistic social formation via the sport-media complex (Messner, Dunbar, and Hunt 2000).

Most of the recent research on sport, media, and militarism has taken September 11, 2001, as a rupture in modern history when "everything changed." For instance, Kyle Kusz wrote, "[O]ne notable difference between the post-9/11 incarnation of White cultural nationalism and its dubious forbearers is that the post-9/11 version rests squarely and comfortably in the center of the American mainstream and does not seem to be regarded as an extreme ideological expression at all" (Kusz 2007, 81). Similarly, Samantha King argues that since 2001, "sport culture has moved beyond its customary role as an ideological support to the corporate state" and has become a structural element of the political economy of war (King 2008, 528). While situating contemporary sport media within the Global War on Terror has tremendous value for sport scholars, a dehistoricized approach to U.S. imperialism and the operation of militarism can mistake the current wars as a purely Republican problem rather than an outcome of the structure of U.S. society and history (Bacevich 2005). Indeed, sport was a key institution within civil society that was used to promote militarism and U.S. expansionism long before 2002 (Gems 2000).

For this reason *Discipline and Indulgence* examines sport media when U.S. militarism was in the process of ascendance, namely the early period of the Cold War (1947–1964). This examination of Cold War popular culture reveals that the militarization of civil society did not begin after September 11, 2001.[5] What *Discipline and Indulgence* reveals is that white cultural nationalism was solidly within the mainstream during the early Cold War. Moreover, because of the intertwined history of sport, media, and the state, sport culture was never merely "an ideological support to the corporate state" but rather part of the interlocking institutional nexus of Cold War militarism.

*Discipline and Indulgence* explores the relationship between sport and militarism during the early period of the Cold War through an analysis of college football in sport media. This approach is attentive to both the institutional structure and representational strategies of sport media during the early Cold War. Although the linkages between sport and militarism did not begin in the 1940s, focusing on the Cold War makes sense since it was a key moment in the "American Century" when the U.S. ascended to world hegemon. The early Cold War also saw the concomitant emergence of the military-industrial complex and the sport-media complex. Furthermore, the early Cold War and Global War on Terror are intense moments of anxiety, patriotism, conformity, and militarism that saw the rapid proliferation of new media technologies profoundly affect social life. Most importantly, the Cold War and the Global War on Terror are moments when military interventionism as a response to fear of external threats was used to expand U.S. political and economic force abroad as well as to neutralize opposition to expansionism at home.

Since *Discipline and Indulgence* focuses to such a degree on college football, with some focus on physical education, a reader may reasonably ask why it does not focus more on other sports, such as baseball, the "national pastime," or the Olympics, that put the United States in direct competition with the Soviet Union. Certainly, there are many ways in which Cold War culture can be studied through sport (see Allison 1994; Beamish and Ritchie 2005; Domer 1976; Hunt 2006; Kemper 2009; Massaro 2003; Thomas 2002; Wagg and Andrews 2006). American Legion baseball, for instance, is a great example. The American Legion was a politically powerful anticommunist movement in the United States during the early to mid-twentieth century (Campbell 2010). The Legion established both youth baseball programs and adult teams that traveled the nation teaching the virtues of Americanism and anticommunism through baseball athleticism (Krause 1998; Nehls 2007). What made Legion baseball so powerful was the way in which this patriotic, anticommunist program affected national politics through grassroots cultural activism. But *Discipline and Indulgence* is a study of sport media during the Cold War and not a study of grassroots social movements. And while baseball was the national pastime, it was eclipsed during the early Cold War as the dominant spectator sport in the nation. Moreover, football was far and away the most significant and popular spectator sport in the United States, which gave most Americans a qualitatively and quantitatively different relationship with football than with the Olympics. Football's power was so significant at the collegiate level that the NCAA used it to cartelize during the television age of the 1950s (see chapter 5). And, as is argued throughout *Discipline and Indulgence,* the symbolism of football that harkens to technology, mass production, territorialization, and militarism is a more powerful metaphor for the Cold War than baseball's nostalgic imagery of the small town that never really existed (see also Gems 2000; Hoch 1972; Neilson 1995; Phillips 1969; Real 1979; Trujillo 1995; Weales 1959).

## A BRIEF HISTORY OF COLLEGE FOOTBALL AND PHYSICAL EDUCATION IN THE UNITED STATES

This section provides a primer on college football and physical education prior to the period under study for readers unfamiliar with those histories. The emergence of the National Collegiate Athletic Association (NCAA) is addressed in more detail in chapter 5. This brief history, beginning in the nineteenth century, shows that in many ways football and physical education ran parallel in their development, even though one is a spectator sport and the other is participatory, before they intersected in the mid-twentieth century. What football and physical education have primarily in common is that both have been associated with building men and the nation. During the Cold War, football and other team sports were viewed as a useful form of physical education, and organized PE was seen as ameliorating excesses of big-time football.

Big-time, that is commercialized and professionalized, collegiate athletics began in the United States in the 1870s. Initially crew attracted the greatest attention and was heavily covered by the media. As the regatta slipped from favor, football became more popular and more commercial (Smith 2001, 7–10), especially the Thanksgiving Day "big games" such as the Harvard-Yale game (see Oriard 1993; Watterson 2000). Football was initially played in the United States at elite northeastern universities that would later form the Ivy League. Students played intramural ball games based on "soccer" before Princeton and Rutgers played the first intercollegiate game in 1869. In the autumn of 1875 Harvard introduced rugby-style football to the United States, which it adopted from McGill University in Montreal (Watterson 2000, 17–18). The fast-paced game of rugby became popular and quickly displaced soccer in the United States. Increasing intercollegiate competition and preference for rugby led to the establishment of a single, standard game during annual rules conventions attended by representatives from Columbia, Harvard, Yale, and Princeton. "Fewer than a dozen young [white] men, all representing elite universities and relatively privileged classes, controlled the game during these crucial early years of its development" (Oriard 1993, 30). For this reason, Michael Oriard argues that "American football" was not born on the field but in the rules conventions of 1880 and 1882, when the line of scrimmage and the five-yard rule were created (Oriard 1993, 25–34; see also Watterson 2000).

The development of college football is characterized by a shift from an informal, student-run cultural formation to a structural component of the political economy of major universities (Oriard 2009). Initially, football was a form of student resistance to the controlling and effete culture of nineteenth-century academia. As such, it created a space for wealthy young men to express and develop a business-class manhood (Oriard 1993). As the game's popularity grew, it increasingly drew large crowds that were the nucleus for profitable spectacles. And it was not long before colleges began to embrace football as a recruiting tool. Even some faculty supported football since they believed it channeled students' youthful, manly energy into prosocial behaviors and built loyalty among the alumni (Watterson 2000, 43–45). As football's popularity continued to grow on university campuses in the late nineteenth century and entrenched football cultures formed, especially at Yale, Princeton, and Harvard, alumni and some faculty increasingly took control of the game from the students.

As the game moved away from student control, it became increasingly institutionalized, bureaucratic, and run as a business adventure by nonstudents. The development of full-time, professional coaches shows the growth of nonstudent authority in college football. Up until the 1880s, team captains (student leaders) prepared their teams for upcoming games, which meant that students expressed authority over other students. This began to change when Walter Camp, "the Father of American Football," took on the role of "graduate advisor" to the Yale football team in the 1880s. Although coaching was not a full-time, paid occupation for Camp, he helped lead training sessions and design plays that he taught to team leaders. In this sense, Camp was an amateur coach who displaced the student-player-coach (Watterson 2000, 20–21).

Yale was so dominant under Camp that schools around the country emulated his strategies and training regimes. When William Harper, the president of the University of Chicago, wanted to use football as part of a strategy to make Chicago the best-known university in the Midwest, he followed Yale and hired Amos Alonzo Stagg to coach his team. Stagg, an All-American football player at Yale in 1888, became the first full-time professional coach and athletic director in 1892.[6] Watterson suggests that Harper made Stagg a tenured member of the faculty and placed him at the head of the athletic department not only to import the Yale system to Chicago but also to maintain a degree of control over Stagg that Yale did not exercise over Camp (Watterson 2000, 40–41). Although ensconcing coaches like Stagg into the university may have been a failed attempt to maintain control over a football program, it was one among several steps that made big-time, profit-oriented football central to major universities and their destiny.

By the 1890s big-time football largely modeled on Yale had spread throughout the United States. For instance, the University of California and Leland Stanford University played the first "Big Game" in San Francisco in 1891, and the University of Georgia played the first "Clean, Old Fashioned-Hate" against the Georgia School of Technology in 1893. By 1896 the Western Conference, later known as the Big Nine before becoming the Big Ten, formed in the Midwest as an attempt to control excesses in big-time football and would serve as a model for other regional conferences (Watterson 2000, 50). The popularity of Thanksgiving Day big games allowed schools to raise large sums of money from ticket sales and offset a school's early season costs. For instance, Harvard brought in $15,409 from its 1893 game with Yale alone (Watterson 2000, 10).[7] And since big games were generally held off campus in cities like Boston, New York, Chicago, or San Francisco where they attracted large crowds of students, alumni, and other people interested in the spectacle, they also created a multiplier effect, generating significant revenues for the train lines, food vendors, and of course the press that provided publicity for the schools.

Critics within academia since the nineteenth century have argued that commercialized athletics are incompatible with the mission of the university and any association between the two hurts higher education (see Sperber 2000; Watterson 2000; Zimbalist 1999). Football did not escape this concern. The primary concern was that big-time football, with its attendant professionalism and commercialization, leads to an overemphasis on competition, winning, and profits that in-turn leads to violence on and off the field, cheating during games and in classes, hooliganism, and diminished scholarship. Robert Hutchins, former president of the University of Chicago, stated in 1954, "This business, like any other, has to pay. The only paying football is winning football. If you are going to win, you have to have the material; there is no substitute" (Hutchins 1954, 35). An example in the early days of how big-time football was inconsistent with the goals of higher education is the so-called "vagabond players" who traveled the country playing for the highest paying schools. Vagabond players rarely took classes and would leave campus as soon as the season ended, or even midseason if boosters for another team offered them more money than the previous school. Essentially professional players, these nonstudents presented a real danger to actual students on the other side of the scrimmage line (Watterson 2000, 46).

Violence and injury on the field led to two crisis periods in big-time football that resulted from the progressive press sensationalizing injuries on the field as well as overstating the number of football deaths. The first crisis ran from 1893 to 1897 and the second from 1905 to 1911. The crisis of the 1890s was quelled with minor reforms, such as banning the most notorious mass-momentum play, the "flying wedge," but not mass-momentum plays in general. The crisis beginning in 1905, however, led to the establishment of the Intercollegiate Athletic Association in 1906, which later became the NCAA. A slew of reforms minimized the game's most obvious dangers, but as John Watterson argues, they may also have made the game more deadly given a surge of deaths in 1909. Although the reforms may not have made the game any safer, they did make it faster paced and easier for fans to understand, which were important for bringing in new fans less steeped in the game. And the spike in deaths of 1909 also triggered new reforms that not only made the game safer but also opened up the forward pass, which established the modern game of football (Watterson 2000, 72–81, 108–129; also Oriard 1993).

## WARRIOR TRADITIONS—FOOTBALL
## AND PHYSICAL EDUCATION

Although Theodore Roosevelt's role in establishing the NCAA is often overstated (Watterson 2000, 65–81), his actions are in fact indicative of a relationship among football, U.S. geopolitical ambitions, and the desire for vigorous masculine citizens. Teddy Roosevelt was one among several expansionists following the Spanish-American War who supported football since it fostered "manly" characteristics in university men whom people like Roosevelt saw as necessary for U.S. expansionism. As chroniclers of Princeton athletics stated, "The aim of the American University is not merely the production of scholars, but the development of men" (Dyke 1901, 16). In a 1907 speech at the Harvard Union Roosevelt made clear his vision of athletic collegiate men in a modern nation: "We cannot afford to turn out of college men who shrink from physical effort or from a little physical pain. In any republic, courage is a prime necessity for the average citizen if he is to be a good citizen. . . . Athletics are good, especially in their rougher forms, because they tend to develop such courage. They are good also because they encourage a true democratic spirit, for in the athletic field, the man must be judged not with reference to outside and accidental attributes, but to that combination of bodily vigor and moral quality which go to make up prowess" (Roosevelt 1909, 349–350). Indeed, the Rough Riders were composed of cowboys and college athletes (Gems 2000, 77; Watterson 2000, 58), the very archetypes of manliness in a modern, industrial America. As Watterson wrote, "Like his fellow advocates of a tough, manly character, [Roosevelt] worried that Americans would fail to develop the physical and mental strength to stand up to predatory powers and third-world hordes" (Watterson 2000, 65). Roosevelt's attempts at reform were not aimed to remove violence from the game but to *harness violence* in order to produce college-educated leaders with a disciplined, sporting masculinity.

Roosevelt's concern with expansion and rugged masculinity suggests that despite style and appearance, football is not so far removed from the playing fields of Eton.[8] Beyond General Douglas MacArthur's inscription on the West Point gym that draws a connection between "fields of friendly strife" and victories on the battlefield, warfare has played an important even if indirect role in the development of football and physical education. Although college football practically shut down during the First World War, it was widely used as part of training regimes to condition recruits and raise their morale. As a result of football's systematic use during the war, non-college-educated classes of men were exposed to the game, which sparked an enormous boom in football's popularity in the 1920s (Watterson 2000, 139–140). By the time of the Second World War, football was a well-established sport throughout the country, and most top players spent the war years playing for military teams. Although attendance was down during the war, it came back quickly after the war without any significant alterations to its political economy or the intense emphasis on winning that led to the earlier excesses (see Harbrecht and Barnett 1979; Mennell 1989; Reimann 2004). What is most significant about football during the Second World War is the way that it intersected with physical education.

Programs of physical education have developed across Western and U.S. history in relationship to movements of warfare. Arthur Weston (1962) suggests that physical education developed in complex societies that produced leisure time for its population and had military-expansionist tendencies, such as Classical Greece, Rome, Prussia, and England. The working class became subject to physical education in the United Kingdom in order to produce a stock of healthy soldiers ready for war mobilization in 1881 following defeat in the first Boer War (Kirk 1998, 30). And medical examinations became a standard practice in physical education and prenatal care in Britain in order to engineer a healthier white race among citizens and workers (Kirk 1998, 23, 52). Physical education developed in the United States between 1850 and 1900, roughly the same period as football's development, from competing European gymnastic systems (Welch 1996, 113–124). The two most important gymnastics system for the development of physical education in the United States, the *Turnverein* (Turner Movement) and the Ling system, were responses to military-national crises in their home countries. The *Turnverein* began in Prussia as a way to restore national identity and unite a greater Germany following its defeat to Napoleon. And Pehr Henrik Ling developed the Ling system of gymnastics, following Sweden's military loss to Russia and Napoleon, and "had as its aim the instilling in Swedish children and youth a spirit of nationalism reminiscent of their Norse forbearers" (Weston 1962, 17).

Physical education programs in the United States developed rapidly during wartime and postwar periods when concerns over the masculinity of the nation's male youth were triggered (Welch 1996, 134, 175). The announcement that a third of U.S. males called up for service during World War I were rejected created concerns that the nation was not adequately developing its youth physically; chapter 3 shows this anxiety recurs throughout U.S. history including the 1950s. Physical education programs then moved away from dull, repetitive, military-style drilling that was common in the nineteenth century. By 1930, thirty-nine states required physical education as a part of their educational curriculum (Welch 1996, 177). During the Second World War physical education became more organized and based around competitive team sports, contact sports, and other sports such as swimming, track, and hiking that develop physical conditioning.

From the start of the twentieth century educational administrators saw athletics as a means of inculcating discipline and teamwork within students, both of which were seen as valuable traits for citizenship and military service in a modern industrial society (O'Hanlon 1980, 89). World War II was important in the development and organization of physical education in the United States since it was seen as a way to build a better fighting force. It was also argued to save lives by giving men the strength and stamina to withstand the hardships of combat (Lee 1983, 228). As Carl A. Jensen of the U.S. Office of Education stated, "[H]ard soldiers cannot be developed by soft methods" (cited in Welch 1996, 179). Similarly, Jimmy Conzelman, coach of the Chicago Cardinals football team, stated in a 1942 radio address, "Democracy makes us a pacific people. The young man must be toughened not only physically but mentally. He must become accustomed to violence. Football is the No. 1 medium for attuning a man to body contact and violent physical shock. It teaches that after all there isn't anything so terrifying about a punch in the puss" (cited in Peterson 1997, 139). During the Cold War, the *Journal of Educational Sociology* argued that violent sports provide effective training for citizenship and the military because athletics "develop team spirit and the importance of carrying out individual assignments as part of and essential to team success" (Larson 1955, 259). The philosophy of vigorous sports as paramilitary training for (male) youth was also reiterated in the 1951 Coronet Instructional Film *Getting Ready Physically* (the fifth installment in the Are You Ready for Service? series) that outlines recommended fitness regimes for freshman, sophomore, junior, and senior high school boys so that they would be prepared to enter the army upon graduation and withstand the rigors of combat. The militarization of physical education was extended as citizenship and military service were linked during the Cold War and military physical educators started teaching physical education in public schools following the Second World War (Welch 1996, 181).

Football during the early Cold War provided a symbolic and material regime that trained young men for citizenship and the military. At the same time, big-time collegiate football was also seen as part of the problem of post–World War II male youth growing soft. Critics argued that twenty-two elite men on the field received all of the benefits of exercise while twenty thousand to ninety thousand men sat "passively" (and hence effeminately) in the stands growing "soft." President John F. Kennedy stated at the National Football Foundation and Hall of Fame Banquet in 1961, "Football today is far too much a sport for the few who can play it well. The rest of us—and too many of our children—get our exercise from climbing up to seats in stadiums, or from walking across the room to turn on our television sets" (Kennedy 1961). A 1954 article in *Sports Illustrated* titled "How Fit Are Our Kids?" assailed the "big-time sports concept" that put too much competitive pressure on too few students. The author wrote, "Of 242 doctors who were recently questioned about interscholastic football for [the twelve to fifteen] age group, all but 22 were against it" (Morse 1954, 42). The banning of unlimited substitutions in 1953 caused people like Clarence "Biggie" Munn, athletic director of Michigan State University, to argue that the "one-platoon game" restricted access to athletic resources to even fewer young men (Munn 1954). So while football was heralded for its violent, manly training and symbolism, physical education was seen as an efficient way to strengthen and discipline the many average men who would serve the nation as warriors and workers while still participating in its consumer culture.

As I look back now on watching football with my father and learning to be an American, I realize those Saturdays in Memorial Stadium are among my favorite childhood memories. I also realize that I watched far more games, whether with my father or alone, on television. In fact, the first time I went to Memorial Stadium, the game seemed surreal since I was so accustomed to watching football on television. Looking at college football in the early Cold War is instructive for sport sociology because television broadcasting was new for most people and the professional league had not yet eclipsed college football. The ideological power of sport as a vehicle of citizenship also highlights its potential instability.

If sport's power emerges from its ability to link people's lived realities to larger abstract forces, then it is also open to numerous meanings and interpretations, as seen in the playground movement at the turn of the twentieth century (see Azzarito, Munro, and Solmon 2004; McArthur 1975; Spencer-Wood 1994; Stormann 1991) and the 1968 Olympic protest movement (Bass 2004; Edwards 1969; Hartmann 2003). Indeed, sport has the potential for conservative or progressive politics, such as my father's refusal to stand during the national anthem. Michael Oriard (2009) argues that football itself is not inherently conservative or nationalistic as it was portrayed by the counterculture movement of the 1960s. Instead, specific people from Teddy Roosevelt to Jimmy Conzelman worked very hard to construct football as a masculine symbol of the nation. *Discipline and Indulgence* is in fact very concerned with the representation of college football as a masculine symbol of the nation, but it also argues that people like Roosevelt and Conzelman built institutional linkages between college football and the military and the media. And it is those institutional linkages that made football such a powerful symbol of the nation and imperialism that were so despised by the counterculture.

## OUTLINE OF CHAPTERS

Rather than telling this story as a single linear narrative, I attempt to weave together a complicated picture of how modern sport worked to produce masculine citizens that could assimilate into the Cold War political economy at a time when the United States ascended to the position of world hegemon. Chapter 2 introduces what I call "fortified masculinity" to capture the deeply contradictory nature of both the Cold War's political economy of military-industrial Keynesianism (MIK) and the masculine citizenship that emerged out of MIK. Drawing upon the theory of governmentality, the chapter argues that MIK and the theory of containment that guided U.S. foreign policy throughout the Cold War produced a social landscape split between a tendency toward militaristic order and a tendency toward consumerist individualism. And it was upon this contradictory social landscape that men performed masculine citizenship as workers, warriors, and consumers. The chapter concludes by defining fortified masculinity as a paradoxical form of manhood that emerged during the Cold War and argues that sport media helped men to negotiate the Cold War's contradictory landscape.

Chapter 3 builds on the concept of fortified masculinity by looking at a moment of intense anxiety over young men's bodies that flowed from contradictions in MIK governmentality that was known as the "muscle gap." A primary contradiction arose from the simultaneous need to build the nation's military-economy and consumer culture. The need for disciplined warriors and workers butted up against the postwar consumer culture. Critics saw consumerism as producing an affluent society and a generation of soft youth unable to fulfill the national heritage of constant economic and political expansion. The fear of U.S. youth growing soft and susceptible to communist penetration created a desire to close the muscle gap but without lessening consumerism. The solution to the perceived softness of postwar youth was the implementation of mandatory national physical education. Physical exercise was viewed as a kind of therapy for the nation that would allow citizens to enjoy the consumer culture that was the basis of the American way of life while still preparing young men for industrial labor and military service.

Chapter 4 applies the concept of fortified masculinity to early college football television broadcasting. Television transformed an aspect of the American way of life—spectating college football—from a live participatory public ritual into a sponsorship-driven broadcast experience. The success of television broadcasting extended college football's business model from being based on ticket and concession sales to also selling fans in the form of television ratings to advertisers. The new model made television sports fans the objectified subject of football broadcasting. Based on analysis of technical writing about college football broadcasting, I argue that the subjective experience of the stadium was packaged and represented on television by adapting aspects of the classical Hollywood style of cinema (Bordwell, Staiger, and Thompson 1985), especially clarifying and intensifying the game. The subjectivizing style of broadcasting that developed in the late 1940s reproduced football games as exciting patriotic pageantry and created a subjective experience from a process of objectification. Broadcasting also served the pedagogical function of teaching fans not only about the game but also about the nation. In this sense, television broadcasting not only extended college football's business model but also extended the ethical space of the stadium to any place with a television that could receive the broadcasts.

The fifth chapter shows how anxieties around fortified masculinity were mobilized to legitimate the NCAA's process of cartelization in the early Cold War. After years of latency, the broadcasting of college football on television exploded in 1950. The emergence of television broadcasting triggered market instability and a crisis resulting from contradictions between the material forces and the social relations of football production. The crisis precipitated tremendous anxiety among schools already struggling in a market based on stadium revenues. The NCAA then put forward a plan to regulate the broadcasting market and thus contain television by limiting broadcasts and redistributing television revenues. In actuality, the regulations transformed the NCAA from a loose confederation of schools into a powerful cartel that accrued monopoly profits by limiting supply relative to demand. Wealth and power generated by the regulations also allowed the NCAA to gain institutional control of college athletics and football broadcasting. Chapter 5 shows how the NCAA framed its strategy to rationalize market disorder through a prism of Cold War anxieties so that market regulations would appear as serving Cold War national objectives. In effect, the NCAA used the cultural conditions of the Cold War and anxieties around men's bodies to stabilize the development of a new political economy in college football based not simply on ticket and concession sales but also on the selling of broadcast rights.

The sixth chapter spatializes the analysis of Cold War sport media by looking at how *Sports Illustrated*'s coverage of college football in 1954 helped to construct a geographical imagination, or a way of conceptualizing space and one's relationship to other places (Bialasiewicz et al. 2007; Gregory 1994; Klein 2003; Powers and Crampton 2005; Said 1978), consistent with the broader U.S. Cold War strategy. Rather than providing information on geopolitics, football's patriotic pageantry provided a powerful medium through which U.S. citizens could learn new ways of imagining the nation and its place within world history. The power of sport was not lost on Henry Luce, a leading Cold War internationalist and proponent of a muscular foreign policy, who founded *Sports Illustrated* in 1954. Chapter 6 provides a study on how the rhetorical use of images and maps could shape a Cold War imagination. The analysis focuses on the construction of three scales or magnitudes of space (nation, region, and suburban neighborhood) that parallel the organization of collegiate football (league, conference, and team). Within *Sports Illustrated* narrative style, a reader could then locate the Cold War family within national space. The analysis finds an ambiguity within *Sports Illustrated*'s discourse of space that emerges out of competing Cold War narratives. The articles constructed warrior narratives focused on courage, discipline, homosocial bonding, ritualized violence, and intense competition. At the same time, they also produced personal narratives rooted in specific communities and lived experiences that were profoundly emotive. Through *Sports Illustrated*'s coverage, fans could make a personal connection to mass culture and translate intimacy into the abstraction of national space. What ultimately unified the dual narratives was a construction of national space made palpable in football's patriotic pageantry and the norms of a universal white middle class.

The concluding chapter of *Discipline and Indulgence* relates sport media in the current War on Terror to the early Cold War. This history shows that the present is not a rupture from the past; in fact, from the muscle gap to Pat Tillman, the young white male athletic body has been a site of national identification and anxiety through which people can make personal investments. In other words, a raced and gendered construction of both individual bodies and the national body provides ideological sinew that links and allows different institutions to articulate within a broader organization of militarism. Since the 1950s, sport and militarism have articulated along the conceptual linkage of masculinity, race, and nation in media narrative and rhetoric (Jansen and Sabo 1994; Messner, Dunbar, and Hunt 2000). While the linkages between sport and militarism certainly did not begin in the 1950s, the sport-media complex and the military-industrial complex share and proliferate a corporate-capitalist worldview. Sport media operate as a political technology that moves a disparate group of individuals into a unified body of consumers who form a broader sport market. So just as newspapers did in the nineteenth century (Oriard 1993), electronic media of the Cold War *invented the fan* (see Cruikshank 1999) as an imaginative community held together by discourses of manhood, race, and nation that intersect in football broadcasting and where militarism operates in the symbols and assumptions of the institutions.

Despite important transformations that occurred between the early 1960s and the 1990s—such as the dissolution of the "liberal consensus", the emergence of the counterculture, the dismantling of the Keynesian state, and the fall of the Berlin Wall—the first Persian Gulf War (1990–1991) manifested a renewed muscular foreign policy and the reintegration of sport and U.S. militarism in sport media narratives and rhetoric (Jansen and Sabo 1994). These narratives help people situate themselves within time and space in order to form identities and interpret the world they live in from a particular discursive framework. All-American Pat Tillman served as a poster child for U.S. government and NFL propaganda because he gave up a lucrative professional football career to serve as an Army Ranger in Afghanistan, only to be killed in action. His commitment, patriotism, and sacrifice moved people throughout the nation. His service allowed them to project their own hopes, dreams, and aspirations onto Tillman's body, and many were understandably dismayed to learn how his body was used to shore up flagging support for the wars. The roots of Tillman's story, however, lie in a range of texts from the Cold War era, including *Sports Illustrated* and the many educational films of the 1940s and 1950s that solidified an image of citizen-athlete-soldier. Whether framed as patriot or victim, Tillman as citizen-athlete-soldier remains heroic and a symbol of abstract political forces.

# 2 · FORTIFYING THE CITY UPON A HILL

## College Football and Cold War Citizenship

In the fall of 1948, Hildegard Binder Johnson published "Football as Seen—An American Vignette" in the *American-German Review*. Binder Johnson wrote the article as a German immigrant in the United States trying to understand the Midwestern state of Minnesota where she was living and, by extension, all of America. Through her eyes, the colors of the season and the landscape of the Midwest blend with the people as they come together in the stadium. She describes how the flow of people into the stadium "merge into multi-colored pools, and the pools become lakes, and the lakes enlarge until there is one surging ocean, the football crowd, that rises and subsides like waves" (Binder Johnson 1948, 20). When players huddle she sees a flower in bloom, and built-up tension is released with thousands of balloons after the home team's first score. Not even the forces of nature can contain the exuberance of the football season. On rainy days the stadium is awash in the gay colors of umbrellas, which she contrasts with the somber colors of German umbrellas. American football creates a Technicolor dreamscape in which the nation comes into being through its weekly rituals.

Binder Johnson expresses both a nearness to and distance from the Midwestern football world she describes since she was doubly alien to it. As a German immigrant living in the United States since 1934, she was alien to the land and culture. As a woman in a Midwest football town, she was also alien to a sport that had been the proving ground for middle- and upper-class manhood since the late nineteenth century (Gems 2000; Oriard 1993). Binder Johnson, a historical geographer who studied German immigrants in the United States (Lanegran 1994), uses college football in the article to examine her own experiences of marrying an American and living in Minnesota in the early post–World War II era. She concludes that no one is "born a football fan" (Binder Johnson 1948, 20); instead it is passion that one learns through intensive training, whether as child or adult. But once one learns the strategies, tactics, history, lore, and rituals, one can then participate in America the society and the nation. By the late 1940s, as she demonstrates, football opened up an avenue of national incorporation to a person willing to learn the game and participate in its rituals.

Attached to the article is Binder Johnson's hand-drawn illustration of a football stadium on game day (fig. 2.1). In the background is a concrete stadium, perhaps the University of Minnesota's Memorial Stadium, with pennants flying from the top, and in the foreground are streams of people filing into the stadium. Floating godlike in the sky above the stadium is a giant leather-helmeted football player who stares beyond the scene and out toward the person reading the article. The illustration is oddly reminiscent of the upper part of the frontispiece to Thomas Hobbes's *Leviathan* (1651), where the sovereign rises up from the land and embodies the people themselves, except in Binder Johnson's drawing an archaic football player rises from the stadium and seems to embody the *Geist* (spirit) of the community and by extension the nation. Literary scholar Gerald Weales commented more generally in 1959, "When this god is considered in the abstract, he seems to be of the patriarchal galaxy of gods. His celebration is strongly masculine. . . . [During the celebration] the participants and the spectators are expected to assume an air of excess heartiness which is the external evidence of spiritual investiture" (Weales 1959, 104). College football, for Binder Johnson, was a microcosm through which one could both understand and participate in the nation. "Football is not just a sport," she wrote, "but an expression of American life like baseball and roadstands and ice cream" (Binder Johnson 1948, 19). Thus if a person wants to understand and participate in America, the great American spectacle and ritual of college football is the avenue through which he or she participates in and becomes a member of the nation.

Binder Johnson's essay is compelling because it expresses several of the points developed in *Discipline and Indulgence*. College football, as a ritual and symbol of the nation, provides a set of practices that integrate a person into the nation. Integration into the nation requires a person to learn not only the details of the game (its technical knowledge) but also the customs and lore of the game (its cultural knowledge) to achieve cultural citizenship. So to participate in the larger sociocultural formation, a citizen learns a set of values and norms that he or she puts into practice through college football's various rituals. Once a person masters appropriate levels of football knowledge and achieves cultural competence, he or she can conduct himself or herself in the ritual space of the nation and teach others to do so as well. We can thus understand college football as a technology of citizenship where people produce themselves as competent cultural citizens. The ritual and, we should add, commercial space of college football forms an ethical space where people can take pleasure in producing themselves as subjects of the nation. College football's ritual process involves external directives in the form of norms and internal desire as people find pleasure in the ritual itself.

FIGURE 2.1 Untitled drawing by Hildegard Binder Johnson. *American-German Review* 21 (October 1948).

What Binder Johnson does not address is the fact that in the early Cold War, college football formed an uneven sphere of incorporation. In fact, as I argue throughout this chapter, college football in the early Cold War was most effective in opening an institutional path to men of ethnic European descent, whether as players or as fans. This has to do with the unfolding of Cold War foreign as well as domestic policies in the United States and the fact that the American way of life needed to present a *pluralistic image* more than a *pluralistic reality* (Dudziak 2000, 13). The presence of white women and African Americans, as fans or players, in the stadium created tensions. In this chapter, I use the concept "fortified masculinity" to theorize how white ethnic European men were privileged by the conditions of the early Cold War and what it cost them. In the rest of the book, I apply fortified masculinity to a study of college football in early Cold War media.

## CULTURAL HISTORY AND GOVERNMENTALITY IN SPORT SOCIOLOGY

*Discipline and Indulgence* tells a cultural history of college football in the United States during the early period of the Cold War (1947–1964) through the lens of cultural citizenship and governmentality. By placing football within the context of the Cold War, the research takes a historical approach to problems of culture and politics. Football and physical education helped to produce what I call fortified masculinity, which is the social construction of masculine, white citizens who could fulfill the state's Cold War needs as disciplined, patriotic workers, warriors, and consumers. The citizenship frame highlights the simultaneity of race, class, gender, and sexuality as embodied, socially produced aspects of identity that articulated within U.S. global imperialist strategies. As we will see in chapter 6, citizenship also spatializes processes of self-formation or subjectification since citizenship is ultimately about tying self-directed actors to a society that is embodied in a liberal nation-state and that acts purposively within international networks and alliances.

The focus on citizenship and governmentality connects *Discipline and Indulgence* to a larger movement within cultural studies. Since Tony Bennett (1992) called for a greater focus on cultural policy within cultural studies, a growing literature has emerged, guided by Michel Foucault's (1991) notion of governmentality (Bratich, Packer, and McCarthy 2003). This literature's central concern is how allied forces within the state and economy manage populations in liberal and neoliberal regimes of governance through institutions of the state and civil society. College sport is an institution of civil society (Allison 1998) that explicitly bridges the fields of education and commerce (Zimbalist 1999), which is to say that although sport is itself an institution with its own history and norms, collegiate athletics connects sport to the broader institutions of education (such as physical education, extracurricular activities, and inter- and intramural competitions) and media (such as sports coverage in print or electronic media, events staged as media spectacles, cross-promotional marketing with sporting goods manufacturers, video games, and online events). College football, whether in the stadium or on television, is fruitfully studied from a governmentality perspective because it links state, civil society, and market institutions and creates an ethical space where fans produce themselves as cultural citizens.

Cultural studies scholarship has long championed research on popular culture, but sport has largely been sidelined in the literature (Andrews and Carrington, in press; Carrington 2010). *Discipline and Indulgence* is therefore situated within a movement to bring sport to cultural studies and cultural studies to sport sociology that is often called physical cultural studies (PCS) (see Andrews 2002; Andrews and Giardina 2008; Carrington 2010; Cole 1994; Giardina 2003; Ingham 1997; Kirk 1998; McDonald and Birrell 1999; Miller 2001; Newman 2007; Newman and Giardina 2010; Silk and Andrews 2011). By analyzing a moment of liberal governmentality known as military-industrial Keynesianism, *Discipline and Indulgence* takes a historical approach to the physical cultural studies literature, which is very presentist in its nearly exclusive focus on neoliberalism and post-Fordism.[1] Indeed, there was not a single article in the *Sociology of Sport Journal's* 2011 special issue on PCS that used historical analysis. Furthermore, analyses of sport within the context of the Cold War are almost entirely absent from the sport sociology literature and rare in the literature on Cold War culture (Kemper 2009).[2] By drawing upon cultural studies, my approach to sport during the early Cold War attempts to develop a theoretically informed, critical analysis that is sensitive to the interrelated processes of gendering and racialization.

In order to explicate the concept of fortified masculinity, I first outline the theory of governmentality. Then I argue that as military-industrial Keynesianism organized the state and economy for warfare, it was also a Cold War formation of governmentality. Military-industrial Keynesianism in the United States emerged out of the strategy of containment that governed how the country fought the Cold War. Therefore, the following sections of the chapter describe how the strategy of containment and military-industrial Keynesianism interlocked to foster militarism and the effect that containment had upon popular culture. The chapter concludes by building upon the previous sections to define fortified masculinity and show how it operated in Cold War football media.

## PRODUCING AND MANAGING MODERN SUBJECTS

Governmentality describes the relationship between subjects and states in the modern era as a managerial relationship that simultaneous fosters citizens while increasing the power of the state. In its modern configuration, government becomes concerned with the health and welfare of its population so that issues of economy, public health, education, culture, and so forth fall under the purview of government policy (Foucault 1991). The location of modern liberal governmentality is the capitalist state, a bureaucratic state that strives to create the conditions for stable capital accumulation (Jessop 1990, 354–355).³ Since liberalism traditionally distrusts government and sees direct state intrusions into society as inefficient, hence the axiom "government that governs least governs best," liberal regimes tend to move governance into institutions of civil society and the market, such as schools and media. These institutions therefore take on the ethical function of fostering self-regulating and economically independent subjects (see Lewis and Miller 2003; Miller 1993, 1998, 2007; Miller and Yúdice 2002; Popkewitz 2000; Yúdice 2003).

The citizen then is a self-regulating subject in that he or she participates in the governance of society and freely follows externally imposed rules and laws. Since the citizen is a person who governs and is governed, a person who is the subject of and subject to the state, citizenship is a project of governance (Cruikshank 1999). But government should not be understood in narrow political terms; "government" also signifies problems of self-control, guidance for the family and for children, management of the household, directing the soul, etc." (Lemke 2001, 191). The problem of liberalism then is producing subjects who identify their interests with those of the state and society so that they willingly perform roles necessary for the state and society to function with minimal overt state intervention (Rose, O'Malley, and Valverde 2006, 84), which is why both state and nonstate institutions govern by teaching citizens self-conduct and how to direct the conduct of others (Lemke 2002, 50–51). This means that governance involves both ways of thinking (rationalities) and interventions into people's lives through political technologies, or sets of structured forms of action by which we exercise power over ourselves and others (Gerrie 2003, 14; Lemke 2001, 191).

Political technologies combine specific governmental practices with knowledge of the state and its population to take the whole of society as its object to foster, discipline, and individualize citizens.⁴ For instance, cultural policy, or policy that regulates the flow of ideas, values, styles, and genres (DiMaggio 1983), helps produce self-regulating citizens through disciplinary pedagogies. Cultural policy creates "a complex movement between self and society" of practices, social norms, and strategies of economy for running both the state and individual households (Miller 1998, 15). As a result, subjectification and the kinds of cultural repertoires a person develops occur not randomly but within patterned relations of the institutional dynamics of cultural policy (Bennett 1992, 26). Governmentality thus refers to technologies of governance derived from detailed knowledge of populations that unfold through state, market, and civil society institutions to foster, discipline, and individualize citizens while simultaneously accumulating wealth and power within the capitalist state (see Foucault 1988a, 1988b, 1991; see also Bennett 1992, 1995; Gorski 2003b; Miller 1993, 1998; Miller and Yúdice 2002). Government's flexible management of abstract space and the things within it evinces an alliance between the population (labor power) and the state (regulator of accumulation) so that the population's welfare is tied to the state and the state's strength rests in the welfare of the population. In the next section, I argue that the specific form of liberal governmentality that occurred during the early Cold War incorporated Fordist and Keynesian principles at its core, and I call it military-industrial Keynesianism (Isaac and Leicht 1999, 33).

## MILITARY-INDUSTRIAL KEYNESIANISM—EARLY COLD WAR GOVERNMENTALITY

Military-industrial Keynesianism (MIK) is generally understood as a set of macroeconomic policies that use military spending to create economic conditions that support stable capital accumulation (Custers 2010; Isaac and Leicht 1999; Johnson 2008). The British economist John Maynard Keynes argued to policy makers that "the level of consumption among a society's working population is not a matter to be discounted or ignored but is in fact of crucial importance in the maintenance of corporate profits and in ensuring that society's entrepreneurs can sell their produce" (Custers 2010, 81). In terms of MIK, military spending creates economic conditions where consumers not only will have increased income but also will be more likely to spend a larger share of that increased income on consumption and thus create a multiplier effect (Custers 2010, 81). Military spending can be used for short-term stimulation, known as "pump-priming," in which case a government might choose to stimulate economic activity by going to war and making numerous small purchases or achieve a long-term multiplier effect by investing in complicated weapons systems that unfold over several business cycles (Custers 2010, 83). The United States gained a long-term multiplier effect through massive military building during the course of the Cold War, and that ultimately transformed the political, economic, and manufacturing face of the nation (Markusen et al. 1991).

MIK is only one governance paradigm for applying Keynesian principles. For instance, the New Deal was a form of civilian Keynesianism in that spending on social programs was intended to stimulate new business cycles (Custers 2010; Waddell 2001; Wehrle 2003). By revealing the normally opaque levels of class exploitation, the Great Depression created conditions for labor to make tremendous gains through federal policy. However, civilian Keynesianism gives the public leverage over hegemonic capitalist class fractions through increased regulations and that triggered intense resistance (Waddell 1999, 2001). "Conservative capitalists feared that this degree of government intervention would delegiti-mize capitalism," argues Chalmers Johnson, "and shift the balance of power from the capitalist class to the working class and it unions" (Johnson 2007). As a result of divisions generated by civilian Keynesianism, the welfare state remains controversial in the United States since it expands democracy, limits hegemonic class fractions' range of action, and places limits on capital accu-mulation (Waddell 2001, 116–117; also Wehrle 2003). MIK resolved the crisis of the 1930s by making enormous state investments in industry "without the national state interfering with market relationships nor with corporate mana-gerial prerogatives" (Waddell 2001, 122).

The promise of economic growth that was seen during World War II united liberals and conservatives during the Cold War behind MIK. MIK smoothed both political and class antagonisms at the same time that it legitimated the growth of a strong central state and built a military-industrial complex that sub-sumed the interests of a large, affluent group of people in the military-industrial state (Cypher 2007; Markusen et al. 1991; Waddell 2001, 123). The political and economic success of MIK also fostered a powerful sense of militarism as "the prism through which global political events and U.S. foreign policy are inter-preted" (Cypher 2007). In chapter 1, I defined militarism as a set of values and beliefs in the efficacy of the military that emerge out of a complex of political and economic institutions and that are generalized throughout a population to the point of becoming a banal aspect of everyday life. While this certainly describes the early period of the Cold War, which I return to in subsequent sections, for now I want to emphasize that a discourse of national security allowed for the amalgamation of Keynesianism, corporate internationalism, and militarization to form the liberal consensus that unified different sectors of the state and a class-divided society in the early Cold War (Waddell 2001, 122).

The golden age of U.S. capitalism during the Cold War resulted then from a gov-ernance paradigm of MIK with some aspects of civilian Keynesianism retained in a political environment hostile to labor (Wehrle 2003). As Isaac and Leicht (1999) point out, MIK at its core contained Fordist and Keynesian principles. Its Ford-ist elements included expansion of mass production industries such as the auto-mobile, steel, and electric industries; the limiting of collective bargaining to mass production enterprises and to management prerogatives; and a capitalist state offensive against labor, such as the 1947 Taft-Hartley Act, which contained and weakened the labor movement. In terms of Keynesianism, MIK helped to avoid massive economic downturns around the world following World War II through macroeconomic stabilization policies that included military buildups, allocated state spending that provided for social needs (such as housing, highways, agri-culture, medical care, and defense) and subsidized corporate capital unavailable on the market, and directed some state spending toward fostering welfare and producing a margin of economic security (Isaac and Leicht 1999, 33). Ultimately, MIK resulted in a corporate-state alliance that Waddell (2001) describes as a *strong warfare state* and a *weak welfare state* that tilted power disproportionately toward hegemonic capitalist class fractions. The next section details how MIK as a governmental formation operated through Cold War culture.

## COLD WAR CULTURE AND THE MANAGEMENT OF MODERN SOCIETY

This section looks at the theory of containment that structured U.S. foreign policy throughout the Cold war since containment reveals the intertwining of warfare and welfare in MIK governmentality. The beginning of the Cold War marks a transformation in geopolitical power that brought the United States and the Soviet Union into direct competition (Brands 1993, 3–4; Nadel 1995, 74). The imperialist struggle between the United States and the Soviet Union known as the Cold War involved a confluence of factors including political and strategic factors, economic factors such as the cost of the war and the need for foreign markets, and programs of domestic control and policy that generated political capital until the 1980s (Brands 1993, vi–vii). This led to two important outcomes during the Cold War: an unprecedented level of peacetime military buildup known as the arms race that drove the postwar political economy and continuing albeit decreased investments in the welfare of the population (Waddell 2001; Wehrle 2003).

### The Strategy of Containment—Fortifying the Warfare State

The "strategy of containment" guided U.S. Cold War policy from Truman to Reagan. The formal strategy of containment attempted to contain Soviet hegemony to limited spheres of influence while developing networks of commercial exchange within a "Free World" system (Klein 2003, 16; Nitze 1993, 41, 71; also Gaddis 1982; May 1999; Nadel 1995). In this sense, containment was a dual strategy: military and economic. The political-military prong of containment led to conformity, the arms race, and repeated "police actions" throughout the decolonizing world (Brands 1993; Horne 1999; Slotkin 1992). Indeed, NSC-68 led to the militarization of society that was simultaneously a project of capitalist development.[5] As James Cypher states, "NSC-68 made the then novel argument that the U.S. economy had excess capacity and that high levels of military spending on a permanent basis would act as a stimulant to the economy—creating multiplier effects on employment and spending by absorbing the unemployed and the untapped production capabilities of U.S. industry" (Cypher 2007). This points to the political-economic prong of containment that was waged by forming the Free World as a system of trading alliances led by the United States and buttressed by a pluralistic image of the American way of life (Klein 2003, 28; von Eschen 1997, 109–114; also see Alba and Nee

1997; Kazal 1995). The political-economic prong promised to raise quality of life in noncommunist nations through capitalist development and the production of consumer goods. This led to the Marshall Plan, the GI Bill, the centralization of production in large factories, and the proliferation of consumerism. The political economy of containment ultimately produced a military-humanitarian foreign policy (Dean 1998) based as much on consumer goods and a consumerist lifestyle as on bombs, missiles, and soldiers (Klein 2003).

The Cold War had an enormous impact on the cultural landscape of U.S. society. As Christina Klein states, "[T]he Cold War was as much a domestic endeavor as a foreign policy one—and as much an educational as a political or military one" (Klein 2003, 28). Part of Klein's statement refers to the "domestic containment programs" of the early Cold War symbolized by the image and politics of Joe McCarthy (Friedman 2005). But containment also took on a cultural face and formed "containment culture" in the tiny bits of everyday life that were structured by the politics of the Red Scare and that influenced gender roles, self-surveillance, and how to act like an American (Nadel 1995, x). Examples include atomic bomb movies, music, and toys like Kix Cereal's "Atomic Bomb Ring" (Boyer 1994, 10–12); James Bond and Mike Hammer novels (May 1999; Whitfield 1991); civil defense films like *Duck and Cover* (1951) and *What You Should Know about Biological Warfare* (1952); and a series of trading cards called "Children's Crusade Against Communism" (1951) by the Bowman Gum Co. (Walker 1994, 68–69). Containment culture highlights how Cold War policy was disseminated through the media and in civil society to educate citizens on the postwar's twilight world and to normalize anxieties about the Soviet Union.

## Integrating Consuming Citizens—The Welfare State

Klein's statement in the previous paragraph points not just to the surveillance, alienation, and insecurity of containment culture but also to the nurturing, integrative aspects of the cultural Cold War that were concerned with people's welfare. At the international level, integration is symbolized by the formation of an U.S.-led coalition of nations called the Free World constructed in binary opposition to a "Slave World" that existed behind the Iron Curtain. The Free World integrated nations into systems of trade and reciprocity that could demonstrate capitalism's superiority in providing for its citizens (Klein 2003). Holding the coalition together was a notion of the good life, most clearly symbolized by the American way of life that offered an image of racial and gender pluralism basking in the wealth of consumer culture (see Crawford 2004; Thomas 2002). Chapter 4 provides greater detail, but the American way of life and its consumer comforts were to serve as antidote to the social-psychological malaise and economic depression experienced throughout the world following World War II, which was believed to provide fertile ground for communism.

The political-economic prong of containment led to a cultural Cold War where U.S. wealth and culture were the key weapons of war. Indeed, spreading capitalism in the form of the American culture was seen as the most effective antidote to communism's siren call for people in poor and depressed nations. Henry Luce, for instance, in his famous essay "The American Century" (Luce 1941/1969a), argued that the United States could fulfill its destiny of world leadership not militarily but by spreading American popular culture throughout the world (see chapter 6). This meant that U.S. Information Agency (USIA) programs for exporting American culture throughout the world in forms such as jazz music and Hollywood films (see Cohen 1983; Dudziak 2000; Klein 2003) were as important as the Marshall Plan abroad and the GI Bill at home (see Goldman 1960; Schlesinger 1949; see also Brands 1993; Lipshutz 2001; Walker 1994; Whitfield 1991). Athletics was also one of the most important U.S. cultural exports because it was globally popular and did not appear propagandistic (Domer 1976; Thomas 2002).

The success of the United States as leader of the Free World was predicated on a pluralistic image of the American way of life, which made assimilation an unquestioned good and "the embodiment of the democratic ethos" (Metzger 1971, 629). However, the pluralistic image of the United States was often confounded by a cultural and institutional reality of white supremacy (Borstelmann 2001; Dudziak 2000; von Eschen 1997). The need to produce an image even if not a reality of pluralism supported the melting pot as the dominant model for explaining race relations in the United States because it "offered an idealistic vision of American society and identity as arising from the biological and cultural fusion of different peoples" (Alba and Nee 1997, 832). Generalized from the experience of ethnic Europeans (Metzger 1971; Omi and Winant 1994), the melting pot emphasized consensus and the orderly incorporation of diverse ethnic groups into the American way of life, where liberal ideology would serve as the basis of national unity (Kazal 1995, 459–460). Midcentury assimilation theory envisioned a process of Americanization where ethnic groups assumed a single core culture, what Milton Gordon called "identificational assimilation," that provides an entrance into the nation's "imagined community" and access to political and economic rights of citizenship (Kazal 1995, 440). Assimilation and the expansion of citizenship were important to the construction of the Free World since citizenship was understood as synonymous with liberty and freedom and opposed to patriarchal relations of servitude, whether as serf, slave, or colonial subject.

Situating assimilation within the broader history of whiteness in the United States points to the limits of citizenship as a practice of freedom.[6] Whiteness as a broad coalition formed through the actions of white workers, government policy that privileged white families, and discriminatory business practices during the mid-twentieth century (Brodkin 1998; Katznelson 2005; Lipsitz 1998; Roediger 2006). Whiteness thus provides social and material benefits for those people willing and able to take on the full measure of U.S. citizenship, which is why George Lipsitz (1998) argues that people make a "possessive investment in whiteness." The expansion of citizenship rights to women and people of color was not a linear, inevitable progression but a herky-jerky process arising from crises in the capitalist state and strategic social movements that invariably incited conservative reactions by existing citizens (Glenn 2002; Omi and Winant 1994).[7] Whiteness also, as a result, suggests loss as well as gain where ethnic and national identities are exchanged for a white racial identity that differentiates ethnic Europeans from immigrants and stigmatized racial groups (see Brodkin 1998; Frankenburg 1993; Glenn 2002; Hill 1997; Ignatiev 1996; Lipsitz 1998; Roediger 1991, 2000). The social construction of citizenship is not simply a racialization or gendering process but always already both and more. In the next section, I characterize the coming together of race, gender, and sexuality in Cold War governmentality and its relationship to college football with the term fortified masculinity, inspired by Elaine Tyler May's seminal work on Cold War culture.

## FORTIFIED MASCULINITY AND PARADOXES OF COLD WAR CULTURE

What I call fortified masculinity draws upon an ambiguity expressed in the title of Elaine Tyler May's book *Homeward Bound* (1999) that is illustrative of early Cold War culture. May shows how the broader international policy of containment transcended domestic life and policy.[8] Within the Cold War's cultural focus on "the domestic" that signifies the home, the family, the nation, and the rise of the postwar cult of domesticity, May traces out a newly invented, traditional domestic life embraced by young white Americans that she describes as homeward bound. On the one hand, this generation was going home in ever-greater numbers: not just buying homes but also lowering the average age of marriage as well as the divorce rate and raising the birth rate after years of decline. But on the other hand, this generation was increasingly bound by home life. The trappings of postwar domesticity created confines that made the home a container of hopes, desires, and labor power, especially for women.[9]

May begins her book by describing a *Life* magazine article about a newly married couple that planned to spend their honeymoon in a backyard bomb shelter. Photos show the lovers surrounded by consumer goods as they prepared to descend into their bunker of domestic bliss. "This is a powerful image of the nuclear family in the nuclear age: isolated, sexually charged, cushioned by abundance, and protected against impending doom by the wonders of modern technology" (May 1999, x). May's description suggests that Cold War culture constructed a kind of fortified home that held out a double promise of security: (1) it was fortified or enriched with an abundance of consumer goods that signified economic security and (2) it was fortified or equipped with bulwarks that signified security from the physical and symbolic violence of the outside world. The fortified home became both a sanctuary enhanced and rewarded by consumer culture and a compound that isolated the nuclear family within the larger Cold War political economy.

In looking at college football during the early Cold War, I suggest the emergence of a version of manhood that I call fortified masculinity that like Cold War domesticity was paradoxical. Fortified masculinity was an identity made available primarily to white, heterosexual men in the early Cold War culture that carried both rewards and costs. By the early Cold War, white men enjoyed an institutional structure of privilege and wealth far less available to white women and all racialized minorities. Postwar domesticity and government programs of MIK enriched white men with increased power at work, at home, and throughout society.[10] The gendered power of white men also accelerated with the postwar return of GIs to the industrial sector, higher education, and the housing market (Brodkin 1998; Katznelson 2005; Lipsitz 1998; Roediger 2006). At the same time, investments in the patriarchy of white men regardless of ethnicity compensated for submission to the alienating regimes of MIK and the growing need for soldiers of the empire to police the world and keep it safe for capitalism under the auspices of "democracy" (see Williams 1962), as will be explored in chapter 3.

The rise of consumer capitalism and the enrichment of white men's social identities had an ironic and paradoxical effect of also destabilizing Cold War manhood. The idea of masculinity as paradox is not new in the critical men's studies literature (e.g., Boon 2005; Brod 1990; Capraro 2000; Jewkes 2005; Kaufman 1999; Kimmel 1994; Pleck 1983) and is typically understood as resulting from how the institutional organization of patriarchy makes men as a group powerful, but the competitive dynamics of the male peer group makes men as individuals feel isolated and vulnerable (Capraro 2000). While competitive dynamics in male peer groups, or what some scholars call fratriarchy (e.g., Brod 1990; Jewkes 2005; Loy 1995; Remy 1990; Sabo, Gray, and Moore 2000), both empowers and disempowers, I want to add that the paradox in Cold War manhood also emerged out of contradictions in the political economy of the Cold War (MIK) and was expressed in popular culture (see Brod 1990). In this sense, fortified masculinity was tied to Cold War governmentality.

Consumerism and domesticity transformed the way in which men produced their masculinity, and changing gender relations made many men uncomfortable.[11] For instance, Jerome Weidman, in a 1954 Sports Illustrated article, tells a story about attending sporting events at Madison Square Garden during his youth but not as an adult, linking suburbanization with television and emasculation (Weidman 1954). On the one hand, Weidman suggests that he had realized the American

Dream by moving out of the city and buying a home in the suburbs, a powerful image of manhood in 1950s America (Gilbert 2005; Griswold 1993; Kimmel 2012; Spigel 1992). On the other hand, living in the suburbs forced him to drive into the city and pay a man named "Dominick" to protect his car. Ownership of commodities that symbolized manhood and independence, a home and a car, made him dependent upon Dominick, a lower-class man he found distasteful, which caused Weidman to stay home and watch sports on television (Weidman 1954). In fact, many people in the 1950s found television a disruptive force in their homes since it symbolized changing gender relations brought on by consumer culture (Spigel 1992). Instead of liberating people from alienation, as promised by consumerism and Cold War liberalism, the fortification of masculinity compensated for men's submission to the alienating regimes of industrial production and militarism. Fortified masculinity provided a sanctuary from the physical and symbolic violence of a competitive capitalist society by providing patriarchal privilege in segregated communities, job opportunities, and spaces of leisure at the same time that it paradoxically aligned men with the designs of the capitalist state that not only limits expressions of self but also drives men to endure physical and symbolic violence as part of their identities, what Don Sabo (1994) calls the "pain principle."

College football provided working-class men, especially of ethnic European descent, access to civil society, which made college football a powerful symbol of Americanization and proof of U.S. pluralism. Michael Oriard argues that although football was initially a preserve of wealthy northeastern elites, it became a powerful means of opening up institutional access for men of all races (Oriard 1993, 2001). The very names of players painted a picture of U.S. popular culture as an integrated ethnic mosaic that could counter other images of racial discrimination.[12] A 1954 *Sports Illustrated* cartoon shows an injured player being carried on a stretcher to the locker room. Trailing along side of the player is a reporter taking notes. The caption reads, "Bugscinski . . . B, as in Battered . . . U, as in unnecessary roughness . . . G, as in gouged . . . S, as in spiked . . . C, as in concussion" (Levinson 1954).[13] This cartoon suggests that ethnic European men used football as a mechanism to assimilate into U.S. citizenship, but that process of assimilation also came with a physical and mental price that was valorized in terms of toughness and violence. Indeed, John F. Kennedy's touch football games staged as media events on the White House lawn served to construct a vigorous, youthful image of the first Catholic president participating in the American way of life despite debilitating back injuries he probably incurred during the Second World War (Altman and Purdum 2002; Massa 1999).

Commentators in the 1950s called the embodiment of an identity that suppressed empathy for self and others a "suicidal cult of masculinity" that made men the objects of government for themselves, their wives, medicine, leisure and recreation institutions, and the state. According to critics of the suicidal cult of masculinity, the cultural and economic conditions of the early Cold War created a "rat race" where middle-class white men attempted to be outstanding workers and great fathers, with the result that they were unconcerned with their own health and happiness.[14] These men were the embodiment of what David Riesman (1950) called other-directed. Claims of a suicidal cult of masculinity were partially a protest against the rat race of MIK governmentality. A 1957 article by Lemuel C. McGee, medical director of Hercules Powder Company,[15] in *Today's Health* featured a picture of a middle-aged white man in a grass field wearing a baseball glove and squatting behind a young boy with a baseball bat in his hands. Text overlaying this image of the companionate family (see Griswold 1993) read, "Companionship in recreation is a lot healthier and more fun than trying to live up to the iron man tradition by driving yourself on or off the job" (McGee 1957, 29). This image of companionate fatherhood goes beyond the popular adage "the family that plays together, stays together" to suggest that healthful leisure and recreation in an alienating society keeps men alive.

Despite the concern with how the norms of middle-class white manhood drove men to endure forms of violence against the self within an industrial society, this was not a feminist-inspired men's movement. As Dr. Robert H. Felix, director of the National Institute of Mental Health, argued, "Each year thousands of able, ambitious, hard-working men are cut down in the prime of their careers by psychological and physiological ailments. Aside from the human tragedy which this entails for them and their families, *the cost to their business firms in terms of lost executive talent—is incalculable*" ("How to Live with Job Pressure" 1965, emphasis added).[16] Within the institutional realities of MIK, this discourse, like the field of psychology (Deleuze and Guattari 1977), was primarily concerned with organizing middle-class lifestyles in order to adjust men to the alienating conditions of the postwar political economy. The concern with men's health was directed not only at men; a 1953 article in *McCall's* provided wives with a ten-point plan instructing them on how to manage their husband's health (Stare 1953). Thus, white men were encouraged through allied articulations in media to remain goal oriented but also to manage their health (with a wife's aid) so that they could remain productive workers.

Football as public rituals in staged media events, whether on the White House lawn or in Memorial Stadium, constructs powerful, nationalistic imagery of a fortified masculinity. In the rest of the book I attempt to understand how sport and media intersected in the early period of the Cold War and participated in the governance of citizens during a period of economic expansion and growing militarism. I do this by looking at interlinked discourses on college football, broadcasting, and the Cold War across a range of different sources including newspapers, magazines, broadcast manuals, popular and academic texts, and educational films from the era.

# 3 · DUCK WALKING THE COUCH POTATO

## Exercise as Therapy for a Consumer Society

It is paradoxical that the very economic progress, the technological advance and scientific breakthroughs which have, in part, been the result of our national vigor have also contributed to the draining of that vigor. Technology and automation have eliminated many of those physical exertions which were once a normal part of the working day.

—John F. Kennedy, "The Vigor We Need," 1962

IN *THE AFFLUENT SOCIETY* (1958) John Kenneth Galbraith warned that a constant focus on material production would have dire consequences for wealthy societies like the United States. *The Affluent Society* was largely a polemic against dominant economic theories that held constant economic growth was necessary to increase social welfare and security. Galbraith responded to the "conventional wisdom" in economics that the overemphasis on material growth created a social imbalance between investment in the private and public sectors and ultimately lowered a nation's security and quality of life (Kristol 1958). Galbraith put clear voice to the concern that the postwar's affluence and political economy had negative consequences on social life and national security although his specific concern was with developing economic theories appropriate to an advanced stage of industrial capitalism.

*The Affluent Society* presented an original challenge to the conventional wisdom within economics, but his concern that postwar affluence carried social costs was echoed by other public intellectuals of his day. The 1950s saw the publication of several classic social critiques that argued the rise of large corporations as the employers and engines of postwar affluence had profound and often negative effects upon social life, including David Riesman's *The Lonely Crowd*

(1950), C. Wright Mills's *White Collar* (1951), William Whyte's *The Organization Man* (1956), and Vance Packard's *The Hidden Persuaders* (1957). Historian James Gilbert (2005) argues that the mass culture critiques of the 1950s saw the affluence tied to employment in large corporations, the middle-class movement into the suburbs, and the rising consumer culture as impeding the development of rugged individualism and ultimately effeminizing postwar men. In other words, the social, economic, and demographic transformations that took place in the postwar era triggered concerns about the loss of middle-class men's masculinity (see also Spigel 1992, 61).

The concern that postwar affluence led to a national loss of manhood for professional class men expressed in these classic texts was also attached to the bodies of young white men. Anxieties regarding the manhood of U.S. youth expressed a concern for the nation in the present and future since the nation's destiny is generally viewed as resting upon the shoulders of the young (Miller and Leger 2003). The anxiety that young white men were effeminized by postwar culture took on a Cold War coloring when it received the name "the muscle gap," suggesting that U.S. youth were physically falling behind Soviet boys. Muscle gap discourse was produced by politicians, academics, physical educators, doctors, and journalists who were united only to the degree that they agreed consumer culture was simultaneously central to waging the Cold War, since it symbolized the American way of life, and was a key barrier to winning the Cold War, since consumerism took away the rigors experienced by previous generations, as seen in the quotation by John F. Kennedy at the beginning of this chapter.

Muscle gap anxieties were infused with assumptions regarding race, gender, and national destiny in the context of changing U.S. class relations. These assumptions become clear in how muscle gap rhetoric framed U.S. history within a Manifest Destiny metanarrative of progress and expansion. The nation was born out of the wilderness, muscle gap critics claimed, through the purposive efforts of strong brave men, what Riesman called inner-directed. The efforts of our rugged forefathers, the argument went on, led to the establishment of the wealthiest and most technologically advanced civilization the world has ever known. Now, the security of the nation and its historical mission of constant territorial and political expansion lay upon the shoulders of the young. Postwar affluence had flattened class differences, but it also removed the rigors of daily life that the earlier generations of men had experienced. As a result, postwar affluence was causing white America to grow too soft to carry out the nation's historical mission. Consumerism and consumer comfort, it was argued, was cultivating a generation of soft youth who, if not corrected, would ultimately deplete the masculinity of the nation at a moment of intense geopolitical competition with the Soviet Union. Stated crudely, consumerism was producing soft youth and a soft nation open to communist penetration. During the muscle gap period, national programs of physical education became the means to ameliorate contradictions in the Cold War political economy and fortify the manhood of the nation's young men.

## ORIGINS OF THE MUSCLE GAP

The muscle gap began in 1954 when Philadelphia businessman and former national sculling champion John B. Kelly was "horrified" by the results of the Kraus-Weber Minimal Fitness Tests. The crux of the findings was that out of 4,264 U.S. children given the Kraus-Weber tests (six exercises that test strength and flexibility), 57.9 percent failed to meet minimum standards. Out of 2,879 European kids of comparable socioeconomic background from Switzerland, Austria, and Italy, only 8.7 percent failed to meet the minimum standards ("Is American Youth Physically Fit?" 1957; also Prudden 1956, 5). Kelly had led an underfunded, unsuccessful national fitness campaign in 1947 (Prudden 1956, 4) and saw the Kraus-Weber tests results as creating an opportunity to expand physical education. So he passed the report to Senator James Duff of Pennsylvania, who in turn took the results to President Dwight D. Eisenhower, who reportedly was "shocked" (Boyle 1955). In addition to the Kraus-Weber results, selective service statistics reported that out of 4.7 million draftees called up between 1950 and 1957, 1.6 million, or "roughly one-third," were "found unfit for duty" for physical or mental reasons ("Is American Youth Physically Fit?" 1957).

The publication of the Kraus-Weber results and selective service statistics created an image of declining physical fitness among young Americans relative to European youth. At the same time, the rapid rise of Soviet athletes to dominance of the Summer Olympics following Helsinki in 1952 made the Soviet Union appear like a nation of red muscle men (see Beamish and Ritchie 2005; Massaro 2003; also Domer 1976). The debates surrounding the Olympics indicated not only that athletics was perceived as a cultural arena of geopolitical struggle in the early Cold War (Thomas 2002) but also that bodies were weapons in that struggle and the United States should invest in developing its human resources to meet the Soviet challenge. The fear of Soviet muscular advantage led to calls for a strategy to "close the muscle gap" (e.g., Eastman 1961).

The muscle gap, like the missile gap that began after the Soviet Union launched *Sputnik* in 1957, emerged from contradictions inherent to Cold War foreign policy and culture. U.S. foreign policy throughout the Cold War was a two-prong endeavor called the strategy of containment, described in chapter 2. The two prongs worked together to highlight weaknesses in the Soviet system by first fostering markets for the circulation of Western commodities and second by limiting Soviet activity in order to shrink its markets and ability to provide for a growing, dissatisfied population (Klein 2003, 16; Nitze 1993, 41, 71; also Gaddis

1982; May 1999; Nadel 1995). According to the theory of containment, the military and economic prongs of containment together would lead to the internal collapse of the Soviet Union and the global hegemony of U.S. capitalism.

The primary goal of the economic strategy was to demonstrate capitalism's ability to "win of the hearts and minds" of people throughout the world by raising standards of living. Economic development was seen as necessary to create an affluent society that would shore up support at home and abroad for the U.S.'s larger Cold War objectives. As a result, the U.S. saw its struggle with the Soviet Union as akin to a fencing match where "the weapons are not only the development of military power but the loyalties and convictions of hundreds of millions" (Gaddis 1982, 50). As John F. Kennedy wrote in his famous "Soft American" article in *Sports Illustrated*, "We face in the Soviet Union a powerful and implacable adversary determined to show the world that only the Communist system possesses the vigor and determination necessary to satisfy awakening aspirations for progress and the elimination of poverty and want" (Kennedy 1960). Containment made U.S. consumer culture a powerful ideological tool that could demonstrate capitalism's ability to fulfill the promise of modernity as well as create a sphere of life where citizens could demonstrate loyalty and participate in the Cold War without sacrifice (Sturken 2007, 58). Ideally, capitalism would bring "the good life" to people around the world through the proliferation of consumerism and provide citizens with the freedom to choose from a bevy of brands (Cohen 2003). In other words, consumerism became a model for citizenship and consumption the measure of liberty.

Building free markets that excluded the Soviet Union led containment to envision a world that was simultaneously open and closed. While containment encouraged receptivity to foreign access in "open societies" (i.e., capitalist countries), isolating nations of the Warsaw Pact made penetration and defense of valorized space a key concern for Cold War foreign policy (Costigliola 1997). Alan Nadel captures this tension by describing the strategy of containment as a sexual narrative of "courtship and rivalry" where the Blob serves as a metaphor for the Soviet Union—a power flow, fluid in nature and running in allowable spaces (Nadel 1995, 5). Consequently, U.S. opposition had to be prophylactic since containing the Kremlin's seminal trajectory would reveal its economic impotence and effect internal change (Nadel 1995, 15–18; see also Costigliola 1997; Cuordileone 2000). The sexualized nature of Cold War discourse expressed deep anxieties not only for the openness of capitalist societies but also for the permeability of soft male citizens. If citizens grew soft, they, like an open society, could become receptive to communist penetration.

The sexualized and homophobic nature of muscle gap discourse points to its key problematic. If consumerism created a sphere of life where consumer citizens could participate in the Cold War without sacrifice, then consumerism could also present a barrier when citizens are called upon to make sacrifices and asked to do what they could for their country. So as much as it was caused by any real or imagined differences in the fitness of youth in the United States and Europe, the muscle gap emerged in the gap between the two prongs of containment. The dual prongs of containment made imperialism and consumerism two sides of the same military-industrial-Keynesian political economy, which meant that consumer-citizens were as important to contesting the Cold War as citizen-soldiers. However, the self-sacrificing ethos and Spartan discipline necessary for citizen-soldiers came into contradiction with the self-centered hedonism of consumer citizenship (see Miller 2007, 22–25).

The split between hard-disciplined and soft-indulgent citizens within muscle gap discourse constituted Cold War youth as what Toby Miller terms "ethically incomplete," where "ethics" refers to a person's ability to draw upon "moral codes to manage one's conduct" (Miller 1993, xii). In a social context characterized by indeterminacy, Miller suggests that citizens become aware of and see in themselves profound ethical dilemmas that lead them to rely on the advice of experts in order to self-govern. Contradictions in the political economy of the Cold War produced a paradoxical cultural environment in which youth were taught to see themselves as incomplete and in need of physical, mental, and moral improvement. The construction of youth as incomplete and in need of improvement necessitated cultural policy that would teach youth, their parents, and their educators how to constantly work upon and adjust them to the contradictory needs of the capitalist state. In this sense the call for physical education as a strategy to close the muscle gap was in fact a regime of subjectification that could manage the bodies and energy of citizens by teaching them to manage themselves (see Markula and Pringle 2006). And in this way Cold War imperatives became inscribed upon the bodies of youth as they produced themselves as citizens.

Given that the burden of soldiering and working in the factories of the military-industrial Keynesian political economy fell largely on the shoulders of young white men, the bodies of white boys became the site where the contradictions between militarism and consumerism produced the greatest angst. Cultural policy in the form of national, mandatory physical education programs was held up as the means to close the muscle gap. Physical education as the solution to the problem of government had historical precedent in both the military and public education as a cultural technology for managing the bodies of young men since discipline in physical education training is directed at both the bodies and minds of pupils (Kirk 1998; O'Hanlon 1980; Pope 1995). The establishment of a national, mandatory physical education program obscured contradictions that emerged from Cold War foreign policy and allowed young men to be plugged into the Cold War's political economy as workers, warriors, and consumers.

## MUSCLE GAP, MISSILE GAP, AND
## THE LANGUAGE OF COLD WAR FITNESS

In a speech to his troops during the Korean War, Colonel Lewis "Chesty" Puller (U.S. Marine Corps) rested America's destiny on the bodies of its youth in describing the needed preparation for the small wars of the Cold War.[1] "I want you to make 'em [your families] understand. Our country won't go on forever, if we stay soft as we are now. There won't be an America. Because some foreign soldiers will invade us and take our women and breed a hardier race" (cited in Slotkin 1992, 363). Although the Cold War was not always described as a racial war in terms familiar to Theodore Lothrop Stoddard (1920), Colonel Puller's quote makes clear how the Cold War's "police actions" were often understood in frontier terms that were familiar from the United States's own history of Manifest Destiny, pitting a white man's burden of spreading democracy and civilization against the threat of racial contamination (Slotkin 1992, 363; see also Borstelmann 2001; Horne 1999; Klein 2003; von Eschen 1997). Puller further suggests that the American way of life itself as it had developed in the post–World War II era created a threat to U.S. democracy. Therefore, to protect U.S. democracy and racial purity a strategy was needed to harden America's young men to fight the many small wars that made up the Cold War.

The emergence of the muscle gap in the early Cold War should be understood within two historical frames. First, we can understand it within a cyclical pattern of postwar reactions to the rate of wartime draft rejections and a general concern that modern culture feminizes male citizens (Huyssen 1986, 47), which had formed the tenor of Teddy Roosevelt's 1899 speech "The Strenuous Life." A similar pattern followed the Revolutionary War, the Civil War, World War I, and World War II (Dean 1998, 35; Lee 1983, 228; Welch 1996, 175). Dissatisfaction with potential wartime draftees in postwar periods has been a major impetus for the development of physical education in public schools (Kirk 1997; Weston 1962). As early as 1946 commentators expressed concerns about the physical fitness of U.S. soldiers during the Second World War as measured by draft rejection rates and discharge rates based on injuries (Hershey 1946; Rusk 1947). Major General Lewis B. Hershey, the director of the Selective Service System, argued that the lack of a national physical education program cost the nation enormously as a result of the number of rejects for physical, mental, or moral reasons. He also argued that the private sector was depleted of talent since it made up for the high rejection rates. Hershey thus called for a national, mandatory physical education program. "This training should not be reserved alone for those who are physically able to assume the full responsibilities of military duty. It should be given to all male citizens able to participate in it and to benefit by it. The best in citizenship will come only when the citizen has given of his time and his effort—a part of his life as it were—to prepare himself for the protection of his country" (Hershey 1946, 54). In a dawning era of MIK, militarists like Hershey saw the constant preparation of citizens for wars as a necessary part of everyday life and education.

Educational and civic leaders throughout the early twentieth century saw physical education as an effective means to manage the bodies of youth because it used popular recreational activities to "cultivate desirable attitudes and behaviors" in the process of building bodies for citizenship (O'Hanlon 1980, 89). Sport and physical fitness have been embraced by the U.S. military since at least the Spanish-American War as a means for training and managing the bodies of recruits (Pope 1995). Figure 3.1 is a World War II–era recruiting poster that links the physical and mental development of young men to the military and the military to developing the bodies of young white men. The poster suggests that exercise has the ability to organize, manage, and harden young boys' bodies as they become men. Interestingly, none of the boys shown are actually old enough for conscription. The poster further suggests a unity of mind and body, which was a recurring theme of muscle gap discourse, so that physical development and the hardening of bodies lead to mental and moral development. Therefore, when U.S. prisoners of war were "brainwashed" in Korea, it signified physical and mental weakness on the part of "our boys" (Mrozek 1995, 258).

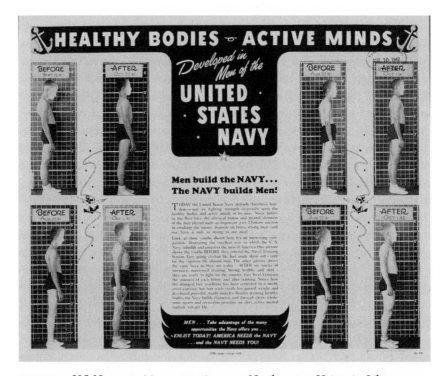

FIGURE 3.1 U.S. Navy recruiting poster, circa 1942. Northwestern University Library, http://www.library.northwestern.edu/govpub/collections/wwii-posters/img/ww1646–84.

This first frame underscores enduring cultural schemas that defined a hard, aggressive masculinity as central to national security. Robert Griswold points out, "The concern for physical fitness [during the muscle gap], at its core, set about redeeming manhood, reenergizing masculinity, and restoring force, dynamism, and control to males in a culture full of doubts and contradictions about men's future" (Griswold 1998, 325). Donald Mrozek makes a similar point in describing imagery of physical education during the muscle gap as expressing a ritualization of pain that was central to the fortification masculinity (Mrozek 1995, 266). Griswold's and Mrozek's use of terms like "manhood" and "masculinity" to construct men as a universal category, however, obscures much of the racial and class anxiety coded in the language and the imagery of the muscle gap. The anxieties driving the muscle gap did not simply focus on male bodies; they responded to a culture of affluence and adhered to middle-class white male bodies—the archetypal U.S. citizen (Glenn 2002) upon which the national heritage is constructed.

If we employ only the first frame—modern culture effeminizing male youth and postwar reactions to deficiencies in wartime draftees—then we would theorize the Cold War reaction as a passive repetition of history structurally indistinguishable from previous or later cycles. However, the Cold War coloring of the discourse suggests a need for greater nuance. Therefore, I suggest a second frame that is less passive and contextualizes the focus on white male bodies within the period. So while imperialists like Teddy Roosevelt have historically fetishized hard white men, Cold War homophobia complicated muscle gap discourse by seeing soft white male bodies as open to communist penetration. During this period, homosexuality was imagined to be a hidden and subversive other that negatively defined and disciplined a hard masculine norm (see Corber 1997; Johnson 2004; also Friedman 2005). Furthermore, this second frame clarifies how government intervention in the social body drew upon familiar cultural schemas to foster a new cultural formation based on the deployment of modern technologies of health and fitness in socializing institutions. Cultural policy deployed physical education, which I term "political technologies of bodily transformation," in the arena of health, fitness, and lifestyle in order to fortify self-regulating masculine citizens consistent with Cold War imperatives.

The second frame complicates the contention that the state made decisions and the people got in line. Rather, it highlights how an interaction between government and citizens through institutional dynamics led to clear transformations in lifestyle and popular culture. Gorski's (2003b) metaphor of state formation as a "top-down" and a "bottom-up" process is useful. On the one hand, state mandate extended and professionalized physical education, as when Eisenhower created the President's Council on Youth Fitness (PCYF) that Kennedy later expanded into the President's Council on Physical Fitness (PCPF) (Weston 1962). On the other hand, by defining itself as the "leader of the Free World" in opposition to the "Slave World" of the Soviet Union, the United States and its Cold War liberalism eschewed policy directives obligating citizens' compliance since that is inconsistent with fostering self-regulating, independent subjects. Moreover, people at both the national and local levels saw the muscle gap as creating opportunities for political and professional advancement. So U.S. cultural policy supported institutions in civil society and the economy such as schools, the Boy Scouts of America, Little League baseball, the Amateur Athletic Union, Wheaties Sports Federation, and Union Oil's 76 Sports Club that maximized citizens' self-direction and self-regulation. Furthermore, nongovernmental actors, such as fitness experts and fitness institutions like the YMCA, helped direct and structure the field of physical education and the habitus that citizens developed through fitness regimes. What we see during the muscle gap period is a moment of hegemony when national and local-level leaders used commonsense understandings of manhood and national purpose framed by the immediacy of the Cold War to direct state power at the bodies of young men through the implementation of cultural policy.

## LOCATING AND DELINEATING MUSCLE GAP DISCOURSE

The muscle gap was a discursive formation that emerged out of a variety of popular, academic, and scientific texts and led to cultural policy concerned with creating self-producing citizens consistent with Cold War imperatives. So my analysis draws largely from close textual analysis of print media and is supported by other relevant texts, particularly from the field of education. For this chapter, I coded 473 articles drawn from a combination of newspapers and popular magazines for repeating themes. I then organized the many subthemes into three larger categories inclusive of most articles.[2] A total of 231 articles were called "muscle gap" since they clearly supported government recommendations. A second group of 164 articles were called "concern not direct" since their framing was consistent with muscle gap discourse, though not directly aligning with it. These articles tended to focus on health and fitness in less overtly political terms, such as when physical educators or medical professionals invoked rhetoric of scientific objectivity to discuss businessmen's health. The use of phrases like "fragile male" and "flabby American" in the 29 "businessmen's health" articles highlights how closely this category parallels muscle gap discourse. The 43 articles in the third category, "skeptical," were critical of the exercise and fitness craze. Figure 3.2 shows the publication pattern of the three main themes over a twenty-year period. We see muscle gap discourse emerge at the conclusion of the Korean War and slowly increase in output throughout the fifties before climaxing with Kennedy in the early sixties. Muscle gap discourse quickly receded after Kennedy's death and the breakup of the liberal consensus of the early Cold War period (1947–1964).

One of the overwhelming impressions one gets when reviewing muscle gap articles is how they couch emotional pleas in scientific and otherwise realist language. Diplomatic historians argue that policy develops not just from rational determinations of national and economic interest but also from the

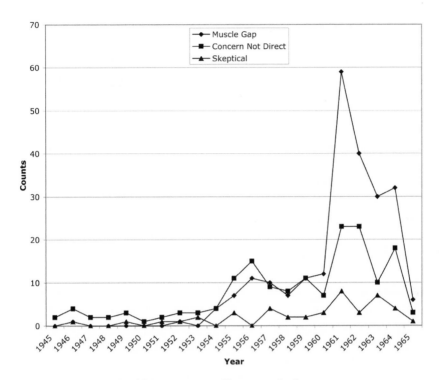

FIGURE 3.2 Publication pattern of fitness articles from 1945 to 1965.

emotion-laden cultural frames of embodied subjects in decision-making positions (see Costigliola 1997; Cuordileone 2000; Dean 1998; Horne 1999; Walton 2004). Enduring cultural schemas of masculinity and race mired in a hard/soft crisis and set in the context of postwar decolonization and confrontation with the Soviet Union gave a Cold War frame to the muscle gap (see Costigliola 1997; Cuordileone 2000). Furthermore, these schemas informed the cultural repertoires, or sets of knowledge that direct strategies of action in the material world (Swidler 1986, 2001) that oriented and united both political leaders' and citizens' perceptions during the early Cold War.

With the postwar framed in terms of modern society effeminizing those male citizens responsible for upholding the national heritage of political, economic, and territorial expansion, government enacted cultural policy that disciplined citizens with technologies of bodily transformation. Following a series of government-sponsored conferences on national fitness and Eisenhower's creation of the PCYF in 1956, a strategy to close the muscle gap began to form. Four themes guiding muscle gap discourse and policy emerged in my textual analysis; I call these dissemination, surveillance and transformation, development of infrastructure, and social movement building.

Theme 1—Dissemination

Without a national program of education, citizens would neither be conscious of the muscle gap nor have the appropriate cultural repertoires to close it. Media during the muscle gap took on the pedagogical function of teaching the Cold War (see Klein 2003, 13). Therefore, the dissemination of the Kraus-Weber results and Korean War draft rejection rates framed by Cold War anxiety defined the muscle gap discourse. Fear has the political expediency of converting beliefs into prescribed actions (Glassner 1999), and muscle gap discourse came with specific recommendations. I coded 139 articles with recommendations on exercise and/or diet and nutrition, 55 articles addressing lifestyle, and 62 articles making practical suggestions for parents and community leaders on hardening "our boys." The primary method of dissemination was print media, though television shows like the *Flabby American* (Gould 1961) disseminated muscle gap knowledge, as did community- and national-level sports festivals and clinics (20 articles covered events).

Dissemination also occurred through scientific, educational, and popular literature channels. An exemplar of scientific discourse is Hans Kraus and Wilhelm Raab's *Hypokinetic Disease* (1961), which contends a lack of exercise in modern society leads to many of our leading physical ailments, with a chapter that takes up the special problem of youth. Bonnie Prudden's *Is Your Child Really Fit?* (1956) typifies the popular literature targeting parents and educators. Texts like *Is Your Child Really Fit?* warned that despite an appearance of health, postwar kids were growing soft. At the educational level, the PCPF distributed a quarter million copies of the pamphlet *Youth Physical Fitness* (1961), which guided primary and secondary schools in adopting "desirable" age- and gender-appropriate workouts in "their own local situations" that students could complete in fifteen minutes (Wilkinson 1962).[3] Educational films like Encyclopedia Britannica's *Eat for Health* (1954) and Coronet Instructional Films' *Rest and Exercise* (1949) and *Getting Ready Physically* (1951) saw national distribution in public schools. These examples demonstrate multiple levels of knowledge production that utilize different styles of rhetorical address to construct the same muscle gap frame of national strength tied to male bodies in need of health interventions for five different audiences (health professionals, policy makers, school administrators, parents, and students).

Theme 2—Surveillance and Transformation

The creation of national standards tied to a series of metrics (goals, testing, and recording) designed to measure, hierarchize, and place youth within a national matrix of bodies was seen as central to disaggregating a national mass of bodies so that weak ones could be identified and made subject to technologies of bodily transformation. When Kennedy changed the PCYF into the PCPF to target the entire population, not just youth, when he appointed the legendary University of

Oklahoma football coach Charles "Bud" Wilkinson as its director,[4] and when the council disseminated *Youth Physical Fitness*, national programs of surveillance and transformation were given material form. I coded fifty newspaper and magazine articles that highlighted the importance of testing, most of which included illustrated instructions on exercises and tests for parents to administer at home.

Consistent with the postwar embrace of science and technology, much of the muscle gap discourse framed the solution to male softness in medical-scientific discourse. I coded thirty-eight articles as "medico-scientific"; however, the language and assumptions infused many more. In this discourse, a triage model of fitness testing was seen as the way to diagnose and cure a sick society by creating self-surveilling citizens who take charge of their own health needs. Just as a doctor develops a health profile useful to the patient, the phys ed instructor would develop a fitness profile useful to the student. As years pass, the student would compare present scores to past scores to measure successes and failures (Hunsicker 1959). In this way, state surveillance becomes self-surveillance where the imperatives of the Cold War state are bodily inscribed on the life histories and practices of citizens as they produce themselves. The scientifically built white body provided the surface upon which Cold War masculinity was written into citizenship (see Foucault 1984, 83). Figure 3.3 shows how to perform

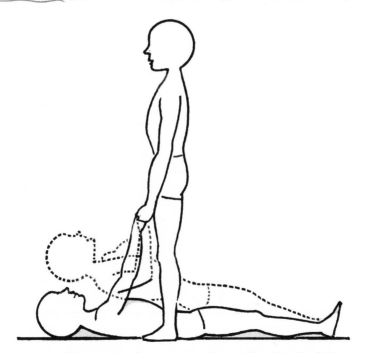

FIGURE 3.3 Illustration that demonstrates reclining pull-ups. President's Council on Physical Fitness, *Youth Physical Fitness: Suggested Elements of a School-Centered Program* (Washington, DC: Government Printing Office, 1961), 30.

a two-person exercise and is an example of the sort of political technology of bodily transformation that filled the government pamphlet *Youth Physical Fitness*. Muscle gap newspaper and magazine articles often contained similar illustrations that were generally directed toward mothers who could monitor the fitness of their children. Figure 3.4 reproduces a fitness chart that teachers could use to organize students into a matrix of adequate and inadequate bodies. Those

SAMPLE RECORD FORM FOR IDENTIFICATION OF PHYSICALLY UNDERDEVELOPED PUPILS

Teacher *Mrs. Bayer*                                    School Year *Fall 1961*

Period or Section *6th Grade*                           Date of 1st Test *9/25/61*

School *Cumberland*

BOYS

| Name of Pupil | Pull Ups Ages 10–13; 1 14–15; 2 16–17; 3 | | | Sit Ups Ages 10–17; 14 | | | Squat Thrust Ages 10–17; 4 | | | Remarks* |
|---|---|---|---|---|---|---|---|---|---|---|
| | 1st Test | | Retest | 1st Test | | Retest | 1st Test | | Retest | |
| | Pass | Fail | Date Passed | Pass | .Fail | Date Passed | Pass | Fail | Date Passed | |
| *Adair, Robert* | ✓ | | | ✓ | | | ✓ | | | *Exceptional* |
| *Bosch, Peter* | | ✓ | *11/6/61* | ✓ | | | ✓ | | | *should exercise at home.* |
| | | | | | | | | | | |
| | | | | | | | | | | |
| | | | | | | | | | | |
| | | | | | | | | | | |
| | | | | | | | | | | |
| | | | | | | | | | | |
| | | | | | | | | | | |
| | | | | | | | | | | |
| | | | | | | | | | | |
| | | | | | | | | | | |
| | | | | | | | | | | |
| | | | | | | | | | | |
| | | | | | | | | | | |
| | | | | | | | | | | |

*Enter here any conditions, e.g., obesity, posture, etc., that may affect physical performance.

FIGURE 3.4 Fitness chart that standardizes groups of students. President's Council on Physical Fitness, *Youth Physical Fitness: Suggested Elements of a School-Centered Program* (Washington, DC: Government Printing Office, 1961), 24.

found to be inadequate through comparison to a scientifically generated norm of physical fitness could then be disaggregated in individualized charts, such as figure 3.5, for increased surveillance and personalized disciplinary regimes.

Theme 3—Development of Infrastructure

Facilities for training bodies and leaders were necessary to successfully inscribe Cold War ideology on the physical and the human landscape of the nation. This meant surveying existing fitness facilities to determine available resources and

INDIVIDUAL PUPIL SCREENING TEST RECORD
(For use with cumulative health record)

This separate form is not necessary if space for recording the screening test is added to the regular health record form.

PUPIL_____

GRADE_____

SCHOOL_____

TEACHER_____

| TYPE OF TEST | FIRST TEST DATE: | | RETEST DATE PASSED: |
|---|---|---|---|
| | PASS | FAIL | |
| SIT UPS | | | |
| PULL UPS | | | |
| SQUAT THRUST | | | |

REMARKS:

SIGNED_____
Teacher or Nurse

DATE _____

FIGURE 3.5 Fitness chart that individualizes students. President's Council on Physical Fitness, *Youth Physical Fitness: Suggested Elements of a School-Centered Program* (Washington, DC: Government Printing Office, 1961), 26.

inform funding decisions; fifty-five articles were specifically concerned with the quantity, quality, and funding of fitness facilities. This also called for training more physical education teachers as well as increased research to inform policy and decision making on the use and the development of fitness infrastructure. A 1962 Associated Press article claimed that with Kennedy's emphasis on targeted funding, "fitness programs [have] more than doubled" (Tolchin 1962). This highlights the role of knowledge production in how governments manage a state's complex ensemble of human and nonhuman resources (Foucault 1991).

### Theme 4—Social Movement Building

Citizen leadership was critical to closing the muscle gap at a minimal cost to the state and to differentiate the U.S. liberal approach to social problems from the Soviet "totalitarian" approach. The primary sites of intervention were schools and homes, but recreation centers and YMCAs took on greater importance, as did extracurricular activities like Little League baseball and the Boy Scouts. Furthermore, participation in government programs by "enlightened businesses," like the Wheaties Sports Federation and Union Oil's 76 Sports Club (Fitness Footnotes 1959), acting as responsible "corporate citizens" (King 2003) was seen as crucial to hardening the nation. In a 1963 *Recreation* article, "Bud" Wilkinson describes a strategy to increase fitness in a community by organizing an urban regime (a grouping of public workers and/or private citizens that forms to influence local policy) of local government, schools, and businesses where as chairman "a real crusader for a cause he deems worthwhile" can coordinate local fitness policy and ensure community buy-in through effective public relations (Wilkinson 1962). Actually this describes a local version of Wilkinson's position on the PCPF that served to coordinate national fitness policy and engage civic support through dissemination of fitness information (Wolf 1964).

Part of the logic of the social movement theme was that citizens' obligation to maintain their health and fitness required that they step outside of the family circle to work on community fitness, and thereby increase the health and strength of the nation. As Wilkinson told parents, "[T]he conditions in our country's schools depend on you. They are your schools, and educators will respond to your whishes" (Wilkinson 1961, 148). In this statement, Wilkinson's direct address interpellates the reader into a body of engaged-citizens working at the grassroots level to improve the nation's fitness infrastructure. The reader of this article, published in *Parents Magazine*, would likely be a mother interested in ideas about childrearing. Wilkinson's parenting advice suggests a modernized version of "Republican Motherhood" (see Salmon 2000, 176) that channels women's political energy into building the nation through domestic concerns such as their children's health. The grassroots strategy of building a fitness movement in a manner consistent with a free society shows how women, through caring for others, can participate in reifying an ascendant form of masculinity.

One outcome of the muscle gap was the rise of national and local-level fitness events. Beginning in the mid-fifties, sports festivals and clinics were held throughout the country to demonstrate the physical fitness of a local school or a Boy Scout troop and to encourage citizens to take up the disciplined ethic of self on display. In 1959, the American Association for Health, Physical Education, and Recreation organized "Operation Fitness—U.S.A." to target youths through schools and community recreation centers for participation in "self-improvement" programs by staging local and national fitness competitions ("A New Lease on Fitness" 1959). Also in 1959, *Sports Illustrated* dedicated twelve pages of coverage to Eisenhower's proclamation that the week of May 3 was National Youth Fitness Week with a photo series demonstrating youth from elementary schools to colleges engaging in a variety of activities in diverse sites that included a Boys' Club, a YMCA, a private all-girls high school, and Purdue University. Consistent with the notion of citizenship that erases difference in universality while simultaneously reifying the very differences it seeks to efface (Warner 1993, 239), in the thirty-two photographs in the article, mostly featuring groups of people, only one boy playing basketball in a Rhode Island Boy's Club is not visibly white ("1959 National Youth Fitness Week" 1959). Despite the racial homogeneity not actually reflective of the postwar United States, the photo series performs "a narrative of the nation" by representing citizens across geography and class simultaneously participating in a national narrative of exercise and good health as rights and obligations of citizenship (Anderson 1991; Bhabha 1991).

For fitness as local-national "street theater," nothing compares to the Kennedy-era hike craze that later returned in the form of "walkathons" (see King 2003). In 1963, Kennedy recalled Teddy Roosevelt's requirement that every Marine be capable of hiking fifty miles in three days without spending more than twenty hours on their feet (Rusk 1963). The public responded, as if challenged, by staging single-day fifty-mile hikes (as well as bike rides) in communities across the nation throughout 1963 (and in memorial to Kennedy in 1964).[5] Sports sociologist Michael A. Messner explains that goal orientation and a desire for public recognition within his school's "Rah! Rah!" Cold War atmosphere drove him over the course of a year to be its first student to earn the "JFK 50-Mile Run Award" despite a personal aversion to running (pers. comm., September 2004). Cold War walkathons as theaters of participatory citizenship mobilized the populace with an ethical fervor to demonstrate commitment to the nation's Cold War mission through personal dedication and sacrifice[6]—a classic example of patriotic pageantry (see chapter 4).

## MILITARIZATION OF THE SOCIAL BODY

The muscle gap desire to make our boys hard led logically to constructing the military as a model for society. The Kennedy-Wilkinson plan for every school in the nation to subject students to at least fifteen minutes a day of calisthenics to train masses of students and single out weaklings for extra attention clearly follows a military model of disciplinary efficiency that has a long history in public education (see Foucault 1979). The Kennedy administration also provided support for teachers to implement the fifteen-minute calisthenics program. In 1962 the PCPF produced "The Youth Fitness Song," commonly referred as "The Chicken Fat Song," for its chorus: "Give that chicken fat / back to the chicken / and don't be chicken again."[7] The environment created by classes of children cheerily performing group calisthenics in unison to the martial sound of "The Youth Fitness Song" transforms the social space of the classroom into a citizen-producing machine where fitness and discipline become synonymous with health and bravery (see Foucault 1979, 147). Or as Kennedy expressed in his "Soft American" article, just as victory on the battlefield was built on "the playing fields of Eton," our American civilization was "won on the playgrounds and corner lots and fields of America" (Kennedy 1960, 15, 16).[8]

The militarization of public education when following the PCPF recommendations were put on display in a 1962 *Look* magazine article that hailed La Sierra High in Carmichael, California. The article features nine photos of white male high school students doing physical exercises while wearing nothing but shorts, sneakers, and expressions of pain (see fig. 3.6).[9] The article claims that physical education director and football coach Stan LeProtti's adaptation of the PCPF's program "popularizes compulsory exercises by giving 'group status' to average, nonathletic youths" (Gordon 1962, 49). The result is a program that uses symbols of hierarchy, like color-coded shorts, to signify fitness rankings and group dynamics to create a hypercompetitive environment where boys gain status from personal achievement in a military-style regime of bodily transformation. The structural dynamics of the program invests increasing status in boys who enthusiastically reproduce themselves through "compulsory exercises" closest to a military model of masculinity. High-status boys are further rewarded, the article explains, by increased admiration of female students who supported the program. The program thus actively mobilizes power dynamics of homosocial and heterosexual sexuality to gain male and female participation in a system of domination that inscribes Cold War ideology upon male bodies.

### Imperial Modeling—Militarized Manhood and White Supremacy

Jean Mayer, in a 1955 *New York Times Magazine* article, "Muscular State of the Union," effectively sums up desired muscle gap interventions as an updated social contract:

La Sierra blues are
required to top Navy
plebes on pull-ups

FIGURE 3.6 Boys at La Sierra High demonstrate strength and flexibility. E. Theisen, "LA Sierra High Shows How American Kids Can Get Physically Tough," *Look*, January 30, 1962, 50–51.

Perhaps the most effective method [to keep the population active and fit] would be to inculcate all young people with the tenet which has long been an effective lesson of British public schools: if society has brought you up as an educated person, it is your duty to keep fit so that in return for what you have received you may be of some use in an emergency to your neighbors and to your country.[10]

Mayer's quote suggests that the United States should take Imperial Britain as a model in building citizens, which was also an argument for football (see chapter 1). Moreover, membership in national society (citizenship) is based on a system of social relations and mutual obligations stemming back to a state-centered socializing process that "inculcates" a disciplined habitus in young people as they become citizens. Schools as local sites of a national educational field inculcating "enduring, transposable dispositions" in citizens suggests Pierre Bourdieu's (1977) notion of habitus forms across local, regional, and national scales. Citizens' habitus does not simply form at their local context but integrates them within larger structural formations of similarly acting subjects (Stoddart 1988). So when cultural policy takes the ethic of British boarding schools (see Mangan 1986; Morford and McIntosh 1993) for socializing U.S. citizens, cultural repertoires consistent with the structural needs of imperialism are inculcated in the habitus at a local level.

### American (Un)exceptionalism

Muscle gap discourse was rife with the contradictions that flowed from the dual prongs of containment. A central narrative emerges from muscle gap discourse, which I call "American (un)exceptionalism," driven by an Orwellian logic of "success equals failure." This narrative states that our national heritage was built through the vigorous activity of "our forefathers" who wrested civilization from the North American wilderness. This civilization gave rise to such a technologically advanced society that its citizens enjoy the highest standard of living the world has ever seen. This standard of living is apparent in vast arrays of consumer goods and measured in the health of its citizens. However, the greatest measures of our success—children who are bigger, heavier, and apparently healthier than previous generations—are also a measure of our failure. Modern technology, the narrative suggests, in producing bigger, healthier kids, also takes away the rigors experienced in the "strenuous life" of previous generations.[11] In essence, the narrative states that "the national heritage" will lead us to decline in the future because of citizens' soft lifestyle in the present, unless cultural policy makes immediate interventions and corrections.

The narrative does not identify the "national heritage" (Manifest Destiny, or the tendency toward territorial and economic expansion) as the problem but the consumer culture of mass society that makes our boys "effeminate." Experts warned that the healthy look of our kids could be deceiving because underneath their big glowing exteriors are "sissies" too soft to fulfill the national mission. Dorothy Barclay wrote in *New York Times Magazine*, "[T]he nation's children this summer presents a picture of general health unmatched in previous history. . . . But what about their fitness, measured in terms of muscular power and endurance?" (Barclay 1958). Critics answered that our effeminate males are getting softer than Europeans, whom we need to lead by example. Max Eastman, for instance, cited a comparative study between U.S. and British youth that showed "in some instances British girls were superior to American boys!" (Eastman 1961). And a New York school official concluded, "All I can say is that it's a good thing our boys don't have babies" since their abdominal muscles are so weak (cited in Boyle 1955, 33).

## Manhood and the National Heritage

The muscle gap's sexualized language is consistent with Cold War ideology deeply concerned with containment and penetration (Costigliola 1997; Cuordileone 2000; Nadel 1995). Cold War discourse was overdetermined by cultural schemas that framed issues of international relations within a common sense of masculinity that sports philosopher Brian Pronger (1999) would describe as simultaneously homoerotic in its desire to penetrate the other and homophobic in its desire to protectively enclose the space of the self. This made gay men appear as security threats since their "deviant lifestyle" made them susceptible to communist penetration through manipulation and blackmail. Furthermore, gay men were constructed as a kind of contagion at the heart of the nation undermining its vigor (see Johnson 2004).

Arthur Schlesinger, in his 1949 treatise *The Vital Center*, initiated the binary hard/soft discourse on U.S. citizens by framing the problem of masculinity as an excess of luxury in a postwar society that produced men lacking the vitality to carry out the liberal-imperialist tradition of Teddy Roosevelt (Cuordileone 2000; Dean 1998). Republicans in the 1950s picked up on Schlesinger's language for a class-based attack on the Democrats' patrician establishment as being too soft on communism, and therefore lacking the masculinity to fight the Soviets (Cuordileone 2000). Kennedy struck back by framing his candidacy and administration in muscle gap discourse that took Teddy Roosevelt's rugged white masculinity as a model of vigorous leadership (Smith 1961). Kennedy, who would famously play touch football on the White House lawn, constructed himself as youthful, vigorous, and healthy in opposition to an aging, unhealthy Eisenhower administration that, like the nation, had grown flaccid (Dean 1998; Walton 2004). Responding to attacks upon his manhood, Vice President Richard Nixon challenged the senator to a fitness test where both candidates would take medical exams and release their medical histories so the public would see who was really more physically fit ("Nixon Issues Health Test Challenge" 1960). At the heart of these cockfights among the political elite was an axiomatic belief that the qualities of leadership in a complex, technological world were synonymous with a British boarding school construction of masculinity: hard, persistent, and plucky (see Mangan 1986; Morford and McIntosh 1993; Stoddart 1988).

## Middle Classes in an Effeminizing Culture

Muscle gap discourse itself reveals a key contradiction in the American (un)exceptionalism narrative. The narrative said that consumer culture produced a soft political body. Therefore, citizens should submit to political technologies of bodily transformation to instill mental and physical discipline so that the empire will be reinvigorated and our democratic heritage protected. This means that two objects in the narrative are infused with anxiety: consumer culture and soft boys. Given the causal ordering, it is revealing that soft boys susceptible to communist penetration were identified as a site of intervention and transformation, but not the consumer culture that produces softness. As Hans Kraus stated in 1954, "We have no wish in trying to change the standard of living by trying to do away with the automobile and TV. But we must make sure that we make up for this loss of physical activity" ("America's Youth" 1960). So rather than addressing the contradiction by restructuring the technologically driven consumer culture or MIK political economy that produces deficient citizens, the solution instituted was additive. As Major General Lewis B. Hershey said, "We've got to learn to stay vigorous and still enjoy luxury" ("Are We Becoming Soft?" 1955, 36). So rather than undermine a culture driven by conspicuous consumption, government intervention would "inculcate" consumer-citizens with discipline and an ethic of self oriented toward public interest rather than self-interest. Indeed, this is the very essence of ethical incompleteness in that citizens are caught in a determined indetermination where cultural policy teaches citizens to manage themselves as disciplined and consuming subjects. This ethical incompleteness became manifest through the strategy of containment that held the American way of life as crucial to winning the Cold War. We must also keep in mind that MIK was a governance paradigm that resolved contradictions in managing an advanced capitalist economy and liberal democracy without undermining the managerial prerogatives or capital accumulation of leading hegemonic capitalist class fractions (Waddell 1999, 2001).

Muscle gap discipline presents an especially modern social anxiety since it linked indolence to postwar affluence, as opposed to earlier periods that were equally concerned with unruly immigrant populations. Baseball commissioner Ford Frick claimed, "Today a youngster will back out the car to go a few blocks to the store for five pounds of potatoes, then have them delivered or get an attendant to lift the bag into the car" (Stull 1956). Frick's concern that modern mechanized society makes young people lazy and soft relative to earlier generations assumes youth have access to expensive consumer goods such as cars, televisions, and laborsaving appliances more typical of upper-middle-class homes. Fifty-four articles expressed analogous concerns about citizens' lifestyle in an affluent society. The assumption that all youth are affluent and indolent hides the many working-class youth, especially racialized minorities, economically forced to work throughout the 1950s and 1960s with limited access to laborsaving devices. Muscle gap discourse thus reified the image of America as a classless society central to Cold War ideology by effacing actually existing class inequalities. The exclusive focus on the symptoms of class privilege in muscle gap discourse obscures the social relations of domination those privileges are built upon.[12] Although internally contradictory, the additive model of muscle gap physical education (consumerism plus exercise equals a disciplined habitus) supported the military and economic prongs of the strategy of containment. Political technologies of bodily transformation would make male citizens hard enough to serve as global cops in the jungles of the Third World or the factories of the military-industrial Keynesian economy and still participate in the consumerist culture necessary to demonstrate U.S. economic and cultural supremacy.

## White Supremacy: The Goal of Empire

The very name "muscle gap" makes clear how a traditionally hard and aggressive version of masculinity became ascendant through allied articulations of state, media, and private-sector forces during the Cold War, but the dynamics of race are less clear. Being the leader of the Free World made the U.S. history of racism and white supremacy a liability to its Cold War objectives. The result was the embracing of some civil rights legislation and the whitewashing of racial rhetoric in favor of clearly anticommunist discourse (see Borstelmann 2001; Dudziak 2000; Horne

1999; Plummer 1996; von Eschen 1996, 1997). Indeed, muscle gap discourse makes no explicit reference to race and cloaks difference in abstract references to citizenship and "national heritage." In order to see the white racial formulation within muscle gap discourse, we must look between the imperialist lines.

The anticommunist stance of the United States was formally nonracial and thus moved away from the racialized language of colonialism. However, calling anticolonial movements "communist" rearticulated the West's imperialist project. As Horne argues, "The tagging of anticolonials as 'red' slowed down the movement against colonialism and—perhaps not coincidentally—gave 'white supremacy' a new lease on life" (Horne 1999, 454). The rearticulation of imperialism necessitates sensitivity to white supremacy in understanding Cold War policies (Horne 1999, 438), a fact unfortunately but understandably overlooked by many African American and labor leaders in the late 1940s when they replaced opposition to colonialism and capitalism with anticommunism for reasons of political expediency (von Eschen 1997, 107–109; also Wehrle 2003). This is not to overlook Cold War tensions or contradictions such as the desegregation of the armed forces as a process of expanding civil rights that made possible increasing deployments of racialized soldiers to suppress Third World liberation movements (Dudziak 2000, 83–88). Few soldiers experienced this contradiction more acutely than American Indians in Vietnam (TeCube 1999), which only points out the fact that civil rights concessions can also serve to restabilize white supremacy (Borstelmann 2001; Dudziak 2000).

In its invocation of "national heritage" that idealized Teddy Roosevelt's rugged masculinity and the nearly exclusive imagery of young white male and female citizens, the muscle gap was clearly concerned with protecting white America's political, economic, and territorial supremacy from Soviet threats, from Chinese attacks coming out of the Orient, and from the rising tide of youthful nations throughout the Third World (Dean 1998, 46). U.S. "national heritage" can be characterized as a series of violent conquests leading to the established of whiteness as the dominant racial category in U.S. social, cultural, and political life (Omi and Winant 1994, 65–66). In situating vigor within the national heritage, Kennedy, in the tradition of Roosevelt, narrates the history of the United States as a history of vigorous men who "subdued a continent and wrested civilization from the wilderness. . . . And today, in our own time, in the jungles of Asia and on the borders of Europe, a new group of vigorous Americans help maintain the peace of the world and our security as a nation" (Kennedy 1962, 12). The connection of Manifest Destiny, or the period of American expansionism that saw wholesale slaughter of native peoples, the slave trade, and repeated incursions in Latin America and Asia, to the contemporary context makes his muscle gap objectives clear. The Cold War–civil rights project that made racially neutral rhetoric synonymous with nonracist ideology hid the rearticulation of American white supremacy as a leader in global imperialism within a black-white domestic binary (see Dudziak 2000; Horne 1999; von Eschen 1997).

Tracing the muscle gap's development, we see a discourse on white masculinity emerge as a crisis in the 1950s from the changing global conditions of the Cold War, domestic conditions of the civil rights movement, and contradictions in containment. Intellectuals like Schlesinger, Eisenhower, and Kennedy, but also Kraus, Prudden, and Wilkinson, addressed the state by enacting cultural policy that created political technologies of bodily transformation to stabilize the crisis with a rearticulated formation of whiteness: hard, disciplined, and anticommunist (see Omi and Winant 1994, 83–88). Consistent with Kennedy's muscle gap image of cultivating an elite corps of self-sacrificing, rugged white men was his creation of the Green Berets and the Peace Corps, which mirrored the military-humanitarian mission of U.S. foreign policy (Dean 1998, 56; Weston 1962, 103). The muscle gap was explicitly about producing young white male citizens who could penetrate and police the Third World while protectively enclosing the nation from similar penetrations (see Pronger 1999).

## CULTURAL POLICY AND UNRULY YOUTH

Without a doubt, the early Cold War was characterized by a heightened sense of anxiety. Popular films like *The Wild One* (1953), *Rebel Without a Cause* (1955), *Blackboard Jungle* (1955), and *High School Confidential* (1958) expressed a broad concern for juvenile delinquency. Many leading intellectuals in the 1950s held that mass media and youth culture created a barrier between youth and adults so that parents could not impress their value system upon their children. And without a clear value system, youth were drawn to criminal behavior (Gilbert 1986, 3). But what the muscle gap shows is that anxieties over the deviance of youth were not limited to criminality. The muscle gap constructed youth as deviant even when engaging in the normative behavior of enjoying the consumer culture of an affluent society (see McLorg and Taub 1987).

The anxieties about deviance born of affluence were most forcefully directed at and adhered to the bodies of young, white men. Muscle gap discourse claimed that the good news of a greater affluence than previous generations had known hid a darker reality; the acquisition of wealth undermines a nation's ability to maintain wealth. Young men's bodies had grown larger and healthier as a result of increased nutrition and wealth, but they were also growing too soft to maintain a national tradition of political and economic expansion. Like the Blob, the bodies of white male youth were imagined to be growing unruly and out of control, which created a danger to national security. Cold War citizenship, however, demanded that young men prepare to serve their nation through productive employment and military service. So without rational planning and discipline, young men would fall short and the nation would go into decline.

Muscle gap discourse coded unruly youth in gendered and homophobic language of softness and loss of manhood to raise anxieties about the spread of communism. The movement from "masculine" citizen to "feminine" consumer was perceived in the 1950s as a significant problem for U.S. society even beyond the young. As James Gilbert writes of *The Lonely Crowd*, "Riesman implicitly wrote the history of character as a story of the decline of masculinity" (Gilbert 2005, 54). Public intellectuals in the 1950s such as Riesman, Whyte, Mills, and others perceived the social and cultural conditions of postwar society tied to the growth of corporations and suburbs as discouraging men from performing a "traditional" masculinity of rugged individualism, what Riesman termed "inner direction." However, consumerism tied citizens to the Cold War through the economic activity of consumption at the same time that consumerism was the medium in which citizens practiced the liberty promised by cultural capitalism (Cohen 2003; Sturken 2007). This meant that the broader social, economic, and demographic transformations thought to emasculate men were also tied to the political economy of the Cold War.

The centrality of consumerism to a Cold War political economy that also needed citizen-soldiers suggests that not only the bodies of youths but also their actions were unruly. This unruliness, or general failure of youth to act correctly, for muscle gap critics was a manifestation of a faulty character born of affluence (see Miller 2008, 4–5). Muscle gap cultural policy addressed the bodies and character of young men. And as I have argued throughout this chapter, physical education was seen as the solution to the maladies of affluence since it disciplined and developed both the bodies and minds of youth without undermining capitalist relations of production and consumption. Physical education as a "conduct of conduct" was effective because its disciplinary regime adjusted citizens to the political economy of the Cold War.

Physical education as a disciplinary regime also invited youth to produce themselves as subjects of the capitalist state, which made it consistent with Cold War liberalism. As Kennedy stated, "[I]n a very real and immediate sense, our growing softness, our increasing lack of physical fitness, is a menace to our security. However, we do not, like the ancient Spartans, wish to train the bodies of our youths merely to make them more effective warriors" (Kennedy 1960, 16). If the United States was to play democratic Athens to the Slave World of the Soviet Union's Sparta, it was imperative that young men had the ability to choose exercise over sloth—to show *character*. The imposition of Spartan exercise regimes, from the perspective of Cold War liberalism, would frustrate independent action and hence make citizens dependent upon the state. Thus direct state intervention in social life would blur the difference between Western liberalism and the

Slave World. So the problem of government during the muscle gap was to create a cultural sphere outside of the state where young men would choose a masculine habitus consistent with the needs of the Cold War political economy. This is why institutions of civil society such as schools, the Amateur Athletic Union, Little League baseball, and the Boy Scouts of America played such a vital role in addressing the muscle gap since they shed the stamp of the state even while receiving state support.

In the looking glass of muscle gap discourse, the results of the Kraus-Weber Minimal Fitness Tests and the selective service statistics constructed U.S. youth as physically inadequate and physical education as a necessary intervention. On the one hand, muscle gap discourse constructed young white men as inadequate and in need of protection from postwar consumerism. And on the other hand, exercise regimes invested social power in white male bodies by defining them as protectors of the nation and its historical mission. By conflating the nation's human geography with its political geography, the muscle gap was concerned not only with the shape of its citizens but also with the shape of the nation itself. Thus the Cold War led not only to an arms race but also to an entire "body race" in that citizens' bodies and the body politic were seen as weapons of geopolitical struggle (Davis 1996; also Griswold 1998). In the next chapter, we will see how early college football broadcasting solved the problem of televising public rituals by replicating the subjectivizing style of classical Hollywood cinema. In doing so, broadcasting opened up the possibility of experiencing an objectified television sports fan as a subjective identity.

# 4 · THE BEST SEAT
# IN THE BALLPARK
## Lifestyle and the Televisual Event

I̶N 1949 *POPULAR SCIENCE* published an article titled "The Best Seat in the Ball Park," which explains how a team of sports journalists and television broadcast technicians worked together to broadcast a baseball game. The article begins by walking the reader through a typical sequence of shots: camera 2 sets an establishing shot of the field prior to the pitch; switch to camera 3 for a close-up of the batter; as the ball screams into the outfield camera 1 uses a telephoto lens to capture the outfielder's play on the ball; switch to camera 3 for a sweep across the stands as fans cheer wildly before panning to the next batter; and finally switch back to camera 2 to set an establishing shot centered on the pitcher (Johansen 1949, 105). Through this sequence of shots, viewers' eyes are kept focused and directed on what the producer feels is the center of action and most engaging in order to create an emotionally powerful reaction to the broadcast. The article then explains that broadcasting a baseball game is technologically very difficult to accomplish since the field is large, the ball is small, and ten to thirteen players can move in different, unpredictable directions at once. The goal of the broadcast crew and the journalists in the booth therefore is to produce the baseball game as clearly and smoothly as possible without losing the excitement fans experience in the stands.

Because the article was written and the games were broadcast for sports fans, the fan is more *subject to* than the *subject of* this technical-sporting discourse. For instance, General Motors' 1955 promotional film *Magic in the Air* treats the sports fan as a problem solved by television.[1] The film opens with scenes of a crowded football stadium and a narrator's voice rings out, "Crowds, music, color and excitement. Who doesn't enjoy a football game? That is, if you are one of the lucky ones to get in." A man holding a ticket in his hand then walks up to a ticket booth that displays a "Sold Out" sign. A group of men who had been loitering around the booth immediately descend upon it and fight for the precious ticket inside. In the tussle, an average-looking football fan—a middle-aged white man in a gray flannel suit—is knocked to the ground. The unlucky fan ends up ticket-less and without access to the stadium, a ritual space of masculine performance (Rinehart 1998). The narrator, however, reassures the viewer that there is a democratizing solution to the fans' war of all against all: "Thanks to television that model of modern science even our unlucky friend and millions of others can sit back in the comfort of their own home and enjoy every thrill of the game without struggle for tickets." Since *Magic in the Air* is a commercial for television, the unlucky fan is not the film's actual subject—he is constructed as a point of identification for viewers of the film. The unlucky fan's story is a framing device that introduces a crisis to be solved by a commodity: uneven access to the American way of life, symbolized by the stadium and football game, creates a crisis of modern civilization for which television is the technological solution since it provides an electronic ticket to the game. Viewers are then taken onto sound stages and inside a television camera to learn about the magical wonders of broadcast technology. In this sense, television is a technology of citizenship by providing men with access to civil society.

*Magic in the Air* and "The Best Seat in the Ballpark" are part of a genre of texts from the mid-1940s to the early 1950s that were didactic commercials for the new medium of television. These commercials generated publicity by explaining the "science of television" through demonstrations of how sporting events are broadcast (e.g., "Life Goes to a Football Broadcast" 1946; Murray 1956; Paxton and Wilkinson 1952; "Soundtrack—Sound and Fury" 1954; Stern 1951). The texts used photographs and detailed illustrations to show and explain the technological complexity of reproducing what most people had previously experienced only as live public rituals. By focusing on the techniques and technology of broadcasting, the genre constructed television as a scientific solution to problems of modernity and thus a commodity necessary for modern life (see Lears 1983). The technological discourse of this genre also produced male sports fans as crucial objects of their technical narratives but objects all the same. Television sport fans did not and could not exist prior to a televisual sport discourse and thus are a product of subjection.

This chapter explores how college football broadcasting created a subjective experience in a controlling commercial medium through an analysis of technical narratives on football broadcasting. The central concern of the chapter is the discursive production of the television sport fan through the techniques and technology of football broadcasting. I first focus on the television sports fan, the objectified subject of football broadcasting, since that construct is illustrative of fortified masculinity. Then I look at television broadcast manuals and news media articles that described broadcasting in the early Cold War to show how broadcasters reproduced football games as exciting patriotic pageantry and created a subjective experience from a process of objectification. This is less a study of real people than a study of how discourses related to media, masculinity, and nation constructed an image of the television sports fan as white, male, and heterosexual. So while not everyone who watched sports on television during the Cold War was white, male, and heterosexual, that referent image (Binder 1993) within broadcast discourse provided a fortified construction of the nation, its citizens, and its political body.

## THE AMERICAN WAY OF LIFE
## AND THE POLITICS OF LIFESTYLE

Beginning in the 1950s, television became the medium through which most fans participated in the national sports culture. As *Magic in the Air* makes clear, television increasingly mediated a fan's relationship to the national culture.[2] This means that television broadcasting expanded the stadium's ethical space. Like radio, television in the United States is a commercial medium, and sports are broadcast to attract viewers who can then be sold to advertisers in the form of ratings (Boddy 1993; Meehan 1990). The television sports fan in this model is not an actual person but a data point on a Hooper or Nielsen rating that is sold to advertisers in a quantified and objective form. But given the fact that *sports fandom is experienced subjectively* (Rinehart 1998; Trujillo and Krizek 1994), the objectified status of television sports fandom produces a paradox visible in the composite graphic that introduces "The Best Seat in the Ballpark" (figure 4.1). The graphic consists of text that describes the article, a photograph of a baseball game, and an illustration that foregrounds a man relaxing at home. With an anonymous man sitting in his easy chair, holding a beverage, smoking a cigar, and earnestly gazing out of a window and onto the photographic reproduction of the ballgame, the graphic operates as an allegory of mid-twentieth-century spectator sport: an individualized masculine subject, located in private space,[3] enjoys a libation of his choice and is happily connected to the national culture by the televisual medium (see Morse 1983). As Barbara Cruikshank states, "[M]odern forms of power tie the subjectivity (conscious, identity, self-knowledge) of the individual to that individual's subjection (control by another)" (Cruikshank 1999, 21). Which means that subjectivity is paradoxical, our desires are our own, but they are also an effect of power (Cruikshank 1999, 33). So although television sports fans are objectified in the broadcast model, they experience that objectification subjectively and enjoy pleasure from a controlling medium.

Figure 4.1 is indicative of the larger discursive formation of fortified masculinity by constructing a white male sports fan as worker and consumer. Although the graphic's masculine subject is largely anonymous, some aspects of his identity are clear. He is a white man with hair cropped short, he has a large jaw, his shirtsleeves are rolled up, and his large body slouches forward

FIGURE 4.1 "The Best Seat in the Ball Park." H. Luckett, "Best Seat in the House," *Popular Science*, August 1949, 105.

toward the object of his desire. The image's iconography suggests the man is a factory worker relaxing at home, enjoying the American way of life. Although he is John Q. Public, a worker in the postwar political economy, the illustration is not socialist realism celebrating the heroic worker as the active agent of history. The man sits passively in his easy chair drinking, smoking, and watching sports. So although he may be a worker and earnest, he did not produce his chair, his libations, or his television set. Rather than suggesting *Homo economicus*, an inner-directed actor rationally maximizing his utility, the image suggests *Homo comedo*, an other-directed consumer passively deriving pleasure from popular culture in the privacy of his own home. As worker and consumer, the television sports fan produces himself as a commodity by selling his labor power outside the home (Marx 1978a) and by watching televised sports in the home. The image thus links the workplace to the home in a way that mirrors the integration of lifestyle into postwar political economic relations of production and consumption (Cohen 2003).

## Lifestyle—Linking Structure and Action

The link here between the objectifying relations of postwar capitalism and the subjective experience of identity that I call fortified masculinity is the idea of lifestyle. Sociologists typically describe lifestyle as sets of distinctive behaviors and beliefs specific to different status groups; for Max Weber, "style of life" was what defined a status group (Weber 1958b, 187–188). Mike Featherstone draws upon Pierre Bourdieu to extend this analysis by describing lifestyle in contemporary society as a field of social and economic relations where uses of the body and acts of consumption allow a person to create a sense of individuality, self-expression, and stylistic self-consciousness (Featherstone 1987, 55). If lifestyle is composed of uses of the body, such as watching televised sports, and consumption, such as drinking a favored brand of beer, then a person produces his or her own self-identity by discriminating between commodities and governing himself or herself in a field of consumer choices. In short, lifestyle is a field of social and economic relations where people experience subjectification, as described in the previous section. Lifestyle can thus be understood as (1) a field of social and economic relations that blurs distinctions between class positions and status groups, (2) a performative social space where people produce themselves by making strategic distinctions between an array of commodities, and (3) a space where people experience internal feelings of desire that are also externally produced. So as college football broadcasting became an aspect of the American way of life, it expanded college football's ethical space into a diffuse, flexible, and transitory commercial-leisure space where people, but mostly men, could produce themselves as patriotic citizens of the Cold War capitalist state (see Miller 1993, 1998, 2007).

The political-economic prong of containment made U.S. commodities and lifestyle a cultural weapon of the Cold War (see chapter 2). Therefore, the image of consumerism evoked in figure 4.1 was central to a U.S. lifestyle that took on political and ethical significance during the Cold War. The American way of life described a lifestyle associated with postwar prosperity that was based on a notion of the good life promised by U.S. liberalism. Suburban homes stocked with a wealth of consumer goods and located in ethnically integrated but racially exclusive neighborhoods symbolized the American way of life (May 1999, xxiv–xxv). Richard Nixon equated freedom and modernity with consumerism when he argued that a modern home stocked with labor saving devices symbolized capitalism's greater ability to provide for its people during the Kitchen Debate with Nikita Khrushchev (May 1999, 10–16). An informed consumer became patriotic by making consumer choices that were construed as small acts of liberty that countered the "Slave World" of the Kremlin. The patriotic construction of consumerism comforted suburban America because it suggested not only that the American way of life was worth defending but also that American affluence was a defense against and challenge to other political systems (Whitfield 1991, 75). In addition, consumption took on an ethical as well as political imperative during the Cold War because, through the lens of Keynesian economics, it was seen as stimulating economic growth, and that meant a good citizen was an active consumer (Cohen 2003).

Television made sports consumption from the Olympics to college football a powerful, patriotic component of the American way of life and hence a technology of citizenship (see Crawford 2004; Domer 1976; Jay 2004; Oriard 2001; Thomas 2002; Wagg and Andrews 2006). Leisure activities like watching football were a "just reward" for men who submitted to the alienating environment of large factories and corporations in order to pay for their suburban homes and consumer comforts. And since suburban homes and the *nuclear* family were central to citizenship and identity during the early Cold War despite also being sites of isolation and anxiety (see Friedan 1963; Gilbert 2005; May 1999; Spigel 1992), sociologists in the 1950s such as David Riesman (1950), C. Wright Mills (1951), and William Whyte (1956) saw the suburbs and consumerism as extensions of an alienating corporate world (May 1999, 16).

Lifestyle, as we have defined it, implies modes of governance active in popular culture since consumers govern themselves and their households by making choices from an array of commodities. Thus the American way of life during the Cold War helped solve a central problem for liberalism, the production of citizens who can and will fulfill the needs of society with minimal state intervention (Rose, O'Malley, and Valverde 2006, 84), by providing behaviors, uses of the body, values, and aesthetics within a field of consumer relations where people produced themselves as patriotic Cold War consumer citizens (see Cohen 2003; May 1999; Sturken 2007). The so-called suicidal cult of masculinity of the 1950s discussed in chapter 2 is an example of lifestyle acting as a field for governance. Allied forces in the state, civil society, and the economy worked together to make middle-class white men's bodies objects of government of themselves and their wives since their "premature" death has economic costs to industry and society (see chapter 2).

Similarly, the anecdote about my father and I attending college football games in chapter 1 shows an operation of governmentality. Through my father's guidance, I learned the historical, cultural, and technical knowledge necessary to define myself as a football fan and produce myself as an "American" who participates in the national culture. Not only did I learn which teams to cheer for and against, I also learned which branded foods to eat. My father guided me into citizenship not as a representative of the state or a corporation but as an authority figure in my life, which highlights Foucault's point that institutions, such as the family, become instruments of government (Foucault 1991, 99) by making interventions in people's lives and teaching specific modes of thought (Lemke

2001, 191). Moreover, the process of becoming a citizen is not always an intrusive state project but is often accomplished through a group's way of life: its patterns of behaviors, beliefs, uses of the body, and consumption choices that produce self-consciousness.

## Teaching and Performing Cold War Citizenship

Like the family, the media act as an instrument of government, however, not so much by direct address and didactic instruction as when Big Brother orders Winston to touch his toes in George Orwell's *1984*. The media and especially sport media create relations of authority that provide a pedagogical guidance on citizenship as well as an ethical space where people can produce themselves through performances of citizenship (see Miller 1998, 234).[4] College football broadcasting makes interventions into people's lives in order to teach a complicated mode of thought and creates an ethical space for performing citizenship. The governmental emphasis on pedagogy and performance thus rejects a simple propaganda or deterministic model of media.

From the perspective of pedagogy and performance, Cold War football broadcasting is best understood as a form of patriotic pageantry. Richard Fried (1998) emphasizes that the politics of Cold War culture were not simply disseminated in a top-down manner in the United States but also required citizens' active participation. Patriotic pageants fashioned a conservative form of participatory democracy that fostered national unity through localized public rituals and demonstrated the nation's pluralistic values while reasserting wartime discipline that many feared was lost in an affluent society (Fried 1998, 19). Local and national leaders worked together to create public rituals like Armed Forces Day, Loyalty Day, Veterans Day, and Flag Day that together formed a patriotic calendar intended to teach Americans the meaning of citizenship. Most of the pageants eventually failed because so many were filled with repetitive, didactic Cold War rhetoric just as postwar affluence was filling people's time with consumerist diversions (Fried 1998, 98, 156–158). However, Fried cites the 1952 movement to have the national anthem sung at all sporting events as probably the Cold War's most successful patriotic pageant (Fried 1998, 97).

Although Fried's examples tended not to be commercially driven, college football is also an excellent example of patriotic pageantry. College football is a nationalistic rite of the harvest season tinged with the carnivalesque (Langman 2003). As such, it performs two contradictory functions reflective of Cold War culture. First, the rhetoric and symbolism of the game are more overtly militaristic and territorial than is the case with most other sports (Gems 2000; Hoch 1972; Jansen and Sabo 1994; Real 1979; Trujillo 1995). The game's militaristic imagery is buttressed by a rigidly bureaucratic organizational structure that is reflected in training regimes that often brutalize players (Meggyesy 1971; Shaw 1972; also see

Kemper 2009; Real 1979; Trujillo 1995; Watterson 2000; Westby and Sack 1976; Whannel 1993). Second, college football is a public ritual filled with pleasurable pageantry. College football is a national rite of the harvest season that symbolizes the American way of life, and as such it presents an opportunity structure regardless of race or class for men who are disciplined and motivated to succeed according to its norms and conventions. This allows college football to present a pluralistic image of the nation as it integrates families and communities into the nation on its highest holy days such as Thanksgiving and New Years Day (Arens 1976; Foley 1990; Langman 2003; Miller 2010; Montague and Morais 1976; Montez de Oca 2013; Oriard 2001; Rooney and Davidson 1995; Watterson 2000).[5] In this sense, college football offers a striking metaphor for the strategy of containment. On the one hand, it offers a highly territorialized image of military-industrial production, and on the other hand it offers a pluralistic image of social integration and commodity spectacle. Television extends football's militarized spectacle of consumption from the stadium to barrooms and people's homes or wherever the broadcast will reach so that people can produce themselves as cultural citizens alone or in groups. We now turn to strategies of representation for broadcasting college football on television in the early Cold War.[6]

## FOOTBALL BROADCASTING AND NATIONAL PEDAGOGY

Although we tend to think of football and television as naturally complementary as peanut butter and jelly,[7] it is only under specific social and historical circumstances that sport and television came to be inextricably intertwined (Barnett 1990, 1). In the early Cold War many people saw broadcasting as highly disruptive to a beloved traditional. One of the fears was that televising college football games subjected a traditionally masculine and nationalistic spectacle to a new field of commodity relations. Jack Gould, a cultural critic for the *New York Times*, saw the commercialization of college football by television as having dramatic and negative consequences on the fall ritual. In a satirical and prescient commentary, he imagined a time when all aspects of the game would have corporate sponsorship, such as Westinghouse Wallops replacing touchdowns, and the networks would not only exert control over which teams could join a conference but also set their schedules (Gould 1951). In a Cold War culture where consumerism and domesticity made many men anxious, the blatant commercialization of such a powerful masculine arena must have added fuel to the fire, which actually says more about the myth that sport exists outside of market relation than about any actual changes that took place in the sport industry.

Sport as commodity spectacle was in fact a precondition for television networks to invest in broadcasting in the first place (Jhally 1984). Indeed, college athletics commercialized and professionalized in the nineteenth century, which means that television and radio broadcasting simply extended and expanded a commercial model that already existed (Smith 2001, 2; also Oriard 1993, 2001; Smith 1988; Watterson 2000; Zimbalist 1999). Televising sports, in the late 1940s and early 1950s, was appealing to networks because sports were popular with male consumers; they were readily available; and the newspapers had already built an indigenous system of stars that early television lacked (Catsis 1996; Oriard 1993; Peterson 1997; Sammons 1990). Thus sport supplied popular broadcast content at a practical cost and circumvented the indifference that established film and theater stars had toward television (Boddy 1993). In a 1947 article titled "Greatest Contribution to Television Supplied so Far through Sports," Harry Wismer, ABC's director of sports, argued that in the television age, "football leads the parade" (Wismer 1947). At the same time that broadcasting extended a commercial sport market, it also made some profound changes to the ways that games were experienced.

The successful introduction of football broadcasting faced two key obstacles. First, it disrupted an economic model based on ticket and concession sales within the stadium that had developed since the late nineteenth century, which I discuss in chapter 5. Second, early broadcasters needed to figure out how to televise a public ritual that previously had been experienced in person without the benefit of technologies that we now take for granted. For instance, instant replay, where the play is immediately replayed in slow motion, did not occur until the 1963 Army-Navy classic (Catsis 1996, 36; Smith 2001, 106–107). The ability to portray athletes as visually heroic and to fortify their masculinity through the use of technology was one of the major concerns of early broadcasters. Once broadcasters were able to successfully capture the spectacle of the games, television created a new way of experiencing and participating in the national sporting culture that differs dramatically from either attending a game or listening to it on the radio.

Broadcasters in the early Cold War found that viewers at home and in bars wanted an experience that approximated the feeling of being in a stadium. The first football game broadcast on television,[8] like the first televised baseball game a few months earlier, used a single camera, and the result was disappointing. The static positioning of a camera with a single lens made the players appear tiny when on the far side of the field and gargantuan when near the camera (Smith 2001, 51). Broadcasters needed to respond to both technical and cultural problems when determining how to reproduce football games so that they could capture the emotional feeling of live spectacles and not undermine the heroic image of the athletes. But how could sport broadcasters capture the effervescence of the stadium through the medium of television? Ed McAuley of *The Sporting News*, while watching a baseball game in a hotel lounge, reflects the astonishment many people felt in 1947 at television's ability successfully to box sports spectacles. "Personally," wrote McAuley, "I couldn't see how a screen of these dimensions could show much of a baseball field without making Lilliputians of the characters, but the white aproned mix-master testified that by altering panoramic shots and close-ups, the operator [broadcaster] achieved satisfactory results" (McAuley 1947, 11). And in 1955 John Lardner argued in the *New York Times* that football was "meant to be televised" because the "set-piece" nature of plays lent themselves to television and sport fans could enjoy a personalized experience in the comfort of their own homes without suffering the discomfort of weather, seats, or rowdy fans (Lardner 1955).

McAuley's comments reveal how broadcasts create a perspective on sporting events (a series of actions bound by time, space, and social norms). That perspective gives viewers an impression and understanding of the event that broadcasters created through their use of broadcast techniques and technology. Harry McMahan, for instance, argued in *Television Production* that good camera work and good editing assemble bits of action into meaningful events that viewers receive on a subconscious level (McMahan 1957, 101, 172). In this sense, broadcasters act as modern-day *scops*, Old English poets who shape or create heroic tales by putting players' actions on the field together into heroic narratives that magnify the athletes' manliness (Marshall 1958, 123). McAuley's explanation of sports broadcasting mobilizes the masculine space of a bar and the masculine figure of the bartender to account for how the operator's use of broadcast techniques and technology fortifies the athletes' masculinity. And his concern that television would turn the athletes into "Lilliputians" (i.e., make the heroic athlete appear diminutive) reveals the scop's desire to fortify athletes' manhood. Similarly, Rudy Bretz in *Techniques of Television Production* consistently advises getting as close to the players as possible because closeness avoids the need for "long lenses" that make athletes look like "unimpressive dwarf[s]" (Bretz 1953, 439; also Stasheff and Bretz 1962, 203).

## Visual Narration—Creating Heroes and Heroic Tales

In order to create a desired emotional effect in viewers, broadcasters reproduced the football spectacle as a pro-filmic event in a style similar to classical Hollywood (see Morse 1983, 49). The classical Hollywood style of cinema encourages viewers to forget they are watching a movie and to lose themselves in the film's diegesis (narrative). This style of presentation emphasizes stories centered on human psychological motivation, such as the will to overcome obstacles. It creates senses of time and space that are linear and character centered. And it relies on an editing style of continuity so that time and space unfold without interruption and so that the film apparatus becomes opaque. Together these elements produce a film drama that encourages viewers to connect emotionally with the film's diegesis and they discourage critical reflection (see Bordwell, Staiger, and

Thompson 1985, 1–59). Since football broadcasting has the two central goals of clarifying and intensifying human action, it is similar to classical Hollywood cinema. Establishing and panoramic shots clarify by setting perspective and spatial relations both among players and between the viewer and the field. These construct a broadcast space that seamlessly draws viewers into a broadcast's *agon* or narrative drama centered on conflict, competition, and struggle (Trujillo 1993, 363). Close-ups create intensity by bringing the viewer close to a player and magnify the emotional effect of the ritual space. Rudy Bretz, who wrote one of the most important broadcast manuals, emphasizes two points when describing techniques for best capturing a football game: (1) maintain the athletes' heroic stature and (2) maintain clarity so that the viewer is never confused:

> The camera on the field is a particularly valuable thing from the dramatic point of view. It is only from the low angle that the *player looks impressive*; and plays occurring on the near side of the field . . . make the most *exciting and dynamic shots*. . . . The ultimate in field-level coverage is the camera mounted on a jeep. . . . Although [this] camera is not used for trucking shots, it [can] easily keep abreast of the line of scrimmage and a very *dramatic* low shot down the line [is] obtained which [can] be used just before the start of each play.
>
> The Zoomar lens, which first began to be used in football and baseball in 1947, is now practically indispensable in covering these sports. The great advantage is freedom from cutting. The moment of the cut is always a moment of *confusion*. . . . The cameraman with a zoom lens may zoom the lens in or out at any time, without running the risk of *confusing the viewer*. Even if the cameraman should lose the ball and zoom in on the wrong player, he can always zoom back out to a wider shot and go into a close-up again only when the position of the ball is *clear*. On a forward pass, the camera can go in for a close-up of the passer as he fades back, stay with him if he decides to run instead, or zoom back out into a wider shot as he passes the ball. (Bretz 1953, 445–446, emphasis added)

Bretz's manual advises broadcasters to balance intensity with clarity. The trouble with using only "impressive" close-up shots is that the viewer looses perspective on the action that takes place outside of the tight frame, something that rarely happens in stadiums. The trouble with using only establishing shots is that they distance the viewer from the action. Distance is a minor issue at the stadium because the public ritual produces collective effervescence, or the idea that as people gather together they experience the energy of the group rush through them and feel a powerful sense of unity as they lose their own sense of individuality (Durkheim 1915/2001, 154, 158). The problem for broadcasters then was not just to create a clear image but also how to reproduce effervescence in a variety of different settings and situations on a small screen. This was an emotional as well as a technical problem. Broadcasters addressed the emotional problem by bringing viewers closer to the game for a more personal and powerfully "real" experience. Thus the emotional problem became a problem of technique where the subjective experience of the stands was re-presented in the subjectivizing style of classical Hollywood cinema.

Bretz's quote also makes clear that achieving a subjectivizing presentation was tied to constantly improving technology. Switching technology gives broadcasters the ability to coordinate multiple cameras in a seamless montage that does not confuse viewers; in effect, switching achieves continuity editing. And the zoom lens allows the television director to frame the context of the action in an establishing shot and then zoom (or cut) to a close-up in order to create a desired effect upon the viewer, heightening the heroic masculinity of the players. In this manner, the viewer can be brought seamlessly into the game's diegesis, the story that the broadcast narrative produces, and drawn to those aspects that the director finds most compelling. Drawing spectators into the diegesis allows them to emotionally identify with the game, its drama, and the masculine athletes as well as perform their dual role of fan and national subject. Thus technique and technology combine to create an emotionally satisfying experience.

The subjectivizing style of Hollywood cinema produces an illusion that Roland Barthes (1989) calls the "reality effect." This is the idea that watching a television broadcast seems more real than actually sitting in the stadium. The illusion is an effect of the techniques and technology of the presentation described in preceding paragraphs, but the presentation results from advance preparations and broadcasters' knowledge of the sport (Bretz 1953, 443; see also Smith 2001). Carroll O'Meara, in *Television Program Production*, explained that in football broadcasting, "[the] director and cameramen must be more alert and provide a much greater effort in the way of teamwork. In the latter category it is imperative that cameramen are well acquainted with the game they are shooting and that they adhere strictly to an established pattern of procedures" (O'Meara 1955, 253–254). We might recall the pattern of shots described in "The Best Seat in the Ballpark" at the start of the chapter that were designed to create both clarity and intensity. O'Meara also suggests that the cameraman "be thoroughly drilled in practice games or in theory before attempting to shoot a major gridiron contest" (O'Meara 1955, 257). Similarly, a 1946 *Life* magazine article claimed that the magic of announcer Bill Stern's "omniscient" style resulted from painstaking focus on detail and teamwork so that at show time he can recognize all the players and pronounce the many Central European names without fumbling any ("Life Goes to a Football Broadcast" 1946). The investment of time and rational planning typical of a broadcast can be seen in an outline of CBS's typical weekly preparation for a college football broadcast: "Monday–Tuesday, filming pre-game shows by advance crew; Wednesday, arrival of production crew; Thursday, arrival of announcing crew; Friday, arrival of technical crew; Saturday, game telecast" (NCAA 1963, 33–34). The net effect of rational planning and style of presentation is the broadcasters re-create the game as a seamless pro-filmic event.

## Aural Narration—Lessons in Manliness

The visual presentation of the spectacle was only half of early broadcasters' concerns. The second major concern for sport telecasters was how to narrate the spectacle. Narration produces a verbal frame of meaning and gives viewers a way to understand the visible action that they can see. The complexity of a football game that unfolds in real time creates the need for spontaneous narration. But it would be a mistake to see narration acting as a neutral technology that simply responds to and reflects a given football reality. The multiple institutions involved in the production of a college football broadcast, including the universities, the NCAA, the network, the sponsors, and the press, work together to create a controlled and controlling image of the game. Ronald Smith (2001) argues that the NCAA wanted only announcers like Keith Jackson who would present a positive image of the game and the nation. And during times of increased social tension and controversy, such as the Vietnam War, support for football from the press box went up (Smith 2001, 131). Moreover, spontaneity in football broadcasting is a product of hours of detailed, advance preparation ("*Life* Goes to a Football Broadcast" 1946; Bretz 1953; O'Meara 1955). The process of selecting announcers and the rational planning for every broadcast produced a desired image of the game, the sport, and the nation.

The style of narration that became ascendant did not happen by coincidence. Bill Stern wrote a 1951 article in *Variety*, looking back on the lessons learned since the first televised baseball game in 1939, and he concluded that the commentator's job is to augment the image on the screen. The commentator should narrate not what the viewer sees on the screen but what the viewer is missing and what the commentator believes the viewer should know (also O'Meara 1955, 260). "Television is like newsreel work," Stern says, "You augment the picture. Explain it; but don't get in its way" (Stern 1951). Narration also solved optical problems created by punts and kickoffs. Announcer Lindsay Nelson explained in *Sports Illustrated* that the commentator and camera crew work together to maintain spatial orientation while magnifying the drama of kickoffs. So rather than a camera following the ball as closely as possible to focus viewers' attention on the center of action, which is disorienting when following a ball's high arc, the camera pulls back and the commentator tells viewers "what kind of kick it is, high, short, squib or shotgun. They see the kicker. Then they see the receiver" (Murray 1956, 60). Similarly, O'Meara explains that "[i]f the tackle has taken place near either side of the field, pan to the nearest yardage marker and zoom in to the limit. Otherwise cut to a shot which will show the linesmen setting their sticks and 10 yard chain" (O'Meara 1955, 257).

In this way, the viewer's attention is constantly controlled and engaged without disruption or distraction through the instrumental use of voice and imagery.

Narration creates verbal frames of meaning that fortify the masculinity of athletes *and* fans. In a study of *Monday Night Football*, Nick Trujillo shows how announcers use language to construct athletes' bodies as metaphorical tools of production and weapons of war (Trujillo 1995). The use of verbal frames of meaning, however, did not begin with *Monday Night Football*. Dennis James was a veteran radio announcer who became one of the first television sports announcers. James was so popular in the late 1940s and early 1950s that he actually drew fans who wanted to see him in person to live events. Part of his fame was for describing what the camera could not catch, such as the blood from a fighter's cut that is lost on a black and white screen ("James of the Telewaves" 1948, 57). But James was most famous for his "Mother" gimmick that he used when announcing wrestling.[9] James created the mother figure in 1946 when he first began announcing wrestling and was insecure about his knowledge of the sport (James 1973; Thomas 1997). But "Mother" also proved useful for explaining wrestling's complicated holds to viewers in bars without challenging men's sport knowledge. "From the start [James] knew that few set owners were hep to wrestling's complicated holds but he was also aware that no sport fan likes to be thought ignorant. . . . Rules, holds, and any other details he carefully explains to 'Mother,' thus preserving the male ego" ("James of the Telewaves" 1948, 57). James's Mother—a mythical older female character—compensated for his own lack of knowledge and soothed male egos in his audience. She also gave male viewers a performative role in the broadcast that fortified their masculinity. James explained in an interview, "So I would say, 'Mother, that is a hammerlock'—so that if [a woman] wanted to say to her husband, 'Is that right, John?' he could say, 'Yes, that is right.' and so he would be a hero" (James 1973, 10). By pretending to speak to an ignorant, older woman, James narrated the sport and fortified male egos all the while building a following of competent wrestling fans.

The inscription of the nuclear family in this broadcasting triad is unmistakable. In constructing a virtual family, James takes on a mediated authority role that didactically positions the spectator as preliterate child and himself as parent in the Enlightenment mold of bringing children to the point of reason through education so that they can function as rational, self-governing citizens (e.g., Locke 1690/1980, 35). However, this is not the father-son relationship imagined in social contract theory, it is a version of consumer citizenship based on the ethical effect of consuming corporate sponsored sport broadcasting and then acting as a competent fan and sports consumer (see Berlant 1997). The media institution itself, although represented by the announcer, creates relations of authority where the technical and cultural knowledge of a complicated sport can be taught and a space created for people to perform an embodied and gendered form of citizenship.

## BROADCASTING, LIFESTYLE, AND SUBJECTIFICATION

I have shown that central to creating the new sponsor-driven model was transforming a participatory public ritual experienced as live events into a public ritual experienced through a televisual broadcast medium. This was no mean feat given the state of broadcast technology in the late 1940s and early 1950s. In part, the transformation involved a commercial program of education typified by "The Best Seat in the Ballpark" and *Magic in the Air*. These didactic technical presentations on the science of television broadcasting presented television as a technological solution to the problems of modernity; television created access to the American way of life symbolized by attending sporting events such a college football. Television and college football broadcasting became part and parcel of the American way of life that in the context of the Cold War was a patriotic space for expressing citizenship. From the perspective of governmentality, it was also a commercial sphere for managing modes of thought and uses of the body as people produced themselves as subjects of the capitalist state. College football broadcasting was not simple propaganda didactically telling viewers to obey and consume; instead, patriotic pageantry facilitated the pleasurable performance of individual and group identities in a nationalistic sphere of commodity relations.

Employing the style of classical Hollywood cinema allowed for subjective connections to an objectifying commercial medium, giving football broadcasts the pedagogical function of teaching fans how to watch, understand, and participate in the televisual spectacle. The greatest benefit of televising games, argue Bretz (1953) and Stern (1951), is the ability to explain and to clarify the game to fans. As one fan stated, "You watched a game on television and, suddenly, the wool was stripped from your eyes. What appeared to be an incomprehensible tangle of milling bodies from the grandstand made sense" (cited in Rader 1984, 119). The subjectivizing style of the broadcasts draws spectators into the spectacle to perform their local fan identity, while it positions them as a member of the viewing public and object of its pedagogical narrative. Television football fandom is not simply an active or a passive role but an ambiguous position that slips up and back between performative subject and pedagogical object (see chapter 5). At the same time, football broadcasting opens up a safe and unquestionably heterosexual public space for the scopophilic pleasure of looking at football heroes whose masculinity is heavily fortified (see Morse 1983; Trujillo 1995). As fans subjectively identify with the masculine heroes through the televisual apparatus, they are simultaneously taught an image of masculinity synonymous with rationality, territorial conquest, and nationalism.

David Harvey (2003) argues that capitalism produces processes of territorialization, deterritorialization, and reterritorialization. These processes can be seen through the production of college football as commodity spectacle. College football went through a process of territorialization in the nineteenth century when the game moved inside of stadiums in order to charge rent upon seats with a view of the action and concessions could be sold to stadium goers. Broadcasting deterritorialized this model by expanding football's ethical space to any location with a box, either radio or television, that could receive the broadcast. However, the process of deterritorialization was also a process of reterritorialization in that a new commercial model was created that expanded and extended the older model. In this sense, television broadcasting extended an existing model of selling rent upon seats and created a new model of capital accumulation that existed in tandem with the older model. The new model made college football a sponsorship-driven spectacle that Jack Gould and others criticized for debasing a beloved masculine tradition. More important, the sponsorship model also objectified fans by turning them into commodities: ratings sold in the commercial marketplace. The process of deterritorialization and reterritorialization did not unfold without conflict and strife, as we will see in the next chapter, because broadcasting revealed the competing interests and positions of different capitalist class segments invested in the production of college football.

# 5 · FORDISM IN THE AIRWAVES

## The NCAA's Use of Market Regulations to Control College Athletics

> Television and the atomic bomb have been hooked up a lot at this conference. Let's wait until the bomb destroys our stadiums, and not let television do it first.
>
> —Asa Bushnell, commissioner of the
> Eastern Colleges Athletic Conference, 1950

THE FIRST FOOTBALL game broadcast on television was played between Fordham University and Waynesburg College on September 20, 1939. Historian Ronald Smith estimates the crowd in attendance was possibly four to five times the size of the television audience that watched what was probably a disappointing broadcast (Smith 2001, 51). In addition to the new medium's imperfect capabilities (see chapter 4), very few people owned television sets, and the broadcast range was highly limited. The further development and expansion of television broadcasting was then suppressed during the Second World War, and as a result relatively few football games were broadcast during the 1940s. The 1950 college season, however, marked an important shift in college football broadcasting. In 1950, the networks began to widely contract with individual schools like Notre Dame and the University of Pennsylvania for the rights to broadcast their games. The number of games broadcast in the 1950 season skyrocketed over previous seasons. This led people in the colleges and the media to perceive 1950 as a watershed season. After years of latency, football broadcasting appeared to offer a new and considerable source of revenue.

Significant structural change will send ripples throughout any industry, but in an industry that is structured by intense competition and great inequalities between participating firms,[1] such as college football, it is likely to trigger a crisis. As we shall see in this chapter, television broadcasting created a crisis in college football. Prior to television, football revenues were derived largely from ticket and concession sales in the stadiums. The ability to sell broadcast rights and accrue significant revenues from those sales radically altered the business of college football. However, laws, norms, and other social mechanisms to govern and regulate these new market relations did not exist in 1950. As a result, schools advantaged by the size of their broadcast market, the wealth of the institution, their team's win-loss record, the region they were located in, and their popularity appeared likely to dominate broadcast revenues and exasperate the already existing inequalities in college football. The development of television broadcast technology and techniques created a new means of cultural production and consumption within a commercial market before the social and institutional systems were established to regulate the new market relations. In short, the rise of television broadcasting created a contradiction between the material and the social relations of football production.

The National Collegiate Athletic Association (NCAA) responded to the crisis by regulating college football broadcasting on television in 1951 with the claim that regulations served the public interest. The establishment of broadcast regulations was monumental since the regulations transformed the NCAA from a confederation of semiautonomous institutions into a powerful governing and policing body that controlled collegiate athletics. Furthermore, the regulations made the NCAA a cartel that limited the supply of football broadcasts relative to demand and thereby inflated the broadcasts' value. The accrual of monopoly profits derived from cartelization fueled the NCAA's ascendance and generated wealth for maintaining the NCAA in a controlling position (Lawrence 1987, 77; Zimbalist 1999, 93). The NCAA's broadcast regulations, in addition to being a bold power grab, addressed contradictions in college football by creating the legal, the normative, and the social systems that could manage and expand a national sports broadcasting market while not resolving the contradictions.

A close look at the NCAA's claim that broadcast regulations served the public interest reveals that the NCAA's actions were more than just an interesting moment in football history. The NCAA was well aware that regulating the broadcast market could lead to a restraint of trade lawsuit under the Sherman Antitrust Act. In order to shield itself from a possible U.S. Supreme Court "rule of reason" test, the NCAA claimed that its regulations served the national interest. To support that claim, the NCAA presented its regulations to the state and civil society through a prism of Cold War anxiety. NCAA publicity drew upon muscle gap discourse, discussed in chapter 3, in order to construct common sense that linked young men's bodies and college football to the nation's Cold War destiny. In other words, constructions of masculinity, football, and the nation were central to how the NCAA addressed contradictions within the political economy of college football and achieved domination of collegiate athletics through control of television broadcasting. When placing the regulations of 1950 into historical relief, we can see that the crisis precipitated by television was actually endemic to the highly competitive, unequal world of college football. And while the construction of masculinity and nation addressed contradictions in college football's relations of production and consumption, it only obscured the structural inequalities in college football itself.

This chapter looks at the historical imperatives that led to the formation of the NCAA and its historical mission within college football. It then places the move to regulate broadcasting within the context of the NCAA's ambition to grow beyond its initial charter. The bulk of the chapter focuses on how the NCAA actually negotiated the social terrain of the early Cold War to successfully implement and defend the regulations so it could undergo a process of cartelization. What this particular history of NCAA broadcast regulations ultimately shows is that culture sits in a tense and dialectical relationship with the political and the economic spheres of society.

## CORPORATE LIBERALISM AND THE FOUNDING OF THE NCAA

To understand the social context that the NCAA negotiated in the 1950s, it is important to understand the importance of football to the colleges that participate in the NCAA and why the NCAA came into existence in the first place. Young men began playing ball games on the campuses of northeastern colleges in the 1860s as an escape from what they perceived to be the effeminizing conditions of academic life. The game of American football then developed during the 1870s and 1880s. By the 1890s, the game had grown in popularity and spread to every region of the United States (Watterson 2000, 40). Although high-pressure football was controversial on many campuses, it was also embraced by most university administrations to generate publicity, to develop loyalty among students and alumni, to fund-raise, and to manage students' behavior (Smith 1988, 23; Watterson 2000, 22–29). The rapid growth and profitability of college football in the late nineteenth century also led to scandals and a sense that the game was out of control. The progressive press sensationalized the cheating and violence that were perceived as rife in the game (Oriard 1993, 164; Watterson 2000, 72–73). And it was criticism of the excesses in college football that created the conditions through which the NCAA would arise.

Higher educational institutions deeply invested in high-pressure football formed the NCAA in 1905 in response to widespread condemnation of college football's brutality and scandals. A group of schools that participated in a high level of intercollegiate football competition created the NCAA. Most, if not all, were motivated by financial and institutional interests (Oriard 1993; Smith

1988; Watterson 2000). As a result, they designed the NCAA as a representative organization to reform the game and quell calls to ban it (Oriard 1993, 164–165; Watterson 2000, 74). In reforming football, NCAA member institutions had no desire to give up institutional control over their teams, high-level competition, or profitability. In fact, schools retained a high degree of individual autonomy in order to compete aggressively with each other on and off the field (Smith 1988, 206–207). The NCAA constitution preserved institutional autonomy through the doctrine of Home Rule, which allowed schools to determine "eligibility rules, coaching salaries, stadium building, ticket sales, and, had they been in existence, radio and television contracts" (Smith 2001, 67). Historian John Watterson claims the creation of the NCAA, like other Progressive Era reforms, insulated an institution from attacks by the state, the media, and citizen groups while preparing it for economic growth (Watterson 2000, 98).

Forming the NCAA produced what Gabriel Kolko (1963) calls market rationalization.[2] Leading football competitors organized themselves to reform an unstable market in order to ensure future economic growth and protect themselves from potential political attacks coming from either the state or civil society.[3] This formation of corporatism within college football is typical of Progressive Era corporate liberalism (Weinstein 1968, ix–xv). The late nineteenth century saw a dismantling of the "free market" and a new regulatory role of the government. Central to the thesis of corporate liberalism is an acceptance by the government and public of greater market controls and centralization of power. Corporatism would ensure the growth of large corporations in a stable economic environment that fostered capital accumulation (Sklar 1988, 15–17). As evidenced by the doctrine of Home Rule, the Progressive Era did not give birth to a fully regulated society, but rather provided the necessary first step of forming alliances between the state and the corporate sector through "progressive" reform (Kolko 1963; Sklar 1988; Weinstein 1968). Indeed, college football enjoyed tremendous growth and prosperity from the 1890s through the late twentieth century despite slumps during the World Wars (see Mennell 1989, 248–260; Reimann 2004, 126–133; Watterson 2000, 140).

As college football became more lucrative, remaining competitive grew more costly. Some of the basic costs of producing a winning team in the early twentieth century included full-time professional coaches who were often better paid than most faculty and some university presidents; fleets of scouts and a feeder system to bring top "football material," that is, athletes, to campus; and both indirect and sometimes direct compensation for the athletes (Watterson 2000, 46, 55–56, 167, 205–207). Whether it was an attempt to appease growing student demand for comfortable seating or a strategy to manage student behavior in controlled campus settings, building enormous concrete stadiums provided ever-greater revenue from gate receipts. As a result, stadiums grew in size during the twentieth century, as did the cost of college football.[4] Schools ultimately became dependent upon stadium-based revenues if for no other reason than to pay down debt on the stadiums (Watterson 2000, 265).[5]

Market rationalization through the creation of the NCAA supported the formation of a tier of elite teams that dominated on-field competition. As the cost of fielding competitive teams soared in the twentieth century, generating revenue through winning became increasingly important. Schools in less significant markets that lacked large stadiums, especially smaller schools, were at a structural disadvantage when it came to purchasing football's forces of production.[6] At the same time, large schools, especially in affluent markets, generated more revenue to invest in maintaining dominance than did smaller schools (Lewis 1970; Riesman and Denney 1951; Westby and Sack 1976). By midcentury, a profitable group of elite football schools had formed. This elite group was composed mostly of public universities like Michigan, Oklahoma, and California as well as some private universities such as the University of Pennsylvania, Notre Dame, and the University of Southern California. Many smaller schools were forced out of the football market by the cost of competition.[7] Even Yale and Harvard, which had created high-pressure athletics in the nineteenth century, "deemphasized" football as a cost savings and a publicity strategy when they could no longer compete with the top schools (Watterson 2000, 243). In short, the early twentieth century saw power steadily centralize in ever-larger football programs.

The NCAA itself began to grasp power in the mid-1940s despite the constitutional constraint of Home Rule. The NCAA quadrupled its dues in 1948 to $100.[8] This increased the NCAA's finances and confidence when added to revenues received from its basketball tournament and the sale of its rule books (Watterson 2000, 209). The doctrine of Home Rule, however, remained an institutional barrier to its consolidation of power. The NCAA made its first attack upon Home Rule with the establishment of the Sanity Code, which attempted to regulate and to police the recruiting of and the subsidies given to athletes (Watterson 2000, 209–277). Adopted in 1948, the Sanity Code allowed the NCAA to expel schools that did not conform to its standards. Economist Andrew Zimbalist argues that the Sanity Code initiated the NCAA's process of cartelization, where colleges colluded to limit compensation given to athletes in order to drive the cost of athletes' labor below the value of their labor power, impossible in an unregulated market (Zimbalist 1999, 10). However, the Sanity Code failed because it limited schools' ability to pursue competitive advantage over other football programs. As a result, a group of schools known as "the Sinful Seven" rebelled, and by January 1951 the Sanity Code was abandoned (Watterson 2000, 214–218). Despite the setback, the Sanity Code was a harbinger of the greater centralization and regulation that television broadcasting would make possible.

The failure of the Sanity Code demonstrates limits on the trend toward market rationalization. U.S. universities exist in a competitive market environment.
Participating in competitive athletics provides financial capital and publicity for
competing in that market (Smith 1988, 4, 10). The Sanity Code attempted to use
calls in civil society for the reform of college football as a means to legitimate
increased market regulation.[9] However, it impeded the ability of leading firms
to compete in the college football market and accrue capital. This suggests that
the desire for reform in civil society alone cannot sustain market rationalization
without the promise of stable capital accumulation for competing institutions.
The establishment of the NCAA in 1905 also suggests that regulations need to
address broader cultural conditions to insulate participating firms from political
attacks (Silva 1978, 345–346). In other words, market regulations must address
the cultural and political interests of civil society at the same time as the economic interests of capital.

## THE TELEVISION AGE AND THE NEW NATIONAL
## COLLEGIATE ATHLETIC ASSOCIATION

The advent of television in the late 1940s created an opportunity for cartelization that the Sanity Code did not. To understand how television created this
opportunity, we need to look at the conditions engendered by television. As
pointed out at the start of this chapter, television broadcasting got off to a slow
and unsteady start in the late 1930s. Nevertheless, the University of Pennsylvania (Penn) invested in and experimented with football broadcasting throughout
the 1940s (Smith 2001, 53). After World War II, when regional networks were
established and vast improvements were made in the techniques for broadcasting mass sport spectacles (see chapter 3),[10] television broadcasting began to look
like a great source of publicity for top football schools. Furthermore, the sales
of television sets began to grow exponentially in the late-1940s expanding from
seven thousand sets in 1946 to one million in 1948 to three million in 1949. By
1954, over thirty-five million television sets had been sold (Zimbalist 1999, 92).
With greater access to television and improvements in broadcast technology,
the popularity of sports broadcasting surged. As early as 1947, cafes in Pasadena
charged $20 for seats next to a television set and $10 for standing room to watch a
local broadcast of the Rose Bowl (Next to Sideline Seat 1947; also see McCarthy
1995). Fan appreciation of televised games was so significant that a 1948 NCAA
survey in the Boston–New York–Philadelphia corridor found that 80 percent of
fans preferred televised games to live performances (Peterson 1997, 197).

The rapid expansion of televisions in the Northeast and Midwest coupled
with surveys indicating fan appreciation of television broadcasting triggered
extreme reactions to the quickly approaching television age. Television network

executives viewed the future through rose-tinted glasses. Robert Saudek, vice president of ABC, claimed in 1950, "[W]e'll have silent football. . . . It will be played indoors under perfect conditions. The weather will always be just right, the grass just the proper height, the ball will never be slippery. In this test-tube football, the players won't be bothered by the roar of the crowd, because the crowds will be watching at home, and they'll be comfortable. There'll be no one at the game except the sponsor—and he'll be behind a glass cage" (Saudek 1950). Saudek's enthusiasm for sterile purity, however, probably owes more to postwar enthusiasm for social engineering and scientific futurism than to fans' actual desire to evacuate stadiums.

Administrators of football programs struggling to survive on gate receipts saw the potential loss of attendance caused by television as a technological threat akin to an alien attack from outer space. Whereas Saudek gleefully imagined a new business model of controlled corporate sponsorship with fans comfortably ensconced at home, many athletic directors felt imperiled. As Asa Bushnell, commissioner of the Eastern College Athletic Conference (ECAC), stated to the first annual ECAC meeting in 1947, "television is the scientific method which has been developed to consign all athletic directors to the Smithsonian Institute and to make football stadiums of interest only to archeologists" (cited in Smith 2001, 59). While holding contrary positions on broadcasting itself, Saudek and Bushnell did agree that television had the potential to transform the business model of college athletics and profoundly affect U.S. society. Implicit in these statements was also a larger concern over control of college football broadcasting and its revenues.

Critics of football broadcasting gained ammunition in 1950 when gate receipts fell into a nationwide decline (Smith 2001, 60; Watterson 2000, 265). Live attendance had increased every year following a slump during the Second World War, and in 1949 ticket sales reached a record high. The 1950 season then saw a surge in television broadcasts as schools like Michigan, Notre Dame, and Penn were free to aggressively pursue commercial broadcasting with the networks in an open market. Fear of television was then fanned by an NCAA-sponsored study done by the National Opinion Research Center (NORC) that found areas broadcasting games had a 4 percent drop in gate receipts whereas areas without broadcasting rose 4 percent in 1950.[11] Though the results were certainly not conclusive, NCAA members saw this pattern as sufficient reason to take action (Lawrence 1987, 77–78).

The television age created new conditions that made old practices appear obsolete to many within the NCAA. The doctrine of Home Rule that previously ensured the tradition of institutional autonomy now limited television revenues to schools that could negotiate broadcast rights with the networks. This disadvantaged not only small schools but also large schools in small markets. For instance, Penn and Notre Dame could negotiate lucrative contracts with the networks in 1950, but Oklahoma, a dominant football program during the 1950s under its coach Charles "Bud" Wilkinson, could not (Smith 2001, 68).

Fear of television's impact on gate receipts provoked a variety of attempts to stave off losses at the gate. Several regional conferences such as the Big Ten and the Big Seven blocked live broadcasts and forced tape-delayed broadcasts of games in 1950. However, popular desire for live coverage led to threats of legislative acts blocking the widespread use of tape delay ("Legis to Force Okla Univ to Telecast Games" 1951; "NCAA Ban on Live Telecasting Studied" 1951; "Western Conf Bans 'Live' TV" 1950). Another strategy was Theater Television—a live broadcast piped into a theater that charged an admission (NCAA 1954, 64). The University of Michigan experimented with closed-circuit broadcasts in movie houses in 1950—as did Illinois and Northwestern—to not only slow the erosion of stadium and movie theater attendance, but also to re-create the gridiron spectacle (Smith 2001, 64). A *Newsweek* article described the presentation of a Michigan-Indiana game: "As at Ann Arbor there were cheerleaders, a band, hotdog and pop vendors. The difference was that the movie crowd—for 80 cents—saw the game, plus a feature movie and a stage show" ("Football and Video" 1950). The NCAA also hoped that pay-per-view systems such as Skiatron and Phonovision would take hold.[12] Both Theater Television and pay-per-view systems followed the older ticket-sales model, and neither provided a sufficiently robust economic model (NCAA 1965, 24–25). The television age had created new social and economic conditions and demanded a new economic model.

## FOOTBALL BROADCASTING AND COLD WAR FEAR

Between the unstable 1950 football market and the attempts by schools to impose stability, television had created the conditions for a larger institution to provide order through market rationalization. The NCAA as an umbrella organization proved to be the best instrument to rationalize the market, which after all was the primary reason for its creation. However, the consolidation of broadcast power by the NCAA was certain to raise antitrust concerns. So the NCAA acted, conscious of a possible Supreme Court "rule of reason" test (NCAA 1954, 34). Under prevailing interpretations of the Sherman Antitrust Act, the Court could allow a restraint of trade if it were deemed reasonable—that is, if a restraint fostered stable capital accumulation (Sklar 1988, 111–117). Therefore, the NCAA constructed its broadcast regulations with this in mind. The NCAA used the conditions of the early Cold War as a prism for the state and civil society to view collegiate athletics and television broadcasting in order to sell its regulations as reasonable in the 1950s.

The early Cold War engendered great anxiety in U.S. society. Three sources are particularly relevant: technology, centralization, and conflict. Nuclear annihilation was certainly a primary technological threat that hovered over the entire Cold War.[13] But the early 1950s also saw a welter of new technologies invading postwar homes that made nuclear warfare only the most glaring and dramatic source of technological anxiety. Prominent in the technological invasion of postwar homes was television. Television historian Lynn Spigel argues that many people in the early 1950s experienced television as an alien force that transformed the social space of their homes. As discussed in chapter 2, debates over television's impact on the home refracted a broader anxiety that modern technological society had an effeminizing effect upon men (Spigel 1992, 61).

As four major television networks began to stretch across the United States,[14] C. Wright Mills lamented that changes in the United States during the twentieth century had led to the rise of a "power elite." Mills saw the centralization of power and wealth in three massive institutions (the military, the federal government, and corporations) as producing the "higher circles of power" that controlled postwar U.S. society (Mills 1956, 3–29; see also Mills 1951), and ultimately formed what Eisenhower named the "military-industrial complex" (Eisenhower 1961). Mills's critique of mass culture joined a chorus of critics warning against the rise of giant institutions that dominated all aspects of social life and that left "the little guy" vulnerable to external control. Historian James Gilbert (2005) argues mass culture critiques expressed and provided a means for working out changing gender relations during the postwar period, of which the critiques of television, mentioned in the previous section, were a part.

Fears of invasion and vulnerability were made most palpable by the U.S. conflict with the Soviet Union. The openness of liberal society evoked fears of a communist invasion that would penetrate deep into the heart of America. In an example of patriotic pageantry, the residents of Mosinee, Wisconsin, staged a one-day takeover of their own town in 1950 to dramatize the dangers of global communism (Fried 1998, 67–86). Similarly, the popularity of science fiction films like *It Came from Outer Space* (1953) expressed a fear of Soviet invasion and nuclear technology (Biskind 1983/2000; Boyer 1994; Nadel 1995; Perrine 1998; Slotkin 1992). George Kennan, the architect of Cold War foreign policy, was keenly aware of the period's climate of anxiety (Kennan 1950, 9). As already discussed, fears of invasion and vulnerability were the very basis of the strategy of containment that guided foreign policy throughout the Cold War, and Cold War historians widely agree the culture of containment transcended all aspects of society in the 1950s (May 1999, 13–14; Nadel 1995, 2–3).

Addressing the interrelated Cold War anxieties, technology, centralization, and conflict was central to how the NCAA framed its regulations. Framing the regulations as furthering institutional interests was unlikely to be accepted by the Supreme Court as a reasonable restraint of trade. Instead, the NCAA framed television and football broadcasting as a technological threat not only to colleges but also to the nation. Television, according to the NCAA, created a "free ticket" that drew fans away from the stadium. The football programs of small colleges would become vulnerable in a market dominated by a "TV aristocracy" where fans enjoy football from the comfort of their own homes (NCAA 1953, 12–13). The vulnerability of small schools is of national concern, the NCAA argued, since they form the foundation of the U.S. system of higher education (NCAA 1953, 12–13; 1954, 18). The NCAA further claimed that football funds physical education and intramural athletics, so the loss of football revenues would curtail the physical training of the nation's business and military leaders (NCAA 1954, 32; 1956, 34)—harkening to both prongs of containment. Furthermore, attending football games historically has been a component of the college experience and therefore a part of the American way of life (NCAA 1953, 16–17). The NCAA did not simply frame television as a threat to schools that had grown accustomed to profiting from the business of college football; it framed television as a threat to the nation and the American way of life. This frame suggested that television's technological threat would increase centralization and impede America's ability to wage the Cold War by undermining the masculinity of its youth. The NCAA's emotion-laden appeal at a time of geopolitical struggle could make a mere restraint of trade seem quite reasonable.

The NCAA's framing of its broadcast regulations did not suddenly spring forth in 1951. Looking closely at the reports of the NCAA Television Steering Committee demonstrate that it crystallized over a period of years even though important aspects were in place at the beginning. Annual reports show a narrowing and clarifying of the frame by subsequent Steering Committees. Framing the regulations was not simply a response to the concerns of the state and civil society; the frames also responded to NCAA member institutions, the networks, and sponsors. The new economic conditions of the television age and the cultural conditions of the Cold War allowed the NCAA to remake itself as a regulatory agency with the power to police its members.

It is interesting to note that a range of possible responses to the challenge of television lay before the NCAA. The NCAA neither embraced nor rejected television; instead, it decided to contain it. The NCAA's strategy of television containment began in 1951 when member institutions voted to regulate football broadcasting by calling for a moratorium—though critics saw it as a ban—on broadcasting to "test the effects" of television on gate receipts ("Ban on Video Discussed" 1951). The moratorium was the NCAA's first step toward becoming an actual cartel (Zimbalist 1999, 93). The defining term of NCAA containment was "limit": limit the number of broadcasts and limit schools' broadcast appearances.[15] The regulations also made the NCAA Television Committee a clearinghouse that the networks and colleges had to work through when setting broadcast schedules, for which the Television Committee asked for 18 percent of the royalties from the 1951 season ("NCAA Committee Recommends Football Video on Limited Basis" 1951).[16]

## NCAA BROADCAST POLICY FORMATION

Creating NCAA broadcast regulations was a three-step process. The first step was negotiating with the myriad, competing parties involved in college football broadcasting in order to win their support for its regulations (NCAA 1957, 3). Therefore, the NCAA took advice and counsel from "networks, stations, TV set manufacturers, pay-as-you-see TV companies, advertising agencies, sponsors, press, TV committee consultants, delegates from conferences, [and] representatives of various areas" to formulate its policy (NCAA 1953, 10). NCAA broadcast policy was written to bring the varying competing interests necessary for broadcasting into a coalition. The financial and publicity benefits of football broadcasting were inequitably distributed among coalition members in favor of top football schools despite the NCAA's emphasis on revenue sharing (Zimbalist 1999, 96, 116–117).

The written policy was then pitched to the association itself. Member institutions, including the ones that had participated in its formation, ratified the policy at the annual NCAA conventions to which the Television Committee reports were presented. The reports were an important tool for wining support for the policy by informing the coalition about the current state of college football from the NCAA's perspective.[17] The reports framed television as a financial threat upon college athletics that only the Television Committee could effectively contain. The reports maintained this position even after 1956, when college football embarked upon decades of stable financial growth. The reports suggested that the NCAA's suprainstitutional position allowed it to provide the solution to television because it acted on behalf of all of the schools without bias. The reports went on to stress that the NCAA formed its policy through the study of the trends in both broadcasting and stadium attendance made available by the NORC reports. The policy also served the greatest number of parties, albeit imperfectly for everyone, because of the democratic participation of a representative sampling of individuals and institutions with vested interests in college football broadcasting. And last, the reports claimed that the policy protected the many small schools that felt more embattled than ever by the emergence of television and that made up a majority of NCAA membership.

Many NCAA members felt that television accentuated the already inequitable distribution of football revenues that had produced the elite tier of winning teams that already existed. The early NCAA Television Committee reports spoke to the fears of small schools when they described, under the subheading of "commercialization," the emergence of a "TV aristocracy" that would dominate on-field competition and monopolize network revenues. The 1952 report states that although protecting the gate is imperative, "there is perhaps an even more disturbing threat to the future of intercollegiate football inherent in the premium financial and publicity rewards which can be realized from live television" (NCAA 1953, 12–13). One of the few things that the NCAA Television Committee stated confidently about television was that it would eventually generate large sums of money and accentuate the commercialization of college football by producing a TV aristocracy. Even large schools, for publicity reasons alone, would support limited measures to maintain competitive balance in a structurally unequal environment (Zimbalist 1999, 117–118).

The final step in the process was selling a policy of limited broadcasting to a public that desired freedom of choice as consumers. This was a trickier step since fans simply wanted to watch the game of their choice whereas members of the broadcast coalition from schools to networks to advertisers had a common interest in stable capital accumulation. As a result, fans and sports writers reacted critically to the NCAA's limited broadcast schedules (Gould 1953; Lohman 1951). Given that Cold War discourse said that freedom of choice in consumption was an expression of citizenship, the controlling nature of broadcast regulations was no small issue. Therefore, the NCAA undertook a program to "correctly inform" the public on controlled broadcasting in order to shape public opinion in favor of its limited broadcast schedule. The article "Why Football on TV Is Limited," by Asa Bushnell, NCAA director of television programming and secretary of the U.S. Olympic Committee, is an example of how the NCAA responded to consumer dissatisfaction (Bushnell 1953). Bushnell defends the NCAA's policy of limiting broadcasts to one game per week against fans' apparent desire for free-market conditions by describing the NCAA as the steward of college football that saved it in 1905. Bushnell argued that fans' unrestrained desire for free football would have "catastrophic" effects upon college football that funds all other intercollegiate and intramural athletics. Therefore, protecting gate revenues against television and evenly extending televisual representation to all regions and schools regardless of size best serves the public interest (Bushnell 1953, 106). The connections that Bushnell draws among football, revenue flows, masculinity, and public interest highlight the NCAA's framing of television broadcasting, discussed in the next section, and resurfaced decades later in Title IX debates (see Sabo 1998; Staurowsky 1998; Weistart 1998).

The NCAA disseminated publicity through a variety of means and methods. One of the stated criteria for selecting a network was its willingness to aggressively promote the NCAA. The Television Committee instituted a "liaison officer" in 1953 who interfaced with the contracting network to ensure clear, consistent, and broad dissemination of NCAA publicity. While the liaison officer dedicated time to producing content like the "will-to-win" packages, his primary charge was organizing an array of publicity channels to educate the public. This included press kits, pregame and postgame packages, newspaper ads and articles, radio interviews and spots, and talks given to special groups, "such as Sportswriters and Sportscasters associations, [and] college booster and alumni clubs" (NCAA 1963, 33). The messages focused on how NCAA regulations serve a public interest that was defined in line with broader cultural tendencies of the early Cold War.

## FOOTBALL AS REMEDY FOR DEPLETED MASCULINITY

The NCAA needed to develop a clear frame in order to present its vision as reasonable. NCAA reports described fans' desire to watch the game of their choice for free without enduring weather conditions, crowds, or parking as a threat to intercollegiate athletics since football financially supported all other athletic programs. Whether college football actually benefits other athletic programs or not is open to question (see Lederman 1988, 1993; Oberlander and Lederman 1988; Zimbalist 1999), and it was questioned in the 1950s.[18] Nevertheless, the NCAA held football's economic beneficence as axiomatic. The NCAA reasoned that since football funds all other athletic programs, any challenge to football's preeminence on college campuses would curtail other sports. And a reduction in intercollegiate and intramural athletics would jeopardize the physical training of U.S. youth at a time of international crisis (NCAA 1953, 7). Therefore, to protect football was to protect the nation at large.

The success of the Soviet Union at the Summer Olympics beginning with the Helsinki Games in 1952 added urgency to the NCAA's claim (Beamish and Ritchie 2005; Jay 2004; Massaro 2003). Critics claimed that the Soviet Union was using the Olympics to wage the Cold War in a cultural sphere. The United States responded by turning its universities into a training ground for preparing athletes to meet the Kremlin on a global stage of Cold War athletics (Montez de Oca 2007, 117; also Domer 1976; Jay 2004; Thomas 2002). The use of university athletics provided a liberal strategy for harnessing the nation's resources during the cultural Cold War by outsourcing athletic production to "nonstate" institutions.[19] But university athletics played a larger role than just preparing elite athletes for Olympic competition, as John T. McGovern, a U.S. Olympic official, made clear: "[T]he most important thing of all is to impress on our young people the soundness of constant training and conditioning" (McGovern 1954). This suggests that university athletics was a site for waging the Cold War, and young people's bodies were weapons in the geopolitical struggle (see chapter 3).

Concern over the declining physical fitness of U.S. bodies reached a heightened pitch during the muscle gap. As discussed in chapter 3, the muscle gap was part of a larger crisis of masculinity during the 1950s manifested in the language of mass culture critiques. At the heart of the crisis was a concern that modern society had an effeminizing effect upon men and that was leading to the replacement of "traditional" masculine characteristics of rugged independence for the passive conformism of the companionate family and large corporation (Gilbert 2005, 48). Despite having a vested interest in becoming a large, controlling institution through the establishment of its broadcast regulations, the NCAA found great cultural resonance with the claim that college football was a part of the national mission at a time of widespread concern over men's physical development. Rear Admiral Tom Hamilton, chairman of the 1951 Television Steering Committee, attempted to cultivate that link when he claimed that football broadcasting created a "perplexing problem, which threatens the maintenance of our national physical training and competitive sports programs" (cited in "NCAA Committee Recommends Football Video on Limited Basis" 1951). Along with Ralph Furey, co-chairman of the 1952 Steering Committee, Hamilton reiterated the connection between broadcast regulations and the physical development of the nation's youth. "As the sports public comes to understand the issues [via NCAA publicity], it will recognize the NCAA efforts in this field as the best and only means of protecting the physical well-being and physical development of the sons and daughters of the nation" (NCAA 1953, 7).

The NCAA continued to cultivate that link in its publicity campaigns by arguing college football supported a broad array of athletic programs necessary for supporting national fitness programs. Robert Hall, former Yale athletic director and NCAA Television Steering Committee chairman in 1955, argued in *Sports Illustrated* that television would siphon off gate receipts from small schools, causing them to divert money from intramurals to support their football teams. Curtailing intramurals is a problem, Hall reasoned, since "[l]ack of adequate exercise is deemed at least partly responsible for the increasing number of rejections for physical reasons by the armed forces" (Hall 1955, 26). By 1955 the NCAA had refined its frame into a seven-point plan intended to structure all NCAA publicity. The plan emphasized public interest and the traditional role of athletics in college education:

1. College football is a character-building activity which performs an essential and worthwhile function in the over-all academic life of the student.
2. Intercollegiate sports competition aids in the development of the youth of our nation and prepares them for positions as future national leaders.
3. The 1955 Plan as devised offers the American public a true cross-section of collegiate football and at the same time protects the athletic budgets of member colleges.
4. Intercollegiate competition—
   a. develops will-to-win;

   b. teaches self-discipline, self-sacrifice, and self-control;

   c. builds sound minds and bodies through mental and physical training and coordination;

   d. develops a spirit of loyalty and team-work which is the foundation of success in American industry, government, and the military.

5. Small colleges have important sports programs, and their football produces keen, close competition.

6. Good attendance at college football games throughout the nation each Saturday will support the year-round campus sports program.

7. College football is the original football; it is great football. (NCAA 1956, 34)

A clear though complicated image arises from the NCAA's framing of college football. First, it suggests that football serves an important academic function in cultivating desirable characteristics in (male) citizens, including the desire to work as a team to dominate others while remaining loyal to authority (Messner 1992, 10), the development of a hard body and mind, and the development of ambition to lead peers. Second, college football as both a local and national practice represents the many diverse regions of the nation. For instance, the September 30, 1961, halftime program titled "All-American Sport for All Americans" suggested that college football creates a cultural sphere that brings the diversity of the nation together in pluralistic harmony (NCAA 1962, 25). This makes football a pluralistic representation of the nation that allows fans to experience what Homi Bhabha calls the "double-time" of nationalism (Bhabha 1991, 297), in which fans are simultaneously pedagogical objects learning about the nation, its regions, and its people and are performative subjects participating in the American way of life by attending college football games and watching the limited broadcast schedule. Third, point 6 invokes consumer citizenship by suggesting regular attendance at live games sustain the nation's health. Thus citizens have an obligation to act as responsible consumers by supporting the games of local schools. The obligation is based on the assumption that the nation's health is tied to gate receipts because football funds other athletic programs on campus. The "spend locally, act nationally" logic of consumer citizenship offers another way for citizens, once properly educated, to become performative subjects of the nation. My second and third points highlight the active, participatory nature of sports fandom. Not only does fandom produce football, participation in the American way of life simultaneously produces the nation and a fan's position in it. Fourth, point 7 brands college football as original and authentic in opposition to its primary economic rival, the National Football League (Oriard 2001, 200–201; Smith 2001, 94). When put together, the list constructs football as a tradition of college life that expresses national spirit and produces masculine subjects who will participate in the Cold War nation as active consumer citizens. All seven points of the plan are expressed in the text of a 1956 halftime message:

> The Army-Navy game, perhaps the most colorful of the hundreds of contests making up the intercollegiate football schedule each autumn, illustrates graphically the many fine features of this greatest of all contact sports. Similarly college football accurately characterizes the diversified competitive athletic program which the NCAA and its member institutions from coast to coast consider indispensable if on-campus training of the country's youth is to be complete, comprehensive, and effectively preparatory for the future. Collegiate football does not need the de-emphasis sometimes suggested for it; but it should not be handicapped by over-emphasis. The correct treatment of collegiate football is its continuing strong emphasis as a worthwhile ingredient of the nation's educational process. (NCAA 1957, 33–34)[20]

Eventually the NCAA believed that its publicity swung the public in its favor. The 1958 report stated, "Although there are indicators that the public would like to see the game of its own choice, the development of understanding by the public has resulted in an acceptance of a controlled program" (NCAA 1959, 3). College football broadcast ratings consistently grew throughout the following decades (Zimbalist 1999, 95). As college football broadcasting experienced steady economic growth, fans became acclimated to the NCAA's controls and limitations on consumer choice. But before realizing that growth, the NCAA needed to quell internal challenges to its cartel.

## POLICING THE COALITION—PENN'S REVOLT

The strongest challenge to NCAA regulations came from an NCAA member institution. Ingham, Howell, and Schilperoort argue that a cartel functions effectively when member firms stick to collusive agreements that are based on mutual interest. However, if a member firm sees greater interest as an individual agent outside of the cartel, that member is likely to bolt and the cartel must act to discipline the transgressor or risk disintegration (Ingham, Howell, and Schilperoort 1987, 436). This is an important point both for the NCAA, which enjoyed new authority following the recent setback of the Sanity Code (Watterson 2000, 263), and for schools that could negotiate lucrative television contracts individually. Notre Dame chafed under NCAA controls since it had the most to gain from Home Rule. However, Notre Dame bided its time and let Penn directly challenge NCAA authority (Smith 2001, 65–66, 68; also Watterson 2000). Flouting the NCAA's policy of controlled broadcasting, Penn struck a deal with ABC worth $250,000 to televise its 1951 season ("Football Heretic" 1951). The NCAA reacted by ruling that no NCAA school could play Penn as long as it acted outside of the cartel. Ultimately, Penn backed down and agreed to work with the Television Steering Committee in scheduling its broadcasts.

The rift between the NCAA and Penn lasted for three years and served as a warning to schools wishing to break broadcast containment ("3-Year U. of P. Feud with NCAA Ends" 1954). The NCAA exerted direct, disciplinary force by blocking Penn's broadcasts and barring its athletes from events like the prestigious Ohio Regatta ("UP May Be Excluded from Ohio Regatta" 1951). But the NCAA also acted more in line with the conditions of the early Cold War than did Penn. The NCAA did not frame its regulations as a restraint of supply that artificially inflates value, but positioned its policies as steps to protect public interest by defending small schools and their overall athletic mission to fortify masculinity in the nation. The NCAA successfully framed uncontained broadcasting as a technological threat to the nation's human resources that would lead to greater centralization of wealth in large institutions. It also situated its regulations as a bulwark of defense against that attack. With the NCAA framing its regulations as protecting youth and small colleges, Penn's actions appeared as crass egoism in the conformist 1950s despite its adherence to the NCAA's tradition of institutional autonomy. Arthur Daley of the *New York Times* chided Penn's actions as poor behavior from a school associated with Ivy League respectability rather than public school ambition (Daly 1951). Critics berated Penn's president, Harold Stassen, for his ambitions in football and politics. One critic wrote to Penn's Board of Trustees that "Mr. Stassen is having difficulty subduing his political tendencies and wishes to ingratiate himself with the Roman Catholics" (cited in Smith 2001, 68). The success of the NCAA's frame was tied to a general tendency during the early Cold War to suppress individual liberty in favor of order and consensus. This tendency was driven by Cold War anxiety and referred to as the liberal consensus (Gerstle 1995, 579; see also Biskind 1983/2000; Murphy 2004; Phillips-Fein 2007).

NCAA broadcast regulations were more consistent with what David Harvey (1990) refers to as postwar Fordism than the entrepreneurial strategy of Penn. Fordism was a logical development of corporate liberalism that involved a high degree of corporate regulation of both the economy and society. It relied on a tripartite pact struck among big business, big labor, and big government. Although Fordism's flowering was contained early in the century, it blossomed following the success of centralized planning during World War II, the rise of Cold War unity against communism, and the establishment of new regulatory schemes for government (Harvey 1990, 127–129). Fordism ensured the formation of a disciplined workforce compensated in rising wages and increased leisure time that was the foundation of the American way of life in addition to consolidating capital in enormous corporations and increasing the nation's productive capacities (see Antonio and Bonanno 2000; Harvey 1990; Pietrykowski 1995).

The state never officially questioned the NCAA's collusive and restrictive regulations until the 1980s. In fact, the NCAA felt emboldened in 1953 by the *United States v. National Football League* decision that upheld the right of a league to limit broadcasts as a measure to protect attendance, especially of smaller institutions (NCAA 1954, 35). Judge A. Grim stated in his decision that the overriding public interest is healthy market competition. "The purposes of the Sherman Act certainly will not be served by prohibiting the defendant clubs, particularly the weaker clubs, from protecting their home gate receipts from the disastrous financial effects of invading telecasts of outside games" (*US v. NFL* 1953). Given the overriding interest of supporting commerce, Judge Grim further reasoned that "[t]he League is truly a unique business enterprise, which is entitled to protect its very existence by agreeing to reasonable restrictions on its member clubs" (*US v. NFL* 1953). In *US v. NFL*, the Court saw protective regulations that fostered stable capital accumulation as reasonable restraints upon trade. Despite *US v. NFL* being a ruling on professional football, the NCAA, correctly, believed that the case would shield its regulations from legal or political scrutiny. The NCAA further claimed congressional support of its regulations in 1961 when the House blocked both live and tape-delayed broadcasts of professional games on Friday evenings and Saturdays during the college football season.[21] The House Committee on the Judiciary explained it acted so that "college football, upon which substantial educational programs depend for revenue, is not unduly prejudiced" (cited in NCAA 1962, 28). In both instances, we see state acceptance of regulations that limit competition as serving public interest in order to stabilize market chaos and foster conditions for predictable capital accumulation.

Originally drafted as a defensive measure to contain television's technological invasion, the NCAA plan provided a stable environment for predictable capital accumulation. The first step in building a robust economic model was the NCAA's effective cartelization of athletics and selling its restrictions as reasonable. The final step was the establishment of an effective sponsorship model. From 1951 to 1953 the NCAA contracted with a single, large sponsor that could afford and benefit from national advertising. However, the NCAA lost General Motors (GM) as its sole sponsor when switching from NBC to ABC in 1954. Unable to find a replacement for GM, the NCAA was forced to cobble together a group of smaller companies interested in regional advertising. It turned out, however, that using several smaller sponsors and a regional marketing strategy lowered the cost to individual advertisers while increasing the pool of potential sponsors. The regional marketing model also matched the regional broadcast model that the Big Ten and Pacific Coast Conference successfully pushed through in 1955 over the resistance of many small and southern schools (Smith 2001, 95–97). NCAA regulations coupled with a multiple-sponsor model set the conditions for accruing significant financial revenues from football broadcasting at the same time that stadium attendance was reaching new highs. The NCAA began to embrace television when it realized that college football and broadcasting could form a symbiotic relationship, what Sut Jhally calls the "sport-media complex," where sport and media become so economically intertwined they form a single structural unit (Jhally 1984, 42). When the NCAA embraced television, discussion of commercialization and a TV aristocracy disappeared from the Steering Committee's reports (NCAA 1955, 30). Control over television revenues bought more than just positive feelings. Broadcast domination produced enough capital for the NCAA to buy support throughout the Cold War and discipline wayward schools like Penn (Watterson 2000, 284–285).

## BROADCAST REGULATIONS END, INEQUALITIES CONTINUE

Dialectical tension and contradiction have been at the center of the NCAA's growth across the twentieth century. The NCAA emerged in the early twentieth century in order to stabilize a chaotic market and legitimate an existing system of accumulation in the face of popular criticism. Over time, the NCAA itself had growing organizational ambitions. The emergence of television created a crisis in college football that the NCAA compared to the period in which it was created. Broadcast regulations were then used to transform the NCAA from a loose confederation into a cartel that restricted the supply of television broadcasts relative to demand in order to accrue monopoly profits. The NCAA structured its publicity with a frame that linked men's bodies to U.S. militarism and national interest. Refracting broadcasting through a prism of Cold War anxiety made the collusive regulations appear reasonable and allowed the NCAA to win consent from the state and the public for its control over college athletics.

Cartelization allowed the NCAA to rationalize and build a broadcast market. Top football schools had enjoyed increasing financial rewards from football broadcasting throughout the 1950s and 1960s. The expansion of the college sports broadcast market made protectionist policies an impediment to elite schools by the 1970s as the U.S. economy shifted from Fordist relations of production and consumption to neoliberal capitalism. These structural changes caused top schools to see diminishing returns from their broadcasts, so they pushed for deregulation in order to unleash the economic power of the broadcast market in the 1980s. Once again a contradiction arose between college football's social and material relations of production as new communication technologies and new promotional strategies transformed the industry (Whitson 1998). Unlike the 1950s, when the NCAA instituted regulations to control and foster an emergent broadcasting market, in the 1980s the capitalist state intervened to deregulate and unleash a highly developed broadcasting market. NCAA regulation of college football broadcasting came to an official end when the U.S. Supreme Court ruled in *NCAA v. Board of Regents of the University of Oklahoma* that NCAA regulations constituted an unfair restraint of trade (*NCAA v. Board of Regents* 1984).

But as Andrew Zimbalist (1999) and others have shown, broadcast revenues in the deregulated era are more inequitably distributed than ever. The case of Notre Dame University, which always stood to gain the most from a return to Home Rule (see Smith 2001, 168), is illustrative. Notre Dame was an original member of the College Football Association (CFA), which led the fight against NCAA broadcast regulations and supplanted the NCAA as a broadcast cartel in the mid-1980s. In 1984 the CFA negotiated a one-year contract with ABC for $12 million, and in 1990 the CFA signed a five-year $350 million TV contract that was split among 64 schools (Siegfried and Burba 2003). That same year, Notre Dame pulled out of the CFA for a five-year independent contract with NBC worth $35 million that has since been renewed through 2015 and is valued at $15 million per season (Sandomir 2009). Without Notre Dame, the CFA's bargaining power plummeted and the organization eventually folded in 1995 (Siegfried and Burba 2003; Zimbalist 1999). The contrast within the NCAA becomes stark when comparing the broadcast revenues of a heavily branded school like Notre Dame to the entire operating budget of a non-BCS school like San Diego State, which survived on a budget of $7.5 million in 2006 (Zeigler 2008).

Since the late nineteenth century we have seen growing economic inequality in college football. At every step, we hear political rhetoric of reform but see material conditions of centralization. In the 1950s, the NCAA argued television presented a technological threat to the nation based on an ecological fallacy— when television sales were up and ticket sales were down, the NCAA presented these general trends as causal of individual action. The NCAA then championed small schools by placing controls on the free market in order to accrue monopoly profits, essentially siphoning revenues away from small schools. The NCAA claimed that cartelization served the public interest by supporting the U.S.'s fight with the Soviet Union when it in fact limited institutional freedom and consumer choice through market rationalization, which is particularly ironic since consumer choice signified the very freedom that the U.S. championed in the Cold War. If we understand ideology as systems of knowledge that produce a particular way of seeing, understanding, and experiencing the world (Hall 1986), then the interlocking of masculinity and nation within a militarist ideological frame has provided a key strategy to support capital accumulation in college football. As we saw during the muscle gap period, the fortification of masculinity addressed certain contradictions to foster capital accumulation and create inequalities, while contradictions that might have interfered with capital accumulation remained obscure and unaddressed.

# 6 · FROM NEIGHBORHOOD TO NATION

Geographical Imagination of the
Cold War in *Sports Illustrated*

THIS CHAPTER RETURNS to the relationship of sport, space, and identity introduced in chapter 1 to argue that the coverage of college football in *Sports
Illustrated* (*SI*) in 1954 helped to teach a Cold War geographical imagination.
According to Christina Klein (2003), media, including film and print journalism,
participated in the U.S. Cold War project by "teaching the Cold War" through
the construction of two images of the world that were homologous to the double
nature of U.S. foreign policy: containment and integration (see chapters 2 and 3).
Two "global imaginaries" were articulated in the media: a *heroic* imaginary of
containment that saw the United States on a crusade in a dangerous world and a
*sentimental* imaginary of integration that saw the world interconnected by emotional bonds of reciprocity. Both global imaginaries circulated within the media
and provided a "common sense" by which people could understand their position within the nation, perceive national destiny, and chart strategies of action
within national and global space (Klein 2003, 14, 22–23).

Like most Cold War scholars, however, Klein does not include sport in her
analysis of Cold War popular culture (Kemper 2009; Carrington 2010). This is
unfortunate because, as Aden and Reynolds (1993) argue, *SI*'s spatial metaphors
help readers understand their specific place within a larger national context and
negotiate contradictions of late capitalism. Similarly unfortunate is the fact that
very little sport scholarship situates *SI* within the machinations of the Cold War.
Most research on *SI* has focused on the way in which its issues, articles, and covers
valorize white male athletes in major sports (Condor and Anderson 1984; Davis
1993, 1997; Fink and Kensicki 2002; Leath and Lumpkin 1992; Levy and Bryant
1993; Lumpkin and Williams 1991; Messner and Montez de Oca 2005; Salwen and
Wood 1994; Shores et al. 2005). The most significant in this regard is Laurel Davis's
(1997) book on the swimsuit issue that sketches the intersection of hegemonic
masculinity and whiteness within the swimsuit issue, consistently *SI*'s most widely

read and profitable issue. And although Davis emphasizes how the swimsuit issue creates an imperial imaginary by shooting in "exotic locales," she, like most other authors, does not connect the Third World locations to a Cold War global imaginary (Klein 2003; Westad 2007). The one exception in the *SI* literature is scholarship by John Massaro (2003), who argues that reporting in *SI* during the Olympic year of 1956 was framed by an anti-Soviet bias indicative of Cold War hegemony within the West. Since the Cold War was waged to a large degree in popular culture and sport is one of the preeminent areas of popular culture, it is worthwhile to follow Massaro and look at *SI*'s relationship to Cold War popular culture. In this chapter, I look at three articles from *SI*'s first volume to tease out how a particular geographical imagination was constructed in text, images, charts, and maps that could help support the broader U.S. Cold War project.

## THE COLD WAR'S IMAGINATIVE GEOGRAPHIES

The concept of geographical imaginations is useful for understanding how popular culture texts like *SI* participate in a territorialization of space. Derek Gregory writes, "[I]maginative geographies are discursive formations, tense constellations of power, knowledge and spatiality, that are centered on 'here' and projected towards 'there' so that 'the vacant or anonymous reaches of distance are converted into meaning for us here'" (Gregory 1995, 29). In other words, rational and precise representations of geographical knowledge in maps, texts, and images allow people to imagine space that really exists but cannot be wholly perceived in one's immediate physical and social surroundings (Deutsche 1995, 169). Understandings of space and people's relationship to space thus arise from multiple forms of knowledge to construct a rationally ordered, productive image of the world that can structure people's understandings of reality and thus their material practices (Hall 1986). The fusing of physical space that people can touch and know to conceptual spaces in a way that appears natural, inevitable, and rooted in experience is central to nationalist projects (Anderson 1991; McClintock 1991). What we see in this chapter is how the presentation of text, images, charts, and maps in the glossy pages of *SI*'s football coverage constructed an image of space and place consistent with the broader imperatives of the Cold War.

The formation of a Cold War global imaginary is important because the strategy of containment necessitated that Americans adopt new ways of conceiving space, nation, and their relationship to national and global space. In short, the Cold War required the ascendance of a new geographical imagination. By looking at *SI*'s football coverage in 1954, I demonstrate how *SI* could help foster an *internationalist* geographical imagination that would displace the nation's previously dominant *isolationist* imagination.[1] As opposed to the constricted imagination of isolationism, Cold War internationalism took the whole world within its field of vision and saw danger embodied in communism and the Soviet Union everywhere (Roskin 1974, 569). The Cold War and the transformation of U.S. foreign policy from isolationism to internationalism produced an extroverted geographical imagination that required active military engagements and economic support beyond traditional spheres of influence (North America, Latin America, and parts of Asia). This new geographical imagination became manifest in containment and integration. The articulations of containment and integration in popular culture helped support an internationalist paradigm in Cold War foreign policy.

Internationalism did not simply spring up with the Iron Curtain. Visions of internationalism on the political right tied to missionary movements, especially in China, and the political left, such as the Popular Front, had presented competing challenges to isolationism back into the nineteenth century. Cultural producers drew upon these earlier strands of internationalism to give a positive vision of the otherwise chilly business of the Cold War. "Like the producers of missionary and Popular Front culture before them, [middlebrow intellectuals] brought to life the abstract principles of a particular form of internationalism by translating them into a concrete body of social practices, aesthetic philosophies, and cultural forms. In the process, they further worked out the synthesis of left and right internationalisms that the Truman and Eisenhower administrations had achieved at the level of political ideology and policy" (Klein 2003, 58–59). Central to the success of early Cold War foreign policy was spreading the idea throughout the public that the United States had not only a historical mission in the world but also a moral imperative to intervene in the affairs of foreign nations. And it was through popular culture, including sport, that these ideas could get worked out.

The United States's history of isolationism and its citizens' hesitancy to provide welfare to other nations were barriers to forming the consensus that the nation's political leaders wanted (Roskin 1974, 566). Political leaders who devised the strategy of containment believed that they needed to shape the public's understanding of the global order and their geographical imaginations in order to win popular support for U.S. Cold War policy. As NSC-68 states, "This process requires, firstly, that sufficient information regarding the basic political, economic, and military elements of the present situation be made publicly available so that an intelligent popular opinion can be formed. Having achieved a comprehension of the issues now confronting this Republic, it will then be possible for the American people and the American Government to arrive at a consensus. Out of this common view will develop a determination of the national will and a solid resolute expression of that will" (Nitze 1993, 43).[2] Thus the authors of NSC-68 believed that the strategy of containment would require an effective educational campaign to build a shared understanding of the new global order.

In forming a unified national self backed by political, military, and economic capital, top-down political leadership alone was insufficient. A concrete and tangible vision of the national self as well as sets of practices were necessary for citizens to participate in the Cold War and thereby consent to its costs and consequences. Part of the solution to this problem, as Klein argues, was the articulation of Cold War internationalism in sentimental narratives so that people could develop a meaningful, emotional connection to abstract foreign policy objectives. So although political leaders during the Cold War articulated their needs through overt propaganda (Sherry 1995), most of that propaganda, such as Coronet's educational films *Service and Citizenship* (1951) and *Communism* (1952), was highly didactic, stilted, and easy to mock. In contrast to didactic propaganda that many people experienced as external to their lives and interests, sport media create patriotic pageantry that balances heroic and sentimental narratives while producing in fans a deep sense of participation in something larger than themselves (Fried 1998; Silk and Falcous 2005).

One of the most popular forms of patriotic pageantry in the early Cold War was college football. Although it was played at colleges across the United States in the 1890s and its popularity expanded beyond college campuses as a result of its use by the military in the First World War (see chapter 1), the rise of television transformed college football into the most popular spectator sport of the early Cold War. Professional baseball was the *national pastime* from the mid-nineteenth century through the early postwar period, which means it was a consumer-leisure industry that served as a unifying symbol of the national self. The symbolic power of baseball during the era of isolationism and industrialization was its nostalgic harkening to an imagined rural life that urban industrial workers could participate in and use to construct a masculine identity separate from but in relationship to the shop floor (Kimmel 1990; Neilson 1995). Football eclipsed baseball on television, in print media coverage, and in people's minds during the Cold War (Oriard 2001). The popularity of college football during the Cold War and its eclipsing of baseball in popularity speak to its power as a symbol of containment and postwar Fordism (see Danzig 1956; Oriard 1993, 2001; Peterson 1997; Real 1979; Trujillo 1995; Westby and Sack 1976; Whannel 1993). As comedian George Carlin's famous "Baseball-Football" (1975) skit suggests, football's militaristic nationalism, its rationalization of time and space, and its expressions of violent masculinity carried greater symbolic currency in an era of containment and MIK than did baseball's lost Jeffersonian past.[3] Containment as the guiding metaphor of U.S. foreign policy is, of course, paralleled as a metaphor for defensive strategy in football, especially the perimeter defense articulated in NSC-68.[4] College football and its media coverage during the early Cold War thus form a consumer-leisure industry that has the political power to help people construct a sense of citizen-self that imagines their destiny tied to the nation as they move together through calendrical time and geopolitical space.

## *SPORTS ILLUSTRATED* AND THE RISE OF NATIONAL SPORTS

Tying a national imaginary to local identity in sports coverage needs a local-national sports discourse. However, until 1957, when the Brooklyn Dodgers and New York Giants went west, the national pastime was contained east of the Mississippi. Besides *The Sporting News*, which exclusively covered baseball, national news coverage of sports was inconsistent. And although the coming of the telegraph had promised the "collapse of time and space" (Covert 1984; Marvin 1988), prewar travel between cities by competitors and spectators was constrained by roads and rails. As a result, prewar sports, other than college football in print media (Oriard 1993), were consistent with isolationism by encouraging a locally focused geographical imagination. The proliferation of communication and transportation technology in the postwar period (especially television and the jet airplane) accelerated the sport-media complex, without which truly national sports leagues and consumption patterns would not be possible. And it was in the expanding postwar moment that Time, Inc. launched what became the most successful national, all-sports publication: *Sports Illustrated* (James 1994).[5]

In 1954, during the heady era of post–World War II prosperity and the anxiety of the early Cold War, *SI* burst onto the U.S. landscape. Market research in the early 1950s had suggested the existence of a significant yet untapped male market of potential sport-media consumers that Time, Inc. and its founder, Henry Luce, sought to exploit (MacCambridge 1997, 11). In planning for a successful launch, Time, Inc. discerned two major obstacles. The first obstacle was the perceived lack of a mass audience necessary to support such an adventure. After all, *SI* would be the first nationally distributed, glossy, all-sport publication that covered a range of both spectator and participatory sports. Although market research suggested male sports fans were a market waiting to be tapped (MacCambridge 1997, 11), they formed a fragmented market of fans loyal to individual teams or players and regional sports. Without nationally unifying sports, Time, Inc. feared *SI* might not generate a significant market base. Indeed, what characterized the development of sport as a consumer-leisure industry in the twentieth century was the reconceptualization of space, place, and identity so that teams like the Fighting Irish of Notre Dame and the Dallas Cowboys could become not just local heroes but also national brands symbolic of the nation (Foster 1999; Whitson 1998). But at the time, those symbols of nation did not yet exist. So although interest in sports did exist and television was helping to consolidate a market for spectator sports, in 1953 television's eventual role was not yet clear to the people charged with this risky new adventure (James 1994; MacCambridge 1997; also chapter 5). Furthermore, previous national sports publications tended to limit coverage to single sports like baseball, boxing, or fishing. Thus the founders of *Sports Illustrated* felt that constructing a unified audience would require consumer education.

The idea of education as central to the construction of *SI*'s audience touches on the second obstacle: the concern that advertisers would avoid the magazine for fear that it would not yield a significant return on investment. The primary reason that advertisers were leery of *SI* regardless of its subscription size was a general image on Madison Avenue of sports fans as drunken, howling denizens of the Ebbets Field bleachers (James 1994; MacCambridge 1997). This classed perception of sports fans saw the potential *SI* audience as working-class men who are less than ideal consumers (see Meehan 1990). Therefore, it was necessary for *SI* to construct not only a mass audience but also the *right* mass audience: a discerning, consuming audience (MacCambridge 1997). The elitism of Madison Avenue and Time, Inc. led *SI* to construct a white, middle-class, male audience through a pedagogical presentation of sport that elided much of the difference that actually existed within the sports covered.[6] Luce, for his part, had never shied away from a pedagogical calling to educate the populace. In seeing *SI*'s role as providing "basic information," Luce stated, "One doesn't want to be didactic. A good rule of pedagogy in any field is 'To teach as if you taught not and things unknown as things forgot'" (cited in James 1994, 242). In order to build a large national audience that could be sold to advertisers, the ideal American constructed by *SI* in the early postwar was a middle-class consumer who implicitly was white and masculine (see Davis 1997).

Although Henry Luce was not directly involved in the day-to-day running of *SI*, he was essential to its founding (James 1994; Massaro 2003) and a significant Cold Warrior (Klein 2003; Walker 1994). For Luce, publishing was part of a project to cultivate a transposable set of enduring dispositions, or habitus (Bourdieu 1986, 1991), in the American public consistent with his own conservative ideology despite a tendency to hire liberal writers (see Griffith 1995; Kobler 1968; Neils 1990; Swanberg 1972). The son of Calvinist missionaries in China, Luce held a right-wing internationalist vision for the United States that he expressed in "The American Century" (Luce 1941/1969a). Luce felt the United States should take a leading role in world politics to spread "American values" and democracy in the fight against totalitarianism. He believed the United States should not hesitate to use military force when necessary, but his vision of U.S. internationalism was not simply coercive, it was also cultural (Luce 1941/1969a, 117). American music, film, and slang already packaged and disseminated by a culture industry that included his publications were teaching Americana domestically and internationally. With the founding of *SI*, sport, and especially American football, could be added to Luce's list of American cultural products that served a pedagogical function consistent with his internationalist vision.

## THE FOOTBALL FIELD—FROM
## HERE TO THERE AND THERE TO HERE

Analyzing *SI*'s football coverage is complicated not only because the articles fuse conceptual space (there) to particular places (here) but also because their spatial construction functions on multiple geographical scales. In geography, the term "scale" refers to measures or magnitudes of space that demarcate units of analysis—similar to periodization in history. Football coverage constructs relational scales that include human bodies, stadiums, towns/cities, regions, and the nation. Players and fans enter football's social relations of production and consumption through institutions homologous to its relational scales—teams, stadiums, divisions/conferences, and leagues. Unsurprisingly, *SI*'s sports coverage constructs three primary scales of space: the national, the region, and the familial-local. The specific scales constructed in the articles discussed here are the nation as a legal-political entity, the four traditional regions of the United States, and the suburban neighborhood. These conceptual spaces are embodied by particular places populated with real and imagined football fans: the United States as a bounded and contiguous social unit, the U.S. South as a product of U.S. social and cultural history, and a specific neighborhood in suburban Minneapolis. By linking space to place in its articles, *SI* football coverage constructs rescaling networks that allow people to conceptually move up and down the relational scales nation, region, and locale. The ability to rescale and link place to space is crucial to the development of an internationalist geographical imagination that would simultaneously conceive of the United States and the Free World in relation to the Soviet Union and the Slave World.

I discuss only three articles from *SI*'s volume 1 (1954) for reasons of space and clarity, though my analysis draws on a review of *SI* throughout the early Cold War period. While constituting a small sample, these three articles sufficiently illustrate how early *SI* football coverage tied space to place across rescaling networks parallel to the institutional order of football's social relations of production and consumption. This pattern describes a sport-media matrix (Burstyn 1999) that ties college football to media, education, economics, and governmental institutions at national, regional, and local scales. Unlike daily newspaper coverage of sport that tends toward simple descriptions of local events and outcomes, the weekly, national coverage of *SI* enabled it to take on a more narrative, pictorial, and personal coverage of athletes, events, and athletics. In doing so, *SI* was able to simultaneously tell heroic and sentimental narratives. The heroism of *SI* coverage is immediately apparent in its article "U.S. Football: In Maps and Diagrams" ("US Football" 1954), which maps the football field onto the nation itself. The analysis then moves to the article "The Solid South" (Hickman 1954), which situates contemporary college football within the historical construction of the South as a region of the nation. The sentimentality of *SI* football is explicit in the article "I Taught Bud Wilkinson to Play Football" (Berg and Kantor 1954), by golf legend Patty Berg, which links the shared professional success of Berg and Wilkinson to playing football in the suburban neighborhood of their childhood. In the end, *SI* football coverage draws upon both cultural and scientific knowledge in its descriptions of football, the United States, its regions, and its localities so that readers can participate in spatialized narrative of the nation.

The Nation as Field of Play

> At the height of the football season, a Monday morning quarterback's map of the U.S. *(above)* looks like nothing so much as a general's battle plan. From one end of the country to the other, the weekly battles are organized like encounters of battalions, regiments and divisions in a system as complex as it is often confusing to the eager football layman. And behind them stand the colleges, large and small, from whose ranks of men and women come the teams, cheerleaders, the bands and all the pageantry which makes football what it is.
>
> Here with the aid of diagrams prepared by L. H. Billing, Sports Engineer for the Falk Corporation's Sports Facts, *SI* presents an over-all view of the national football scene. The conferences are located above, and detailed in charts at right, which lists colleges, their enrollment and football stadiums. The gridiron itself, scene of the weekly battles, is blueprinted on [*sic*] opposite page with all the precise measurements developed from 80 years of play.[7]

I quote the entire text of "US Football" because it encapsulates much of my argument about *SI*'s Cold War geographical imagination. By situating individual football fans at home imagining participation in imperial conquest within a national space that is abstracted onto the territorialized plane of the football field, the article ties individuals to the nation as competent cultural citizens who perform their citizenship as football fans. The militarized social order is so complicated and confusing that pedagogical lessons are necessary to make sense of the nation and to allow imaginative participation in it. The article teaches the reader that the nation and its football league are composed of various regions and locales that bring men and women together into organized, harmonious solidarity through its ongoing practice. This ongoing practice is not a recent phenomenon but has developed over eighty years, and in that it is an organic expression of national spirit.

The text of the article provides an ideological frame in which its graphics should be understood. These graphics include a three-column map of the nation with the forty-eight states drawn across it and the seven regions that compose the fourteen NCAA conferences (fig. 6.1).[8] On the facing page is an equivalently sized map of the "Modern Collegiate Football Field" that details its many boundaries (fig. 6.2). Immediately right of the text and below the two pages of maps is

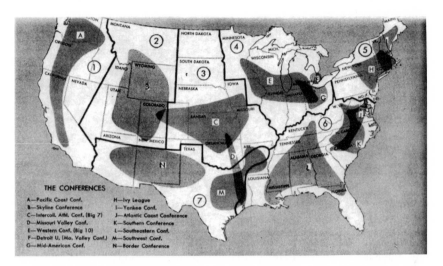

FIGURE 6.1 Map of the United States. Map by L. H. Billing, in "US Football: In Maps and Diagrams," *Sports Illustrated*, November 15, 1954, 4.

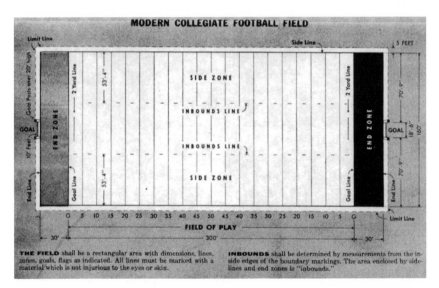

FIGURE 6.2 "Modern Collegiate Football Field." Map by L. H. Billing, in "US Football: In Maps and Diagrams," *Sports Illustrated*, November 15, 1954, 5.

a chart of the conferences organized by region with school names, their location, the number of students broken down by sex, and the capacity of their stadiums. Thus the article maps the NCAA's demographics and market potential in a clear matrix of human geography for readers and advertisers. Once taught the NCAA's composition of men and women tied to specific locales by the detailed chart, the reader can use that knowledge to participate in a national football discourse.

Although they are clearly distinct in most regards, there is a similarity between modern maps and modern football when they are viewed as spatial technologies. Both maps and football present a world of apparent chaos abstracted onto a rational plane of perception.[9] This point is more obvious in terms of maps, but both need some elaboration. Although generally viewed as an objective technology, maps do not simply reflect a naturally given world; they are rhetorical devices for constructing a particular geographical imagination that brings space otherwise beyond cognition into human perception. Whether a satellite photo, a computer model, or an illustration of a childhood memory, maps turn space frozen at a particular moment in calendrical time into visible landscapes inscribed by the power dynamics of territoriality (Holloway and Kneale 2000). The development of maps figures prominently in the history of Western modernity since capitalism has always been a "geographical project of spatial expansion and spatial integration" (Swyngedouw 2004, 27) that produces processes of territorialization, deterritorialization, and reterritorialization (Harvey 2003). Modern maps were a crucial spatial technology in capitalist development because they made possible predictable navigation in trade and commerce, imperial conquest, and clear demarcation of property boundaries. As a result, maps have transformed people's understandings and experience of space (Harvey 1990, 241–246; see also Brealy 1995; Harley 1989; Monmonier 1991).

Similarly, the history of modern football unfolded as a history of increasing rationalization of bodily practices tied to capitalist development and nation-state formation (Brohm 1978; Dunning 1972, 1975; Guttmann 1978). Like maps, football transformed free-form communal places of play into clearly demarcated, precisely measured, standardized, and enclosed abstract geometric spaces that fans must pay to access (Bale 1994; Clarke 1993; Eichberg 1998; Ingham, Howell, and Schilperoort 1987; Morford and McIntosh 1993; Whitson 1998). In football, the ordering of chaos is most apparent in the markings on the field that make up the gridiron and the fetishization of measurement. What we learn from the map of the field (fig. 6.2) is that football is a battle over a territory of 120 by 53.33 yards broken into ten 10-yard zones and two 10-yard goals. The clock measuring play runs only when the ball is kept within the measured space of play, forcing "play" time to be grossly out of sync with "real" (abstract calendrical) time. And in a sense, a team's score is a measure of geometric space within the confines of rational time, that is, the number of times one team penetrates the space or end zone of the other while resisting penetration of the space of the self (Dundes 1978; Pronger 1999). What ultimately makes maps and football comparable spatial technologies is the underlying Cartesian logic that rationally plots people, things, and representation along points of a geometrical grid that is visibly displayed and experienced socially (see Lefebvre 1991).

The conflation of the nation and the football field as a site of imperial play implied in the article's text is highlighted in the juxtaposition of the map of the nation that details the various NCAA conferences with the map of the football field that details its various boundaries. This comparison is highlighted beyond simple juxtaposition by the rational divisions of space visible in overlaid grids that order segments of space into individual, defensible territories. Although the gridiron that demarcates ten-yard zones of contestation is more obvious, the map of the nation is overlaid with two grids: the primary grid of football regions marked by solid lines and the secondary grid of states marked by dotted lines. While the sovereignty of the states and regions on the national map is not contested in the manner of a football field (bracketing the "Solid South" reference discussed in the next section), the rationality of the grid orders space as contained, defensible territory. Indeed, this is exactly what Lefebvre means by the term "abstract space," which envisions space as empty containers waiting to be filled by people, things, and representations (Lefebvre 1991).

## Traveling the Nation by Region

Creating a sense of the nation as an imagined community through representation was central to *SI*'s strategy of creating a real market of subscribers and advertisers. For *SI* to construct a single national market out of the many individual possible subscribers, they needed to bridge a multitude of diverse, lived localities with a single national imagination. A necessary step in their strategy was moving the mass of disparate individuals who could potentially purchase the magazine into a solidified body unified by a common love of sport. This ability to transcend social difference produces a central discourse of the nation: *e pluribus unum*, or "out of many one" (Anderson 1991; Bhabha 1991; Miller 2007). In "US Football," the multitudes of lived places around the nation are represented through text, maps, and a chart as unified on Saturdays through the social relations of competitive football—we might call this a solidarity of rivalry and difference. However, capturing the lived experience of real people within the abstract and heroic space of the nation required not only constructing relational scales but also placing those scales within a sentimental narrative that appeals to the subjectivity of emotion and experience. As we will see in the next section, Patty Berg provides a sentimental description of her childhood suburb as an American urban ideal—one neighborhood out of the many found around the nation—that draws heavily on emotion and experience. But as we rescale from the abstraction of the nation to the particularity of the neighborhood, we arrive at the interim scale of the region that unifies the heroic with the sentimental in its narrative.

In volume 1 and subsequent seasons, *SI* broke the nation into jigsaw-like pieces that seem to naturally fit together through its regional roundup of the nation. While there are many ways the various colleges and teams can be organized, *SI* spent a month highlighting the four traditional regions of the nation: the Midwest (September 20), the West (September 27), the South (October 4), and the East (October 11). In circumnavigating the nation, readers are taken on an imaginary tour from the comfort of their own home. This imaginative tour constructs a pedagogy of rivalry and difference that prepares readers for the upcoming broadcast season by educating them on the myriad different schools they could see competing on television. It also prepares fans for what Homi Bhabha (1991) calls pedagogical and performative functions of nationalist discourse. In the former, the reader is a pedagogical object of the nation being taught what the nation is, in this case four contiguous regions composed of various localities that have mutually exclusive characteristics. As discussed in the following paragraphs, the construction of regions plays upon differences stemming from the regions' unique histories, but those differences are not only contextualized within a larger U.S. history; the individuality of the regions adds emotion to football competition that fuses them within a larger national space that is united in rivalry. Football lore naturalizes regional distinction by equating style of play, such as run orientation and pass orientation, with environmental conditions of the respective regions (see Bourdieu 1991). As performative subjects, the readers can then participate in and feel they have a stake in the nation through their virtual tour of the various regions—identifying with their own and imagining differences from the others. At the end of the tour, the readers are prepared to continue their performative role in the national discourse by following a favorite team's progression across calendrical time toward a bowl game.

While the tour is imaginary, the stops are real places made manifest through the use of text, photos, and maps. Figure 6.3 shows a two-column graphic that introduces *SI*'s article on the southern region of the United States. This graphical allegory or visual narrative can be read through its three parts: the text that describes the region, the illustration that maps the region, and the photo that gives an example of who the reader might see there. The descriptive text is also the title of the article: "The Solid South." I return to the political meaning of the phrase "the Solid South," but since the author states "solid" is the best possible description of the "football world" in this region, it is worth noting what the term "solid" signifies in football.

Solid is a compliment in any sport, but especially in football. When applied to a team, it means that the team is talented, is disciplined, and performs plays in a synchronous manner. Modern football is a disciplinary technology that

FIGURE 6.3 "The Solid South." Map by L. H. Billing, in Herman Hickman "Football: The Solid South," *Sports Illustrated*, October 4, 1954, 60.

turns groups of people into human machines where individuals perform complicated, precise, and unique movements in perfect unison (Shogan 2002). So a solid team masterfully performs "the fundamentals" expertly, and that makes the group hard to "penetrate." This is important in the territorialized world of sport where one attempts to penetrate an opponent's territory while defending one's own (Pronger 1999). Since a team is composed of its players, by extension solid teams have solid players who through disciplined training are equally difficult to penetrate. It goes without saying that penetration divests a male athlete of his manhood. When players and teams are solid, they are not only likely to resist penetration but also likely to penetrate opposing teams and players. The construction of southern space as solid highlights Brian Pronger's concept of the "libidinal economy of territorial domination" that states competitive sports, for which football is archetypal, are based on a masculine will to colonize the space of the other "while simultaneously protectively enclosing the space of the self" (Pronger 1999, 376). Thus given the Cold War concern with male softness and openness to unwanted penetration (see chapter 3), the term "solid" in reference to football implies southern football players are reassuringly hard.

When thinking about the political formation of "The Solid South" as a reaction to "the party of Lincoln" and intrusion from the North during the Civil War and Reconstruction, this article rescales Pronger's notion of a libidinal economy of territorial domination from the scale of the body to that of the region. In this sense, we can bring the title as a description of a region that resists northern penetration into dialogue with the photo of two white football players and the map. The two players, shot from a low angle to capture the backdrop of clear sky, and their heroic qualities become anonymous representatives of a South that is defined by football. Immediately above the photo is an illustration of the South with the NCAA's conferences superimposed upon it. This triptych suggests that the South is solid and that solid southerners are young white men; the major football programs of the prestigious Southeastern Conference remained steadfastly segregated at this time (Demas 2010). The text in the top-right column juxtaposed to the graphic constructs a geographical imaginary that substantiates the existence of the South: "When Charles Mason and Jeremiah Dixon, those two English astronomers, laid their line along the South in 1763 they drew it for the ages. The Mason and Dixon Line still exists today, and there's no better way to describe the football world below it than as solid" (61). In this passage, the history of the South, involving the conquest of American Indians, the enslavement of blacks, and conquest by the North, is conflated with its football in the present, when the South's history motivates its present football tradition (Woods 1998). Indeed, Andrew Doyle (1996) argues that by appropriating the elite, northern game of football, progressive southerners could simultaneously demonstrate the modernity of the South and express the cavalier myth by seeing their young athletes as modern incarnations of

Confederate warriors. The article then goes on to detail the "fast and fancy" football programs of the different schools, such as Georgia Tech, Alabama, and Mississippi, that compose southern football. Ultimately, the article constructs a set of spatial coordinates in political terms. The South is a social space substantiated as real through spatial representations: a map and a detailed description of multiple locales that exist as a region not only in the present but also historically. Thus "The Solid South" is not simply an objective entity but also a social space of white male resistance to penetration consistent with the strategy of containment (see Doyle 1996; King and Springwood 2001).

### The Idealized Neighborhood

The article "I Taught Bud Wilkinson to Play Football" is a first-person narrative on the shared childhood of professional golfer Patty Berg and University of Oklahoma football coach Bud Wilkinson, who grew up together in suburban Minneapolis. Berg and Wilkinson today are considered to be among the best in their respective fields, and in this article Berg relates their success to playing football in their idealized childhood neighborhood between 1925 and 1930. Berg describes how she coached and quarterbacked their neighborhood football team, the 50th Street Tigers, and how Wilkinson was her best blocker at his position of right tackle. The article describes the neighborhood in great detail with the assistance of photos and illustrations that compares the neighborhood "then" to the neighborhood "now." It should be noted that there is no visible change between Colfax Avenue South when they grew up prior to the Great Depression and the year 1954. In recounting this history, Berg describes the children, the rival teams, and the style of play that they used to dominate surrounding neighborhoods. The effective construction of an idyllic suburb in the article connects the nostalgic past of the narrator's childhood to the glorious present of Oklahoma football and Berg's tremendous success in golf. The familial group represented by football teams becomes a symbolic category that transcends time and space while still firmly rooted in an objective place and location in calendrical time.

The story's main lesson is that through intense competition the children learned the skills of leadership that led to success in their adult lives as citizens. Besides the extraordinary success of Berg and Wilkinson, their teammates all built successful professional careers, according to Berg. The relation of the other boys to the parental-like figures of Berg and Wilkinson positions them as average kids who love to play ball. These "regular kids" can be seen as narrative objects of identification for the reader and therefore serve as pedagogical models of what competitive sports offer a citizen. Berg's narrative suggests that football, with its physical conditioning and violent team play, serves as an effective remedy against the softening of American youth since it not only trained minds and bodies, but also drew upon an authentic American spirit to harden bodies (see chapter 3).

COACH AS WELL AS QUARTERBACK OF THE 50TH-STREET TIGERS, 11-YEAR-OLD PATTY GIVES HER YOUNG LINEMEN A FEW GOOD TIPS

FIGURE 6.4 Patty Berg lectures the team. Patty Berg, "I Taught Bud Wilkinson to Play Football," *Sports Illustrated*, November 8, 1954, 27.

The graphics included in the article give visual form to the territorial abstraction of this Minneapolis suburb. Figure 6.4 presents a three-column image across the top of the page of quarterback Patty Berg lecturing the linemen of the 50th Street Tigers. Immediately below it is figure 6.5, a two-column graphic that includes a photo of the neighborhood now (1954) and a schematic illustration of the neighborhood then (1925–1930). This montage creates a transhistorical allegory of life in an American suburb through the photo of the kids at play (fig. 6.4) and schematic of the households "then" (fig. 6.5) that are linked in time and place by the photo of the neighborhood as it really is "now" (fig. 6.5). This allegory of a transhistorical, idealized suburban neighborhood effaces Depression-era suffering, the recent World War, and the Cold War raging at the time of the article's publication. Instead of focusing on larger sociopolitical processes that might call the naturalness of this exclusive suburb into question, the allegory ties a little girl lecturing well-behaved boys to the present-day suburb and its transhistorical structure. And, as we shall see, the article credits the success of the athletic boys to the idyllic setting of their childhood games as they were able to develop the skills of leadership through the rough-and-tumble play of competitive football.

Patty Berg's idyllic neighborhood presupposes the containment of difference through the exclusion of Otherness. After describing the neighborhood as a place structured by violent competition in football, she states, "[My description] must sound as though we were raised in the midst of an unshaven, slouch-cap, slum area. Colfax South actually was pretty fashionable" (28). So although the football teams function like street gangs competing over neighborhood

FIGURE 6.5 Map of Colfax Avenue South. Patty Berg, "I Taught Bud Wilkinson to Play Football," *Sports Illustrated*, November 8, 1954, 27.

turf, Berg constructs her suburb in opposition to an unnamed, universal "slum area." The unnamed slum area visible in her statements "unshaven" and "slouch-cap" is juxtaposed to their "fashionable" neighborhood, and the accompanying photographs of racial purity negatively defines Colfax South as a middle-class white enclave, which it likely was since exclusivity defined the Cold War suburban ideal (May 1999). Excluding poor whites and people of color from the article makes Colfax South a utopian container of middle-class whiteness at the same time that it constructs sports fans as middle-class and "fashionable" for *SI*'s advertisers.

In naturalizing this ideal white community, although complicated by Berg's authorial position,[10] the article reinscribes a hierarchy that further contains difference. Reading the text in the neighborhood's schematic map, one is presented with an adult's remembrances of a child's view of the neighborhood. The houses lining Colfax Avenue South are represented by a box marked by the inhabitants' familial name. Besides the named boxes are adult Patty's childish evaluations of the inhabitants, which are based on their functional qualities in football. As such, adults are essentially nonexistent, girls are referred to but largely ignored since they serve little function in Berg's football narrative, and unathletic boys are debased. For instance, Berg writes next to the Peterson box, "Jackie and three sisters. He tried but wasn't too strong." Her description of the Morrisey box reads, "The kids who lived here played once in a while. We beat them up most of the time." A comparison with the Pringer box reveals her bias: "Bob was University of Minnesota halfback; now doctor in L.A. Also there was Tippy and Peggy."

The unathletic boys are linked to the girls in Berg's description, and it is their shared subordination within the childhood peer group that produces the athletic boys as idealized. Therefore, girls are a presence but of little significance, so they receive no description beyond their name. Climbing up the hierarchy, we see the less athletic boys whose failed masculinity garners them a name and a subordinate description restricted to the past—the site of their transgression and humiliation where they "tried" but failed, they "didn't play much," and we "beat them up." The competitive boys, on the other hand, receive a full historical treatment. Not only do they exist in the past, but like the neighborhood they also exist in the present. We learn not only that Bob Pringer grew up and went to college but also that he is now a doctor living in Los Angeles. In short, the children who could not participate in competitive neighborhood football by structural exclusion (be it race, class, gender, temperament, or physicality) are subordinated in Berg's recalling of her childhood with Bud Wilkinson. In opposition to the subordinate children, those children who played football with competitive ferocity are meaningful historical actors whose present-day success is rooted in an idyllic childhood of territorial competition.

As my discussion suggests, this article is largely sentimental but also heroic. Patty Berg's remembrances are evocative and emotive in their recounting of how football held the community of children together and fortified the masculinity of the successful men. Her neighborhood experience is told as a universal experience of suburban America that draws connections not only between the characters but also to the reader. At the same time, the human connections exist within an intensely hierarchal world structured by violence, competition, and exclusion. Submitting oneself to the disciplining regime of football, the article suggests, is an avenue to culturally defined models of success that readers could emulate or risk being excluded in the conformist 1950s.

## OF THE NATION AND THE FANS

What I have argued in this chapter is how a war that for most Americans was fought largely in the realm of the symbolic but had repeated material manifestations, like the Korean War, could be understood as meaningful, natural, and inevitable with the aid of spatial technologies that included *SI*'s football coverage. Obviously the historical linkages between football and militarism (see chapter 2) made it a useful tool for fostering a Cold War geographical imagination. For instance, Secretary of State Dean Acheson once used football to explain the Truman Doctrine (Gaddis 1982, 110), and an editorial in the *Freeman* ("Football and Strategy" 1950, 71) suggested that Acheson watch more football to learn better strategies for containing communism. However, it is easy to overstate the linkage between football's territoriality and militarism and its popularity during the Cold War (Oriard 1993, 2009). Football and its coverage are better understood as a prism through which Cold War leaders, such as Henry Luce, could project a vision of the world for popular consumption (Kemper 2009).

Henry Luce was a staunch Cold Warrior famous for imprinting his anticommunist ideology on his publications; however, it would be a mistake to understand *SI* as simple propaganda. *SI* was conceived of as an innovative, risky business adventure that celebrated sport and American sporting traditions. At the same time, Luce did not see his ideology as inconsistent with either his business mission or his mission to reconfigure U.S. culture. The social world was changing during the postwar period, and Luce saw his publications participating in that change (see Luce 1941/1969a, 1953/1969b). This is why the subtle use of education in Time, Inc. publications is so important. Football's territorial and militaristic metaphors are clearly consistent with the politics and culture of the Cold War, but more than that, *SI*'s football coverage could help Americans assimilate a Cold War global imaginary even when focused purely at the scale of the domestic.

U.S. Cold War policy required a reconceptualization of space, and cultural leaders like Henry Luce mobilized their resources to support that vision. This new conception of space is apparent in the internationalist paradigm of containment that defined a new world order structured by global conflict between two superpowers over the decolonizing Third World. This strategy led to global networks of economic alliances in binary relation to a clearly defined opposition as well as military-humanitarian interventions. U.S. spectator sports, aside from the Olympics, are generally conceived of as pure entertainment that resists encroachment by politics. So no one would expect to learn about troop movements in Korea or the building of the Berlin Wall from *SI*, as they might when reading Luce's other publications, such as *Time* and *Life* (see Klein 2003). Rather than directly encouraging U.S. imperialism, *SI*'s football coverage participated in normalizing a Cold War conception of space in everyday life that helped make the costs of the Cold War (unimaginable before 1950) seem understandable, reasonable, and even inevitable.

The connection between *SI*'s football coverage and Cold War geopolitics is not direct, but *SI*'s football coverage did, I believe, participate in a larger sport-media complex from which fans could derive an enduring set of transposable dispositions. This means that the sense of self that people accrue from consuming sport media is largely consistent with its institutional relations that form in the institutional nexus of sport, media, education, business, and politics (see Burstyn 1999). This particular history is interesting because the sport-media complex that includes *SI* and football is not simply a set of institutional relations existing outside of space but is embedded across sets of relational scales.

*SI*'s football coverage becomes an ethical space by its pedagogical function of teaching difference and rivalry as the basis of national solidarity (Miller 1998). This pedagogy had two parts: first as a heroic narrative that constructs a masculinity fortified by competitive football training, performance, and spectacle; second as a sentimental narrative that integrates rival masculinities through participation in football. In this way, football as performance of the American way of life embraces its diversity and integrates even its most wayward region, the South. *SI* in the early Cold War constructed football as a national allegory unifying middle-class white men for the explicit purpose of building a market that advertisers would invest in.

Indeed, this is the power of a liberal governmentality that operates through popular culture. The capitalist state does not need to directly intervene in social life once a market is established that encourages autonomous social actors to act on their own behalf in a manner consistent with the needs of the state and economy. When *SI* as well as other media construct football as a regime of bodily transformation that physically and mentally inculcates the traits of leadership, as we saw in the Berg-Wilkinson article, people are further encouraged to produce themselves in a manner consistent with the needs of state and economy. As the literature critical of assimilation (discussed in chapter 2) suggests, assimilation works best when subjects actively pursue citizenship.

# 7 · CONCLUSION

Football is one of the worthwhile things in life, like your hitch in the Marines. . . . Life is always a challenge and a struggle, and football seems to be a way of condensing the training for it in a short period of time. In meeting a challenge, man finds within himself strength and weakness he never before knew.

—Kilborn Church, Yale alumnus, speech at the 1951 Yale football dinner[1]

*D*ISCIPLINE AND INDULGENCE began with a personal anecdote about attending football games with my father. Watching football was one of the ways that my father introduced me to and brought me into an interlinked sense of manhood and U.S. citizenship. The anecdote highlights how football games operate as moments of what Clifford Geertz (1973) calls "deep play." In his analysis of rituals, Geertz suggests that the mobilization of symbols creates performative spaces that are saturated with social meaning outside of the experience of everyday life. At the same time, however, public rituals are also deeply woven into the networks of social relations and the organization of society, which is to say that they are spectacular, exceptional moments of everyday life. The ritual space of football extends beyond stadiums and into parking lots, public transit, homes, workplaces, and water coolers, where fans can discuss, share, and re-create the ritual experience.

My discussion of Hildegard Binder Johnson's experience of college football in the Midwest and *Sports Illustrated*'s football coverage in 1954 showed how football's ritual space helps construct images of the nation. I have also argued that television broadcasting transforms and extends football's ritual space far beyond the stadium itself. This expansive and diffuse ritual space allows men to express a collective sense of manhood in complex ways where the "sacred" and the "profane" can comfortably intermingle in the spectacle of the event. And although fan performances in the ritual are rule governed, such as standing for the national anthem, following the rules is largely voluntary, which means some fans might protest the national anthem by sitting. This allows fans to both reenact traditional cultural schemas related to notions of race, gender, class, sexuality, and nation as well as author their own enactments in ways that are meaningful and responsive to their specific situation. So like a Balinese cockfight, football is a mundane aspect of social life, except that the highly symbolic, ritual context makes the performance exude meaning until it virtually drips with cultural significance.

At the same time, college football during the early Cold War was different in important ways from Balinese cockfighting. When attending his first cockfight in Bali, Clifford Geertz was forced to flee from a police raid to avoid arrest (see Geertz 1973, 413–414). Cockfighting was illegal in Indonesia because the state, on a developmental path to modernity, saw it as a counterproductive use of its citizens' time and resources. Geertz would not have needed to flee Harvard's Soldier Stadium in the 1950s and hide from the police for attending a Crimson football game.[2] Football had been rationalized and separated from its unruly folk traditions during the eighteenth and nineteenth centuries (Dunning 1972, 1975; Elias and Dunning 1986a; Morford and McIntosh 1993) so that by the postwar period the state deeply invested in football as an extracurricular activity in primary, secondary, and higher education. So although cockfighting in Bali and football in the United States in the 1950s opened up ritual spaces for producing masculinity, nationhood, and cultural citizenship, football was discursively linked to modernity and the U.S. Cold War effort (Kemper 2009).

The construction of football as modern and liberatory in opposition to communist totalitarianism is visible in popular and academic writing on football during the Cold War. Popular and academic writing constructs football's history and social function as an allegory of the nation; the game serves as a metaphor for the nation itself. In other words, football as a familiar and emotionally powerful ritual within everyday life acts as a metaphor through which the abstract space of the nation and a fortified masculinity become visible. The game thus acts as a synecdoche for the nation, meaning the entirety of the nation is visible in this particular aspect of the national culture: football represents America and an idealized American manhood (White 1978, 73).

The operation of allegory is especially clear in popular football histories from the 1950s, where the game explicitly serves as a symbol of freedom and an antidote to the lures of communist totalitarianism. But the allegorical construction of nation not only existed in popular football histories but also was visible in Cold War academic texts. After showing how national allegory operates in popular history texts, I show how academic texts, especially Allen Guttmann's *From Ritual to Record* (1978), also construct national allegories. *From Ritual to Record* is a seminal text in sport sociology and sport history and is interesting here because although Guttmann distinguishes his analysis from popular histories, his use of Parsonian functionalism ultimately produces a powerful Cold War allegory. Ultimately, the popular and academic texts converge on the political conviction that football offers training in modern citizenship and proves the superiority of the capitalist West over the Soviet East. This chapter then concludes by looking at the operation of national allegory in contemporary media constructions of football during the Global War on Terror.

## THE STORY OF AMERICAN
## FOOTBALL IN POPULAR HISTORIES

The "story of American football" was told in popular histories as an unbroken linear progression of Western civilization. According to these accounts, football was born in ancient Greece; it was adopted by Rome, and Roman legionnaires carried it to Britain; British peasants played a variety of wild and wooly ball games before boarding schools like Eton and Rugby formalized the game; U.S. college students in the Northeast began playing the game in the late nineteenth century; from the Northeast it diffused across the continent; a uniquely American game, expressing a deep American spirit, sprung up on North America soil; and through its development in the colleges and the professional league the game has become the most technological and democratic sport played in the world today (see Buchanan 1952; Cohane 1951; Danzig 1956; Heffelfinger and McCallum 1954; Weyand 1955). The story of football in popular histories operates as a Cold War allegory of Western civilization: football began in Greece, developed in Rome and Britain, and reached its full flowering in the United States. Football thus functions as a microcosm of Western civilization and produces an unbroken continuity from past to present, and, by implication, to future.[3]

Popular histories use a linear model of diffusion in telling the story of football to link the game to some essential aspect of American society and individualism. As *The History of Football at Harvard* states, "The story of football at Harvard is more than a chronicle of collegiate sport; it is part of the history of the United States" (cited in Boyle 1963, 215). Another historian wrote, "The story of American college football is more than a story of fine teams and outstanding individuals. It is the saga of a great nation, and of that nation's enthusiasm and youth and strength" (Buchanan 1952, 9). Chester "Chet" LaRoche, chairman of the National Football Foundation and Hall of Fame, drew an explicit connection between football and the Cold War in the introduction to *This Was Football* (1954), the biography of Yale's legendary William "Pudge" Heffelfinger.[4] LaRoche explains that while he was writing the introduction, the newspapers were filled with two stories: the passing of Heffelfinger and the Viet Minh siege on the French at Dienbienphu. Musing upon Heffelfinger and the Viet Minh siege led LaRoche to ask, "Why is it that every robust American lad tries his

hand at the game?" He answers, "There must be something elemental and satisfying and important to the nation that this is so." Football is a crucial institution
of the American way of life, LaRoche surmises, because it teaches discipline and
a will to power necessary for a democratic civilization. "As long as there are men
who will pay the price for their convictions, as long as there are men who put the
spirit above the flesh, just that long will America be provided with the will to win
this battle [the Cold War] for the integrity and place of all men in the brother-
hood that must come if our way of life is to survive" (cited in Heffelfinger and
McCallum 1954, 15). For LaRoche, the lesson that readers should take from Heffelfinger's life was the same that they could learn from the brave French at Dienbienphu: both showed fortitude and discipline on the field of battle. Therefore,
it did not matter whether the French won or lost the battle; all that mattered was
they stood strong in the face of overwhelming odds. LaRoche was reiterating,
of course, what sporting nationalists had claimed about football since the nineteenth century: the softening forces of modernity and democracy needed to be
contained by exposing young men to violent regimes of bodily transformation
such as football (see chapter 1).

Given the hyperbolic language used to describe the game and the nation in
Cold War popular football histories, it is easy to overstate the power of football
to control people's conscious (Oriard 1993, 2009). The focus on allegory helps to
keep a measured view of how popular texts attempt to influence people's understandings of the world through the construction of game, nation, and manhood. Allegory in literature and history works as metaphor to make distant and
abstract concepts like the nation clear and concrete by reference to something
familiar, in this case football. Moreover, the heroic tales of football gods like Heffelfinger can appeal to and capture the imagination of boys as they become men.
The tales become a piece of a broader cultural formation (*bricolage*) that people
can draw on and creatively use in the act of self-construction (see Hebdige 2002;
Jordan and Cowan 1995).

Football in these stories is not a simple metaphor but a synecdoche, meaning
football is representative of the nation in that the difference between the nation
and a particular slice of the national culture becomes symbolically indistinct
(White 1978, 73). National allegories draw a synecdochic connection between
an experiential thing (person or institution) that one can touch and the abstract
category that exists only in the imagination, such as the nation (Anderson 1991;
Bhabha 1991; Gregory 1994). Football may not in fact be the United States, but
people from Binder Johnson to LaRoche could mythologize that attending a
football game allows a person to experience and participate in America (Barthes
1972). The construction of football history as national allegory is a crucial operation in the production of a geographical imagination, discussed in chapter 6,
but it also does more. Fredric Jameson points out that capitalism structurally

separates public from private, but the operation of allegory reconnects the poetic and experiential with the political and economic, even if in symbolic form (Jameson 1986, 69). In other words, the image of the nation constructed in allegory clarifies the interrelationship of the political and economic operation of the nation-state and the cultural experience of nationness. Throughout *Discipline and Indulgence* we have seen how the nation as an abstract category or imaginative community born of political discourse is experienced through the cultural metaphor of football.

## FOOTBALL, MODERNITY, AND BUREAUCRACY—LIBERTY AS FRUIT OF REGULATION

While one might expect popular histories to sound a nationalistic tone, academic texts also constructed football as a symbol of the nation and practice of freedom in opposition to the Slave World of the Kremlin. David Riesman and Reuel Denney's "Football in America" (1951) uses the concept of cultural diffusion to continue their characterlogical studies begun in *The Lonely Crowd* (1950). By focusing on how the British cultural form of football transformed as it was adapted in the United States, the essay largely adheres to standard histories but sets the starting point of football in Britain rather than Greece. Riesman and Denney argue that football transformed in the United States to fit the cultural needs of a large, heterogeneous nation that never had a landed aristocracy and that was going through the process of industrialization. The transformations were propelled as the United States became increasingly democratic and inclusive of ethnic European immigrants. And they conclude that the game will remain as it is unless it becomes a stronger tool of Americanization. A narrative of American exceptionalism and westward economic expansion thus explains in allegorical form both football and U.S. society. Within the allegory of America's progressive history, football functions as an institution of cultural integration that opens access to the category of citizenship.

Robert Boyle's *Sport: Mirror of American Life* (1963) views sport as a reflection of and metaphor for the industrial spirit of the nation. As he states, "The swift rise of sport between 1875 and 1900 paralleled immense changes in American society" (Boyle 1963, 19). Constant movement, expansion, and growth characterize the national spirit, according to Boyle. Consistent with the muscle gap discourse that he participated in (see Boyle 1955), Boyle connects the contemporary problem of softening youth to increases in civilization and technology (Boyle 1963, 55, 59). As we recall from chapter 3, the muscle gap emerged from contradictions in the operation of the strategy of containment and Cold War political economy. The result was that the United States needed disciplined worker-warrior-consumer-citizens to outproduce and outconsume the Soviet

Union in order to demonstrate the superiority of the American way of life. This put tremendous pressure on youth, especially young men, to enjoy the pleasures of a consumerist society while remaining willing to submit to the alienating conditions of abstract labor in blue- or white-collar professions as well as to police the Third World. The muscle gap call for physical education as a means of disciplining young consumers for citizenship was matched in other areas of education since education was seen as a means to train youth to discipline their desires for the easy pleasures of an open consumer society (Coleman 1965). The containment, intensification, and directed release of inner desires into controlled and productive activity is exactly what order theorists argued was the function of sport, particularly football, during the Cold War.

One of the clearest examples of order theory in sports studies is Allen Guttmann's *From Ritual to Record* (1978). Although *From Ritual to Record* falls outside of my period, I focus on it for two primary reasons. First, it was immediately recognized as a seminal text in the fledgling subdiscipline of sport sociology (Aaron 1979; Hazard 1979; Mandell 1979). Second, as was noted by reviewers at the time (Henricks 1980; Messenger 1981), Guttmann's ebullient analysis of modern sport is more consistent with the noncommunist left that emerged during the liberal consensus than other streams of sport scholarship of his day (e.g., Brohm 1978; Ingham and Loy 1974; Lawson and Ingham 1980; Rigauer 1981; Theberge 1981, 1985). So although *From Ritual to Record* pushed sport sociology forward in many regards, its theoretical assumptions and political concerns were largely rooted in the early Cold War.

*From Ritual to Record* uses a study of sport to offer a Weberian-Parsonian analysis of Western modernization. As such, it disrupts the narrative of continuity between Ancient Greece and contemporary society constructed in popular histories (Mandell 1979). Instead of unbroken continuity, Guttmann argues that the advent of modernity in the West placed sport in a broader process of rationalization whereby sport was transformed from religious rituals into a set of modern bureaucratic institutions. The rise of a scientific *weltanschauung* in Western society created an *elective affinity* between the dominant social order and modern sport, especially football in the United States (Guttmann 1978, 80–87). Therefore, sports that began as cultic rituals in traditional societies were superseded in the modern era by rational-bureaucratic institutions characterized by centralization, standardization, secularization, and extensive record keeping.

*From Ritual to Record* offers a modernization thesis that argues the increasing technologization of society leads to greater specialization and orchestrated cooperation that in turn increases the wealth and freedom of all people. Although Weber does offer a modernization thesis, Guttmann's logic that the growth of technology and division of labor increases freedom is more familiar in Adam Smith's *The Wealth of Nations* (1776/2003) and Emile Durkheim's *The Division of*

*Labor in Society* (1933/1997) than in Weber, who saw the spread of formal rationality to all aspects of modern life as entrapping people in a steel-hard casing (e.g., Weber 1947, 1958a, 2002). For Guttmann, the spread of bureaucratic institutions is a triumph of liberal reason that increases freedom by intensifying social control; formal rules external to the individual open up spaces of play, freedom, and self-expression. The formalization of sport (rigid rule structures that govern social practice) leads to greater specialization and an increase in cooperation that produces greater individuality as well as individual freedom. In this sense, *From Ritual to Record* is more in line with Parsonian order theory (see Guttmann 1978, 16, 69, 80–81) than the conflict theory of Ralf Dahrendorf or C. Wright Mills.[5] As Richard Gruneau points out, Guttmann's belief that bureaucratic social control increases freedom seems less influenced by Weber than Durkheim's dictum in *Moral Education* (1961) that human "liberty is the fruit of regulation" (Gruneau 1983/1999, 23). Ultimately Guttmann, following Parsons, sees rational-bureaucratic institutions such as football producing universal norms that protect the individual and stabilize society in the face of mid-twentieth-century crises in Western liberalism (Seidman 1998, 102–105). And in this sense, his analysis of sport and society mirrors the claims of sporting nationalists like Chester LaRoche in that sport operates as a vehicle of freedom in opposition to both the bonds and fetters of feudalism and communism.

In this vein, Guttmann's analysis of the state is instructive since it articulates with Cold War liberalism. As stated in chapter 2, the problem for liberalism is how to foster citizens who can and will fulfill the needs of the state with minimal direct intervention. This means that the state should not intrude upon citizens' lives because doing so makes them dependent upon the state and hence not free (e.g., Coleman 1965, 97–98). But the capitalist state also supports the conditions for capital accumulation, which include the production of workers, soldiers, and consumers. Thus the state is a powerfully present absence in Cold War liberal discourse. In Guttmann's history of sport, the state is visible only in prohibitions (negative force), not as an enabling (positive force). Therefore, he acknowledges the state in the Middle Ages, when kings passed edicts against football, but does not account for the state in the modern era after sport was rationalized. This raises a question: Can we locate the state in Guttmann's account of modern sport? In fact, we can find the state when reading between the lines in his chapter 5, which discusses American football.

Guttmann argues that people are unmistakably drawn to the spectacular and self-destructive violence in football (Guttmann 1978, 118–119). However, football violence is not violence per se. He argues that if a person suddenly tackled another in a public park it would be violence and the offender would be arrested. In other words, spontaneous tackling in the park is illegal violence. However, linebackers are rewarded for doing the same thing on the field of play. How do we explain this? Football violence is not violence per se but "disciplined vio-lence" that generates pleasure in highly disciplined middle-class fans (Guttmann 1978, 120). Drawing upon figuration theory, Guttmann puts forward a "modi-fied catharsis theory" (Guttmann 1978, 134) that draws a homology between controlled expression of violence on the field and the disciplining of the self in the stands. "Stimulated by the primitive contents of a football game," Guttmann states, "the middle class spectator is better able than others to find a socially acceptable way to simmer down. . . . Games like football provide Saturnalia-like occasions for the uninhibited expression of emotions which must remain tightly controlled in our ordinary lives" (Guttmann 1978, 132–133). In other words, it is not simply in playing the game but also in consuming a game that provides a disciplinary pedagogy on citizenship where fans learn to channel expressive emotions into socially acceptable spaces and forms (see also Dunning 1972, 1975, 2004; Elias and Dunning 1986b; Guttmann 1998).

But Guttmann avoids recognizing the state as a social actor since he never explains why disciplined violence is legal unlike undisciplined violence, or cock-fighting in Bali for that matter. To understand why disciplined violence is not violence per se but legal violence, we need to define the state. Since Guttmann is a "Weberian" (Guttmann 1978, 80), we can define the state as an institution that holds a monopoly over taxation and the legitimate use of coercion in a given territory (Weber 1947, 154). If only the state holds the right to the legitimate use of violence, and if disciplined violence is legal, then the state must *delegate* the right to violence to athletes who act in civil society according to rules prescribed by the state or state-sanctioned governing bodies (such as the NCAA). In short, if disciplined violence is legal violence, then it is also state-sanctioned violence. The state must see the simultaneous promotion and disciplining of male-on-male violence in civil society as a public good.

We might then ask why the state sees the promotion of violence between men as a public good. But Guttmann has already provided an explanation for why the promotion and disciplining of male on male violence is a public good. Football performs an important function in a liberal society, it creates and fulfills desire at the same time that it disciplines and directs desire. Bureaucratized cultural institutions like American football provide a disciplinary pedagogy so that citi-zens internalize a social order that coordinates social action according to liberal norms while minimizing direct state intervention. Liberal states allow cultural institutions in civil society to act as proxies for the disciplining of desire. Key to Guttmann's theory is that voluntary participation in sport leads to the internal-ization of social norms that have emerged out of the West's progressive history.

But one might ask Guttmann how the unfolding of formal rationality in bureaucratized cultural institutions fosters individual freedom if those institu-tions regulate and constrain social action. In answering that question, Guttmann's response is curious and informative. Guttmann distinguishes between two traditions in liberal political theory that "contemporary philosophers" identify as "freedom from" and "freedom to" (Guttmann 1978, 158). The first tradition (freedom from) offers a negative conception of freedom in that "a man [*sic*] is unbound by the restraints and trammels of institutional order," such as when Henry David Thoreau or Huck Finn isolate themselves from society in order to escape social constraint (Guttmann 1978, 158–159). Freedom from is thus negative and based on a lack of external constraint. The second tradition (freedom to) offers a positive conception of freedom in that "a man [*sic*] is free to choose among alternatives and to act upon his choice" (Guttmann 1978, 159). Freedom to choose results from coordinated social action that limits spontaneous freedom (play) but increases the range of actions that one has to choose from, and a quantitative expansion of choices increases individuality. So although the rise of formal rationality in bureaucratic institutions curtails freedom from and people must accept increased self-discipline, we also realize greater positive freedom by achieving what was never previously possible (such as a quantitative increase in sporting forms and new world records) and the euphoria of self-expression (Guttmann 1978, 160–161). Or as Guttmann states, "Under the conditions of modern democracy, society liberates because man [*sic*] in society is free to do what no man [*sic*] ever did alone" (Guttmann 1978, 159).

Guttmann's conclusion about modern sport creating and expressing the flush of Western democracy's positive freedom is ironic in several senses, but for the purpose of space and clarity I focus on only two. In the first instance, Guttmann's conclusion is ironic as a result of his misrepresentation of liberal political theory. Guttmann neglects to cite any of the "contemporary philosophers" who inform his analysis; however, Isaiah Berlin's 1959 essay "Two Concepts of Liberty" (1999) was the seminal statement on Cold War conceptions of freedom (Carter 2008). Close inspection of Berlin reveals that Guttmann oversimplifies and speciously links both conceptions of freedom to the liberal tradition. Berlin does not define negative freedom (from) as the absolute absence of all external constraint since one person's liberty needs to be protected from the liberties of others, such as a minority from the majority. Instead, Berlin argues that negative freedom allows a person to realize his or her potential without *unreasonable* or *coercive* restraint from other people, whether individuals or the state (Berlin 1999, 156–157).[6] Negative freedom that preserves individual liberty stems from the tradition of British liberalism, such as John Locke, Adam Smith, and John Stuart Mill (Berlin 1999, 157).

How then does Guttmann's characterization of positive freedom stand up to close scrutiny? Guttmann theorizes positive freedom as a person's freedom to choose from a quantitative expansion of options in order to best express his or her unique personality. But Berlin does not define positive freedom within a consumerist mode of freedom to choose (see chapter 4). Instead, he argues that positive freedom assumes people are rational and conscious of the choices they make, which means that they are free to the degree that they are conscious of their own freedom (Berlin 1999, 161). Positive freedom emerges in rationally ordered collectivities that foster people's self-mastery and stems from the communitarian traditions of Jean-Jacques Rousseau, Georg Hegel, and Karl Marx. Berlin sees positive freedom as dangerous because it is motivated by a vision of a higher good, and since everyone may not share that vision, it can justify coercion in the name of rationality. Ultimately, Berlin argues both versions of freedom run the risk of creating slavery in the name of freedom, but there is greater historical precedent in the positive conception to split humanity into a universal controlling rationality and an "empirical bundle of desires and passions to be disciplined and brought to heel" (Berlin 1999, 163).

Given Guttmann's polemics against Marxist and neo-Marxist interpretations of sport and society as well as his defense of Western liberalism (Gruneau 1983/1999; also Aaron 1979; Hazard 1979), it is deeply ironic that he misrepresents liberal political theory and that he champions disciplining the passions of individuals by powerful institutions. But this points to a profound irony of Cold War liberalism: the way in which fear led Cold War liberals to invest in powerful, authoritarian institutions as a defense of freedom against the authoritarian institutions of the Soviet Union (Blauner 2009, 2). Guttmann describes the experience of freedom in sport thusly: "I have surrendered myself to the rules of the game and I am, paradoxically, flushed with an ecstatic sense of amplitude and freedom. . . . When we are weary of modern sports, when cooperation falls into conformity, there is always another option" (Guttmann 1978, 161). The sense of freedom that Guttmann evokes is more consistent with Erich Fromm's critique of democracy during the Cold War as "consent manipulated without force" (Fromm 1959, 8).

The freedom that disciplinary institutions within a capitalist state provide is the freedom to consume and the freedom of constrained self-expression within one's consumption choices. Sport sociologist Stanley Eitzen argues that upon reappraisal after the Cold War the clear distinction between the Free World and the Slave World regardless of political claims was far less conclusive given the tendency on both sides of the Iron Curtain toward highly authoritarian institutions in the name of a freedom that could not be realized in actual practice (Eitzen 1999, 94). Rather than fostering independent thought and action, authoritarian institutions foster productivity within highly constrained ranges of action. Self-expression in the controlled spaces of disciplinary institutions like modern sport offers an illusion of freedom necessary to maintain the false binary of East and West, modern and traditional (see Fromm 1941/1994, 33). Disciplined consumption, according to Fromm (1941/1994), is not an act of freedom but an escape from freedom driven by fear and an inability to shoulder the burden of engaged citizenship.

Football in both popular and academic historical allegory operates as a disciplinary institution that integrates young men into a bureaucratic nation-state as citizens. The integration of diverse people into the nation via the category of citizenship is the mystical feat of nationalism—*e pluribus unum* (Anderson 1991)—in which varied regional, ethnic, class, gender, and religious interests are subsumed into the interest of the state. An integrated, orderly, bureaucratic nation-state becomes the mechanism through which diverse interests are ameliorated and national subjects fostered (Foucault 1991). Recall Kilborn Church's claim in the epigraph that football and the Marines provide lessons on how to conduct oneself in order to achieve life pursuits. This will to power is based on self-knowledge—*Know Thyself*. Nietzsche relates this to an "Apollonian" desire for self-control (Nietzsche 1870–1871/1956, 34), and Foucault calls this a technology of self, a means by which people alone or with assistance can make and transform their own physical and mental self (Foucault 1988b). Football, like the marines, also acts as a technology of power that objectifies the subject in order to direct conduct toward specific ends of domination over others. Governmentality forms from the intertwining of technologies of self and technologies of power (Foucault 1988b, 19), which is to say that football, like other sports, fosters self-regulating subjects within a historically specific political economy.

## LOOKING FORWARD AND BACK

In "The Eighteenth Brumaire of Louis Bonaparte," Karl Marx (1978b) famously stated that history repeats itself, first as tragedy and then as farce. Many of the parallels between the Cold War and the Global War on Terror are fairly obvious. Most obvious is the strategic use of fear to push expansionistic military policies and their resultant "small wars" in the Global South that generate tremendous human misery and death.[7] The mainstreaming of extremist anxiety characterizes both periods and supports high levels of patriotism. Indeed, patriotism, or belonging in the fraternity of the nation, provides a sense of comfort in times of heightened anxiety (Sturken 2007, 6). In both periods, the concerns of foreign policy transcend all aspects of daily life so that foreign policy of the Cold War and the Global War on Terror becomes visible in the cultural landscape of everyday life.

But when Marx said that history repeats itself, his point was not simply that we can see parallels—two tracks running side by side in an unconnected manner—but that different moments of history are structurally and dialectically connected across time. As argued in chapters 2 and 6, the Cold War and the interventionist policy paradigm of containment led to the formation of the military-industrial complex. The strategy of containment organized a matrix of social and economic relations with cultural beliefs that were put into material practice in the military-industrial complex and the Cold War's many small wars. I have used the term military-industrial Keynesianism (MIK) to represent the crystallization of the Cold War's forces and relations of productions in large, powerful, and controlling military-industrial institutions. MIK led logically to a series of small wars throughout the Cold War. The term "small war" harkens to U.S. interventions in Latin America in the nineteenth century (see note 83) and indicates that military adventures in the Global South predated and outlasted the Cold War (Klare 1989, 143).

Popular resistance to military interventions in the Global South resulting from the Vietnam War made the continuation of MIK increasingly difficult (Cypher 2007; Johnson 2007, 2008; Klare 1989). For instance, criticism of football doubled as criticism of MIK militarism in the late 1960s and early 1970s (see Hoch 1972; Meggyesy 1971; Shaw 1972). Opposition to interventionism manifested in the Nixon Doctrine that restrained U.S. interventions in the Global South but was seen by many as abdicating the U.S. role as global leader (Klare 1989). This position seemed confirmed by the fall of the Shah and subsequent hostage crisis in Iran, the rise of radical governments in Nicaragua and Grenada, and the Soviet invasion of Afghanistan. As Michael Klare states, "These events, although largely driven by local conditions that were probably beyond Washington's ability to affect, appeared to suggest that America had somehow become *impotent* in the face of overseas challenges. And when President Carter failed to take the sort of aggressive action considered necessary by many Americans to cope with these challenged, he became the victim of public frustration in the 1980 election" (Klare 1989, 157, emphasis added).

Opposition to interventionism and MIK became dubbed the "Vietnam syndrome" to connote a sense of moral loss and a national lack manhood when faced with the difficult task of global leadership (Cypher 2007; Johnson 2007, 2008). In 1980 Ronald Reagan used a political discourse coded in gendered and sexualized language familiar from the muscle gap to suggest the dangers of the Vietnam syndrome. When speaking to the Veterans of Foreign Wars, Reagan stated, "It is the first task of statecraft to preserve peace so that brave men need not die in battle. But it must not be peace at any price; it must not be a peace of humiliation and gradual surrender. . . . [L]et us tell those who fought in [the Vietnam War] that we will never again ask young men to fight and possibly die in a war our government is afraid to let them win" (Reagan 1980).

The gendered connotations of Reagan's language attempted to effeminize Jimmy Carter and the strategy of détente by connection to past historical mistakes. "[The Second World War] came because nations were weak, not strong, in the face of aggression. Those same lessons of the past surely apply today. Firmness based on a strong defense capability is not provocative. But weakness can be provocative simply because it is tempting to a nation whose imperialist ambitions are virtually unlimited" (Reagan 1980). In classical Cold War language, Reagan constructed an image of the Soviet Union as driven by a voracious masculine desire against which negotiation and hesitancy to deploy military forces would only invite foreign penetration (Costigliola 1997). In 1986, when pushing Congress for a $100 million aid package for the rebel Contras, Reagan warned that Nicaragua was only twelve hundred miles from southern Texas (Chardy 1986). Weakness, according to Reagan, is provocative to masculine desire. A "muscular foreign policy," on the other hand, contains Soviet aggression and honors the efforts of America's fighting *men*. When he became president, Reagan increased military spending between 1980 and 1987 by 50 percent, and 1987 saw the highest level of actual military spending since the end of World War II (see fig. 7.1).

Michael Oriard argues that football does not *necessarily* have to promote either capitalism or militarism, and has at times been a site of opposition (Oriard 1993, 2009). Given my own practice of sitting during the national anthem at football games, I have to agree with Oriard. At the same time, we have seen in *Discipline and Indulgence* that militarists in the United States since the nineteenth century have viewed football as a potent institution for preparing young men for war and a powerful symbolic system for fostering a militaristic imaginary. As a result, two totally unrelated institutions (sport and war) have become intertwined, structurally homologous, and articulate together. One way we can see the articulation of football and militarism is in what Sue Curry Jansen and Don Sabo (1994) call the sport/war metaphor. Jansen and Sabo argue that the mixing of sport and war metaphors is not a recent innovation because the structural homology between the two provide "government, the military, the sport industry, and mass media with an easily mobilized and highly articulated semiotic system and set of cultural values to advance and justify their respective plans, actions, and interests" (Jansen and Sabo 1994, 1). While the institutions do not have identical "plans, actions, and interests," their interests converge and allow for articulations. For instance, Michael Malec (1993) found during the First Gulf War that many Division I football programs put American flags on their football uniforms since they perceived patriotic pageantry on national television as beneficial to their programs. The point or pivot of articulation between these different interlinking institutions is a fortified image of masculinity where both individual men and the nation can in "President [George H. W.] Bush's own sport/war metaphor, 'kick some ass'" (Jansen and Sabo 1994, 8).

The interlinking of sport, war, and media during the First Gulf War supported a remasculinization of foreign policy and a fortification of the nation at a time when the United States no longer faced an implacable enemy bent on its destruction. The high-technology, televisual nature of the First Gulf War was

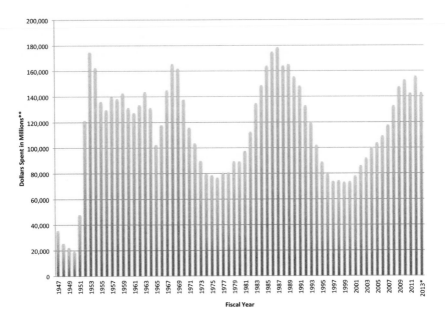

FIGURE 7.1 National Defense Outlays for Major Public Direct Physical Capital Investment: 1947–2013. U.S. Office of Management and Budget, "National Defense Outlays 2012," http://www.gpo.gov/fdsys/pkg/BUDGET-2013-TAB/xls/BUDGET-2013-TAB-9-4.xls.

* Estimated spending in 2012 and 2013.

** All dollar amounts adjusted for inflation to 2012 values. All calculations controlling for inflation were done via the CPI Inflation Calculator http://data.bls.gov/cgi-bin/cpicalc.pl (accessed March 3, 2012).

largely a strategy to mollify opposition to military interventions in the Global South (Klare 1989). And George H. W. Bush proudly proclaimed, "The spectre of Vietnam has been buried forever in the desert sands of the Arabian peninsula" (quoted in Isaacs 1997, 65). He further exclaimed, "It's a proud day for America—and, by God, we've kicked the Vietnam syndrome once and for all" (Bush 1991). As we can see in figure 7.1, Reagan's and Bush's attacks upon the Vietnam syndrome coincided with massive investment in the military-industrial complex even as the Cold War came to an end. During this period football remained symbolically as well as institutionally linked to militarism (Gems 2000; Jansen and Sabo 1994; Malec 1993). The interlinking of sport and militarism, which is always present during the Super Bowl and major college bowl games, was made explicitly clear on January 17, 1993, when an NFL playoff game was *not* interrupted by coverage of a U.S. bombing mission on Baghdad. As Ed Siegel wrote in the *Boston Globe*, "Those who think that TV treats sports like war and war like sports need only have seen NBC's split screen between America shelling Iraq and the Buffalo Bills shredding the Miami Dolphins" (Siegel 1993).

Figure 7.1 shows that the Global War on Terror is a period when military spending matches that of the Cold War despite the fact that a military threat equivalent to the Soviet Union arguably does not exist. We can also see in figure 7.1 that the Global War on Terror in terms of real dollars invested by the United States in the military is not a rupture from the past but is in fact a continuation of militarism that began during the Second World War and continued through the Cold War (Klare 1989). What we see today, according to James Cypher (2007), is MIK minus the limited Keynesian commitment to fostering the welfare of the people, or what he calls global-neoliberal militarism. "In the United States, the objectives of global-neoliberal militarism are served by military spending, which boosts the profit rate of large corporations, creates new technologies such as the Internet, and contributes to policies that confront the onset of recessions. The objectives of lowering the unemployment rate, raising wages, and contributing to workers' economic security are no longer a consideration, as they were in the days of military[-industrial] Keynesianism" (Cypher 2007).

In short, September 11, 2001, did not change *everything*. It did not change the political economy of the United States or the relationship between sport and militarism in fundamental ways. Certainly, this is not to claim that nothing changed during the Global War on Terror. Andrew Bacevich (2005) argues the cost of war is increasingly borne on limited segments of the population, in particular the working class, who are compelled for economic reasons, and members of military families who see military service as an important means of serving the nation (also Pew Research Center 2011; Thompson 2011). The uneven burden of war led Colin McInnes (2002) to argue that since the end of the Cold War, the experience of war for most Westerners has become less direct, especially compared to the World Wars, despite the fact that wars are no less common. Because most recent wars have been fought far from the West in the Global South, relatively few Westerners have been expected to sacrifice, and the experience of war has been increasingly mediated by spectacle, which has made the experience of wars akin to watching sporting events. So rather than states going to war against other states, Western states go to war against individuals (such as Saddam Hussein or Muammar Gaddafi) or regimes (the Ba'ath Party or the Gaddafi Regime), and that allows most citizens to identify with and cheer for the soldiers ("support the troops") without entering the field of battle. As a mediated experience, the spectacle of war and the professionalization of soldiering lead to valorizing the same heroic, manly virtues in soldiers that are seen in athletes and expressed through sport/war metaphors. The dominant experience of war in the West as a technologically mediated spectacle led to Jean Baudrillard's (1995) unfortunate claim that the Gulf War did not take place—the Gulf War did in fact occur, and it revealed profound asymmetries in the experience of contemporary small wars, a game-like televisual spectacle versus living "in the company of death, dismemberment, disease, and famine" (Shohat and Stam 1994, 131).

Using governmentality as tool for guiding analysis has important implications for connecting movements during the Cold War with present-day realities. In an analysis of Fox's 2002 Super Bowl coverage and CBS's coverage of the opening ceremonies of the 2002 Winter Olympics, Silk and Falcous (2005) demonstrate how contemporary sport media recycle Cold War discourse through the use of a War on Terror frame. Highly mediated sport spectacles like the Super Bowl and the Olympics provide platforms for the mobilization of nationalism and the legitimation of policy. Their analysis suggests that Martin and Reeves (2001) were a bit premature in reframing the Super Bowl as a "postmodern carnival" over Michael Real's (1979) "mythic spectacle" of the Cold War. Similarly, Samantha King (2008) shows how the contemporary configuration between sport and militarism produces a synergistic marketing relationship between a militarized neoliberal state and sport. A case in point is the story of All-American Pat Tillman who served as a poster child for U.S. government and NFL propaganda when he gave up a $3.6 million NFL contract to serve as an Army Ranger in Afghanistan, only to be killed in action. His commitment, patriotism, and sacrifice moved people throughout the nation, allowing them to project their own hopes, dreams, and aspirations onto Tillman's body, and many were understandably dismayed to learn how his body was cynically used to shore up flagging support for the wars. Moreover, Samantha King (2008) and Kyle Kusz (2007) show how Tillman was used to smooth contradictions in the operation of neoliberal capitalism without removing those contradictions. But the idealized image of citizen-soldier-athlete that Pat Tillman represents was born a long time ago. It is an image that stretches from *Tom Brown's School Days* (1857) to the Coronet educational film *Service and Citizenship* (1951) to *Fighting Back: The Rocky Bleier Story* (1980). This is why I argue in chapter 3 that sport scholars need to look at structural continuities that repeat across time as well as historically specific manifestations. In this way we do not fall into a trap of seeing either the past as passive or the present as truly unique. Instead we should see all social formations as palimpsestic, where the past is always present even if unrecognizable (Shohat and Stam 1994).

Despite important transformations that occurred between the early 1960s and the start of the twenty-first century—such as the dissolution of the liberal consensus, the emergence of the counterculture, and the fall of the Berlin Wall—the first Persian Gulf War (1990–1991) manifested a renewed muscular foreign policy and the reintegration of sport and U.S. militarism in sport media narratives and rhetoric; the Bell Helicopter Armed Forces Bowl is only the most extreme (see Butterworth and Moskal 2009). These narratives help people situate themselves within time and space in order to form identities and interpret the world they live in from a particular ideological framework. Whether framed as patriot or victim, Tillman as a citizen-athlete-soldier remains a hero and his body a symbol of abstract political forces across a range of political positions. The ideological power of sport as a vehicle of citizenship also highlights its potential instability. If its power emerges from its ability to link people's lived realities to larger abstract forces, then it is open to numerous meanings and interpretations, as seen in the playground movement at the turn of the twentieth century and the 1968 Olympic protest movement.

## FROM BOYS TO MEN—THE PRODUCTION OF DOCILITY

Football during the Cold War was not simply an institution for players and fans to learn about the American way of life; it was also a spectacular way to live it. Elmer D. Mitchell, a prominent physical educator at the University of Michigan, in a 1922 article in the *American Physical Education Review* titled "Racial Traits in Athletics," described the temperaments of different racial groups and their competencies in sport. As Oriard points out, the article presents an index of racial attitudes of the era, so it is no surprise that Mitchell sees Nordic races, especially Anglo-Saxons in the United States, as superior. What makes the article interesting is the way that he conflates political systems with national character and racial competencies. "All through history, democracy has been accompanied by an interest in amateur sports," argues Mitchell. "Team games and democracy are inseparable, the one goes with the other as a training for free citizenship" (cited in Oriard 2001, 257). Football figures into the postwar melting pot narrative of America as a noncoercive technology of Americanization whereby formerly racialized groups gladly become ethnic American citizens. As in colonial contexts, the ability to claim citizenship was coterminous with the ability to claim manhood based on performance in sport, especially football, whether of the Etonian or Rugby tradition (see Fair 2001; Mangan 1986; Shirts 1988). The claim of manhood as a prerequisite to Americanization was especially important in the twentieth century for Jews who were stereotyped as effeminate (see Oriard 2001, 263–265; Riess 1997, 36; also Bodner 1997; Breines 1990; Horowitz 2002; Kugelmass 2007; Levine 1997; Norwood 2009). Football during the early Cold War provided a seemingly open arena, though more open to ethnic European men, and an ethical space in which players and fans could perform masculine citizenship.

In looking at football as a technology of bodily transformation that provided a means to assimilate ethnic European men into the postwar political economy, we can see that sport is less reflective than constitutive of society. Football during the Cold War was not simply a strategy of propaganda in which political elites framed their Cold War agenda. As a powerful form of patriotic pageantry, football works on the conduct of both players and fans. As such, it was part of the uneven, dynamic social structure that makes certain kinds of practices and identities possible while blocking others. Throughout the twentieth century, the capitalist state invested in football and fostered its expansion in public universities and schools, which opened it up to ever-wider audiences as an integrating technology. As a set of institutions that form a market relationship, football is an excellent example of a political technology where the state moves into the background and citizens produce themselves in accord with state needs.

My central concern is how football during the early Cold War participated in producing masculine citizens. But I have also suggested ambiguity in the process with the concept of fortified masculinity: the idea that gendered and racial privilege also comes with costs, sacrifices in the sporting argot. What makes sports like football such an effective regime of bodily transformation is their ability to hearken to people's need for play, camaraderie, and self-expression at a time of increasing contingency. However, need fulfillment occurs within rationally ordered systems and according to prescribed sets of action and behaviors. Thus a regime of bodily transformation provides a social patterning of bodies and desires. Unlike most of the Cold War patriotic pageantry described by Fried (1998), sports such as football have real use value in fulfilling a need for expression, contact, and camaraderie at the same time that they create an internal system of regulation consistent with the needs of state and a broader system of exchange.

# APPENDIX: NOTE ON METHODOLOGY

*Discipline and Indulgence* draws upon a wide variety of primary sources from the era, including newspaper and magazine articles, popular football histories, academic articles, popular and academic books, television production manuals, Supreme Court decisions, and educational films. A cultural studies methodology of textual analysis and coding of articles/texts disentangles narrative themes pertaining to the construction of race, class, nation, militarism, gender, and so on (see Allen 1992; Clayton and Harris 2004; Dworkin and Wachs 2009; Giardina 2003; Radway 1991; Shohat and Stam 1994). Analysis of the articles involved two levels: (1) a focus on the framing argument to construct dominant themes and sketch out broader discursive formations and (2) repeating subthemes within the articles to identify different patterns within the texts. The initial searches for primary sources focused largely on articles related to football broadcasting in published indexes. The main indexes were the *Reader's Guide to Periodical Literature* from 1947 to 1963 and the *New York Times Index* for the news published between 1949 and 1963. I further relied on the *Index of Sports Illustrated Magazine* from its initial year of publication, 1954, to 1968, when Jack Olsen published "The Black Athlete—A Shameful Story," which brought the assimilation era of sports writing to an end. Electronic newspaper searches were done through ProQuest's online newspaper archive of the *New York Times*, the *Los Angeles Times*, and the *Wall Street Journal* from 1945 to 1965. The articles were divided into two primary categories: physical education/health (351) and football (264). The electronic searches generated thousands of citations, most of which were irrelevant to the research. The bulk of the rejected citations were classified advertisements, standard reporting (i.e., game summaries), or articles on soccer and not American football. A search for popular and academic journal articles done in SPORTDiscus using the keyword "football" produced 407 articles between 1940 and 1959, but only 66 were relevant to the project.

Several other sources of information were consulted in researching *Discipline and Indulgence*. Popular histories, such as William "Pudge" Heffelfinger's *This Was Football* (Heffelfinger and McCallum 1954), provide "expert opinion" that frames the meaning of football for a wider population and offer an informative entrée into the world and lore of football, especially for young boys. After consulting the Museum of Radio and Television archive in New York and Los Angeles, the Museum of Broadcast Communications in Chicago, and the University of Southern California's Sports Information Office, I realized that no significant body of broadcasts from the period exists. So instead of watching broadcasts, I studied television production manuals from the period that describe the proper techniques and use of technology for televising football games (see chapter 4). The production manual descriptions were supplemented with articles in popular and trade journals on the techniques, technology, and experience of television broadcasting. I also used LexisNexis to locate and review Sherman Antitrust lawsuits during the period; of special importance was *United States v. National Football League* (1953). Anecdotal research was done at the Internet Archive: Open Source Movies website, where I retrieved educational film by companies such as Coronet and Encyclopedia Britannica on topics related to citizenship, health and fitness, nutrition, communism, television broadcasting, and atomic warfare preparedness.[1]

# NOTES

## 1. INTRODUCTION

1. In *Discipline and Indulgence*, I use the term "football" both generally and specifically to refer to a sporting discipline that involves the use of a ball for attack and defense of rarified space or "goal." At times, I refer to the many versions that have been played throughout history and across geography with the generic term "football." However, *Discipline and Indulgence* is primarily concerned with the version of football that developed in the United States during the late nineteenth century that is often referred to as "American football" or "gridiron football." Primarily, I use the term "football" to refer to the contemporary U.S. version of the game. In situations that call for clarity, I refer to the U.S. game as "American football."

2. This changed significantly after 1984 when the Supreme Court deregulated college football and cable networks expanded slots for broadcasting games.

3. The Thomas Indian School on the Cattaraugus Reservation (Seneca Nation of Indians) just outside of Buffalo, New York.

4. In a seminal essay, Sut Jhally (1984) defined the sport-media complex as the process whereby two distinct institutions, sport and media, became structurally intertwined and mutually dependent upon each other for economic success.

5. The expanded and intensified links between sport and militarism since 2001 have as much to do with developments in neoliberal capitalism, such as the proliferation corporate-state strategic alliances and the mediatization of a whole host of institutions, as they do with the George W. Bush administration.

6. Since Stagg was also in charge of the athletic department, coaching was not his sole responsibility at the time of his appointment. Foster Sanford was named the first single-sport, professional coach at Columbia University in 1899. It should be noted that even as late as the 1920s many schools did not have full-time professional coaches. See Watterson (2000).

7. According to the *Inflation Calculator*, $15,409 in 1893 is equal to $369,064.78 in 2010. See S. Morgan Freidman, *The Inflation Calculator*, http://www.westegg.com/inflation/.

8. A saying attributed to the Duke of Wellington held that "the Battle of Waterloo was won on the playing fields of Eton" since elite British boarding schools, where modern football developed, were training grounds for British officers. Football, whether of the Etonian tradition (soccer) or Rugby tradition, was used as physical and mental preparation for service to the empire. See Clarke (1993); Dunning (1972, 1975); Mangan (1986); Morford and McIntosh (1993).

## 2. FORTIFYING THE CITY UPON A HILL

1. David Kirk is an exception; see Kirk (1998).

2. In addition to Kemper's book, sport historians have produced three dissertations on sport during the Cold War. See Crawford (2004); Thomas (2002); Domer (1976). Also see Beamish and Ritchie (2005); Massaro (2003); Wagg and Andrews (2006). Damion Thomas's book *Globetrotting: African American Athletes and Cold War Politics* (2012) was published too late for review here.

3. Government in a capitalist state manages people and things within its physical and political territory, and its exercise of power is circumscribed by the structure, organization, and dispersion of the state itself.

4. Society is understood here as the complex ensemble of social formations and interactions that compose the population.

5. National Security Council Report Number 68 (NSC-68) was a top-secret document that formalized U.S. Cold War foreign policy by outlining and putting the strategy of containment into practice. NSC-68 thus became a guiding document of U.S. foreign policy for more than the next twenty years. See Gaddis (1982) and May (1999).

6. Citizenship itself as a practice of liberation within Western history has conferred rights upon individual white males in a progressive liberation from traditional patriarchy (master/client relations of dependence) into modern patriarchy or men's domination of women. See Geva (2006) and Fraser and Gordon (1998).

7. Nancy Fraser and Linda Gordon argue that slavery and coverture, subsuming a wife's legal identity into that of her husband, did not simply exclude minorities from citizenship but were the actual mechanisms that white men used to gain citizenship by establishing relations of dependence with minority groups. Fraser and Gordon (1998).

8. As May writes of Cold War culture, "More than merely a metaphor for the cold war on the homefront, containment aptly describes the way in which public policy, personal behavior, and even political values were focused on the home." May (1999, xxv).

9. Postwar domesticity formed partly as a reaction to deprivations experienced during the depression and the world wars with their promises of eventual prosperity, but even more than that, young people feared changes in contemporary society. Those anxieties included the specter of nuclear annihilation and other international threats, racial and labor unrest, rising urban crime and juvenile delinquency, changes in residential patterning, also called white flight, and the political economy of military-industrial Keynesianism.

10. Edna Bonacich's theory of a split labor market demonstrates how economic competition hardened white racial identities when established white workers defended gains on the shop floor against employers' use of new workers to devalue their labor power. Unionization itself has at times provided a mechanism for assimilating ethnic whites into the political economy of the United States while barring other racial groups such access. See Bonacich (1972, 1976), Metzger (1971), and Hirschman (1983).

11. Historian James Gilbert argues that "the effects of conformity, suburban life, and mass culture were depicted [in popular culture] as feminizing and debasing, and the proposed solution often lay in a renewal of traditional masculine vigor and individualism." Gilbert (2005, 4).

12. Mark Massa adds that Notre Dame football helped to assimilate ethnic European Catholics into U.S. citizenship and whiteness during the Cold War. Football as a means of ethnic white assimilation, however, should not be seen as limited only to Notre Dame. See Massa (1999).

13. This cartoon was placed on the page of an article by Otto Graham, quarterback of the Cleveland Browns, on the violence of professional football. Graham (1954).

14. The character Don Draper on the popular television show *Mad Men* during its early seasons provides a good contemporary representation of the suicidal cult of masculinity.

15. It is interesting to note that according to Wikipedia, the Hercules Powder Company was not a medical company but a munitions manufacturer. They were most famous for producing powerful smokeless gunpowder. See http://en.wikipedia.org/wiki/Hercules_Inc.

**16.** Examples include McGee (1957); Lees (1956); Sowder (1954); "Men Are Sicklier Hospital Figures Show" (1955); "How Executives Relax" (1956); "Executive Tensions Aren't All Jitters; They Can Wreck Health Too, Says Doctors" (1956); "Healthy Bosses" (1956); "Bosses Lack Physical Stamina to Cope with Strains of the Job" (1956); "How to Live with Job Pressure" (1965); Snider (1957); Burnell (1956); Glass (1955); Stare (1953).

## 3. DUCK WALKING THE COUCH POTATO

A version of this chapter first appeared as "'As Our Muscles Get Softer, Our Missile Race Becomes Harder': Cultural Citizenship and the 'Muscle Gap,'" *Journal of Historical Sociology* 18, no. 3 (2005): 145–171.

**1.** Lewis Puller would eventually rise to the rank of lieutenant general and remains an icon within the U.S. Marines. He is reputed to have stated during the Korean War, "We're surrounded. That simplifies our problem of getting to these people and killing them."
**2.** In searching for newspaper articles, I used ProQuest's online newspaper archive to search the *New York Times*, the *Los Angeles Times*, and the *Wall Street Journal* from 1945 to 1965. I chose these dates to capture the entire run of the muscle gap and to see if there was a similar media pattern following World War II—there was not. I did three full-text searches on the keywords "physical fitness," "soft American," and "flabby American," which netted a total of 1,936 articles that I narrowed down to 351 by rejecting articles not clearly related to the muscle gap.
    I used the *Reader's Guide to Periodical Literature* to search for magazine articles from 1951 to 1963, under a variety of subheadings like "physical fitness" and "health—men" or "health—women." After eliminating irrelevant titles, I came up with 121 articles.
    Some articles did not clearly fit into any of the three categories, such as the articles I classified as related to "women's health," which take a health-centered, anticompetitive tack.
**3.** Wolf (1964).
**4.** Wilkinson remains one of the most respected coaches in NCAA football history, wining national championships in 1950, 1955, and 1956. His teams also had winning streaks of thirty-one (1948–1951) and forty-seven (1953–1957) games, the latter of which remains the longest streak in NCAA history. See Wilkinson (2004) and Carter (2005).
**5.** Kennedy's hike craze received a combination of praise and ridicule. Much of the criticism was diffracted through praise of Pierre Salinger, the president's notoriously heavy press secretary, who backed out of a scheduled fifty-mile hike. As one article exclaimed, "In a nation suddenly gone berserk, Pierre is a lone voice of reason." Coates (1963). Also see Conklin (1961); "Bob Kennedy Rests after 50-Mile Hike" (1963); Smith (1963); Ryskind (1963); Buchwald (1963); "Marathon Walks Defy State Law" (1963); Rusk (1963); Fox (1963); "Marathon Madness" (1963); Hoffleit (1963); "Substitute for Hike" (1963); Drezner (1963); "College Journalists Get in Shape for 50-Mile Memorial Hike Friday" (1964); "3 on Cross-Vermont Hike" (1964); Buchwald (1964). The result of the marathon craze becomes clear in this final article, "Bicycle Makers Rolling Up Record Sales as Adults Discover New Way to Keep Fit" (1965).
**6.** Since the 1980s, the walkathon movement has embodied an ethic of volunteerism and personal responsibility for maintaining one's health in participatory sports events linked to charitable causes. King (2003, 307).
**7.** According to Internet sources, "The Chicken Fat Song" experienced wide distribution and is indelibly etched, both positively and negatively, on the minds of people subjected to it in childhood. "The Youth Fitness Song" was written by Meredith Wilson and sung by Robert Preston—the composer and lyricist and star, respectively, of the original *Music Man*.

8. In the article "The Soft American" as well as elsewhere, Kennedy's use of "American civilization" works as a euphemism for what could more appropriately be called an empire.

9. When looking at the article, Mrozek concludes that "the authors had associated good grooming with patriotism and toughness with the citizenship appropriate for good Americans." But given the photo series, the *Look* authors don't only suggest that good Americans are well groomed and tough; they are also racially white. See Mrozek (1995, 266).

10. Mayer (1955).

11. What I am calling the American (un)exceptionalism narrative rearticulates Teddy Roosevelt's warning in "The Strenuous Life" that our potential to go soft will make the United States fall behind other imperialist nations. See Roosevelt (1899).

12. When issues of class were specifically articulated, it was in terms of minimizing deviance. A program to control youth offenders in New Orleans, Louisiana, was repeatedly cited as a successful example. It was also the only example cited in my review of the literature.

## 4. THE BEST SEAT IN THE BALLPARK

1. Jim Handy's *Magic in the Air* was originally made in 1941 and sponsored by General Motors. The 1955 version is virtually identical to the original, running about eight minutes in length, but ends with a scene that allows it to double as a commercial for General Motors cars. For more information see "Magic in the Air (1955)," *Prelinger Internet Archive*, http://www.archive.org/details/Magicint1955.

2. Michael Oriard argues that prior to the electronic broadcast media of television and radio, print media had been the primary means through which people engaged with football. See Oriard (1993).

3. Anna McCarthy persuasively makes the case that postwar bars and taverns formed a working-class public sphere that does not remove bars and taverns from the private sector or change the fact that they are privately owned institutions operating within the market. As such, the owner, bartender, or bouncer can remove people from the premises for not purchasing products or for behavior deemed inappropriate in a way that would be impossible in truly public space. See McCarthy (1995, 2001).

4. Toby Miller uses the term "ethical zone" to describe the space within a museum as a technology of citizenship, or a place where people learn the appropriate from the inappropriate, the moral from the immoral, etc. Unlike a specific museum, however, football broadcasting is not tied to a specific place or piece of territory. The broadcast apparatus creates a diffuse, flexible, and transitory space in which people perform their fan identity and participate in the national culture. In this sense, football broadcasting is a technology of citizenship that makes interventions in people's lives and provides a pedagogy on performing citizenship that is less territorially specific than a single museum. See Miller (1998, 234).

5. The deregulation of college football broadcasting coupled with the rise of cable networks and the Bowl Championship Series (BCS) have greatly diminished the significance of New Year's Day through the reorganization of bowl games and spreading them across several different days.

6. This section draws on television production manuals written to instruct prospective broadcasters on the techniques of successful broadcasting. I use these manuals instead of actual broadcasts since broadcasts from the era are no longer extant. See the appendix for more details.

7. Just like sport media, peanut butter and jelly sandwiches have a social and cultural history. Although combinations of sweet and salty food items are popular across global cuisines, the specific combination of peanut butter and jelly is especially popular in North America. Industrialization caused the cost of peanut butter to drop, which made peanut butter and jelly

sandwiches an affordable as well as popular meal for children, especially during the Great Depression. For more information, see Smith (2002).

**8.** Fordham beat Waynesburg College 34–7 on September 20, 1939.

**9.** James's gimmick was so popular that DuMont created a daytime variety show called *Okay, Mother*, which ran from 1948 to 1951.

## 5. FORDISM IN THE AIRWAVES

A version of this chapter first appeared as "A Cartel in the Public Interest: NCAA Broadcast Policy during the Early Cold War," *American Studies* 49, nos. 3/4 (2008): 157–194.

**1.** I use the terms "teams," "schools," and "firms" synonymously even though colleges and universities are nonprofit organizations with an educational mission. The point, however, is that high-pressure athletics blurs the boundary between civil society and the market because colleges vis-à-vis their football teams act as firms competing in market relations. Crosset and Masteralexis (2008).

**2.** Kolko defines market rationalization as "the organization of the economy and the larger political social spheres in a manner that will allow corporations to function in a predictable and secure environment permitting reasonable profits over the long run." Market rationalization is achieved by minimizing competition, planning for future economic growth, and minimizing political intervention by state or civil society. Kolko (1963, 3).

**3.** Although numerous definitions abound, civil society is generally understood as the collection of voluntary civic associations, social organizations, and institutions through which members of society come together to act as citizens and participate in the governance of society. In this instance, I primarily refer to the media and social organizations that might act to constrain the business of college football. Sport sociologists are often concerned with the relationship between sport and civil society. For example, Allison (1998); Houlihan (2001); Ingham, Howell, and Schilperoort (1987).

**4.** For a longer discussion on the development of stadiums in the twentieth century, see Bale (1994); Neilson (1995).

**5.** For more discussion on the economics and politics of stadiums, see Baade and Dye (1990); Baade and Sanderson (1997); Baim (1994); Cagen and deMause (1998); Coates and Humphreys (2003); Eckstein and Delaney (2002); Friedman, Andrews, and Silk (2004); Ingham, Howell, and Schilperoort (1987); Pelissero, Henschen, and Sidlow (1991); Smith and Ingham (2003).

**6.** According to Marx, the forces of production consist of two parts: the means of production and labor power. The means of production include both the raw materials of production and the equipment or tools used in the production process. The capitalist mode of production separates workers from the means of production so that they are forced to sell their labor power on the free market. Capitalists generate profit by purchasing the forces of production in order to produce commodities that will be sold on the free market. In college football, the means of production include stadiums, training facilities, and training equipment. When schools purchase the means of production and the labor power of athletes, coaches, and scouts, they purchase the forces of production. This not only advantages schools over their workers, but also advantages large, wealthy schools over small schools. See Marx (1977).

**7.** The *New York Times* makes several references to teams shutting down their programs in the early 1950s. See "St. Mary's Drops Sport for Duration of National Emergency" (1951); "Duquesne Drops Sport" (1951); "Georgetown Drops Sport" (1951); "Niagara Drops Sport for Duration of National Emergency" (1951); "Sport Dropped by Adelphia for Lack of Student Interest" (1954); "Fordham Drops Sport Because of Financial Loses" (1954).

**8.** The fact that the NCAA quadrupled its dues to only $100 indicates how power relations favored member institutions over the administrative body before the 1950s. The cost of NCAA membership in 1948 was equivalent to $845 in 2005. This calculation was performed at Freidman's *The Inflation Calculator,* http://www.westegg.com/inflation/, on March 17, 2007.

**9.** The following articles are examples of calls to reform college football: "Social Justice for Football Labor!" (1951); "Football Excesses to Be Investigated" (1951); "Football Ethics Scrutinized" (1951); "Touchdowns at Any Price! Discard of Sanity Code" (1951); "What Price Football?" (1950).

**10.** AT&T laid coaxial cables in the Northeast in 1946, just before doing the same in the Midwest. Smith (2001, 54).

**11.** "June 28 Deadline Set on College TV Plans" (1951).While the neatness of the 4 percent rise and fall pattern itself could be questioned, members of the "television industry" criticized the report's "inadequate samples" and "contradictory" results. See "N.C.A.A. Study Attacked" (1952).

**12.** Skiatron required viewers to purchase plastic cards with a hole-pattern punched into them. Every broadcast needed its own card that slipped into a de-scrambler box on the television; cost was either fifty cents or a dollar. Establishing an efficient system of distribution was a major limitation of Skiatron. Phonovision required an AT&T operator to plug a viewer into a given broadcast but faced antitrust concerns until the late 1950s. "Football TV Plan Aides All Colleges" (1951); NCAA (1961).

**13.** Paul Boyer argues that conscious fears of atomic warfare waxed and waned throughout the Cold War in a cycle of "activism and apathy." Apathy describes periods when atomic fears were less conscious than at times when people were moved to social action. See Boyer (1994, 352–367).

**14.** The DuMont Television Network was an important network in television's early days but was pushed out of the broadcast market by 1956.

**15.** The proposed regulations for the 1951 season worked as follows: (1) One game per Saturday from September 29 to November 24 would be televised, generally, in a school's particular region. The bowl games and the Army-Navy game coming after November 24 would not be regulated. (2) At least three games would be blacked out during the season to test the effect of television on gate receipts. (3) No team would get more than two games (a home game and an away game) televised during the season in order to protect smaller schools that did not have the popularity of schools like Notre Dame, Michigan, or Army from being overlooked by the networks. "One Saturday Football Telecast for Each Area Set by NCAA" (1951).

**16.** Westinghouse Electronics Corp. paid $663,142 for the rights to sponsor the 1951 season; out of that total the NCAA collected $119,365 (18 percent), and the sum went to the teams that played in the nineteen televised games. "College Football Limiting TV Again" (1952).

According to Ronald Smith, the NCAA initially wanted to take 60 percent of the revenues to redistribute to nontelevision schools, but top schools like Notre Dame balked. Eventually, the royalties were forced down to 5 percent and never redistributed effectively. Smith (2001, 87).

**17.** Consistency between press coverage of the NCAA's policy and the committee's reports suggest that journalists were also reading the reports.

**18.** While making an argument for football's value in creating social solidarity on an otherwise fractured campus, Ralph Cooper Hutchison, president of Lafayette College, concedes, "But if the accounts were straightened out and the cold facts brought to light it would be found that football and intercollegiate sports are very costly to most of the country's higher schools and are by no stretch of the imagination a device for making money for educational purposes." Hutchison (1952). Also "College Football: Has It Really Gone 'Pro'?" (1956); Hutchins (1954); Jackson (1951).

**19.** While a thorough review of the Olympic debates is beyond the scope of this article, the following selection of citations provides an outline of the discourse during the period under discussion. "A.A.U. Opens Drive for 1956 Olympics" (1953); Black (1954); Blunk (1956); Briordy (1953); Canham (1954); Conklin (1959); McGovern (1954); Perlmutter (1962); Rondeau (1964); Sheehan (1957).

**20.** In postwar debates about the role of football programs on university campuses, the term "emphasis" refers to the amount of capital a university invests in its football program. "Deemphasis" suggests a program of divestment that minimizes the role of athletics in university life, while "overemphasis" suggests a win-at-all-costs attitude that leads to unscrupulous practices.

**21.** Ronald Smith describes the Sports Broadcasting Act of 1961 as helping professional football to expand by giving the NFL a television monopoly on professional football broadcasting. The NCAA claimed victory since the act also gave some protection to college football by blocking the NFL from broadcasting on Saturdays, when college typically played, and Fridays, when high schools typically played. See Smith (2001, 95–97).

## 6. FROM NEIGHBORHOOD TO NATION

**1.** Despite its dominance as a policy paradigm, isolationism always faced internal opposition. Even Senator Arthur H. Vandenberg, a prominent isolationist, began to realize the limitations of isolationism as a guide to foreign policy before World War II. See Gazell (1973, 379).

Isolation was also challenged by competing versions of internationalism. However, it was Pearl Harbor, followed by the collapse of Europe's "balance of powers" and the rise of the Iron Curtain, that forced a reconceptualization of the U.S. geographical imagination. See Roskin (1974); Fensterwald (1958a).

Isolationism refers to foreign policy practices that eschew "entangling alliances" with foreign powers and stress economic practices of self-reliance by developing a national self that excludes and disdains foreign others. The introverted geographical imagination of isolationism is a nation-building strategy that produces its self through internal development, economic self-sufficiency, and territorial accumulation. In practice, it meant isolation from European colonialism and "power politics" while simultaneously giving a moral rationale to Manifest Destiny in North America and foreign adventures in Latin America and Asia. Although legitimated by a dubious moral superiority over Europeans and racial superiority over non-Europeans, isolationism proved an effective ideology throughout the nineteenth century in guiding the foreign policy of a small, relatively weak, and geographically isolated nation that enjoyed the protection of British naval power. See Fensterwald (1958a, 1958b); Gazell (1973); Roskin (1974); Smuckler (1953).

**2.** Experts on the Cold War and containment generally believe that Truman would not have supported the policy recommendation in NSC-68 in 1950 had North Korea not invaded South Korea so shortly after the "loss" of China in 1949. Gaddis (1982); Nitze (1993).

**3.** George Carlin (1975) states,

> Baseball is a nineteenth-century pastoral game.
>
> Football is a twentieth-century technological struggle....
>
> In football the object is for the quarterback, also known as the field general, to be on target with his aerial assault, riddling the defense by hitting his receivers with deadly accuracy in spite of the blitz, even if he has to use the shotgun. With short bullet passes and long bombs, he marches his troops into enemy territory, balancing this aerial assault with a sustained ground attack that punches holes in the forward wall of the enemy's defensive line.
>
> In baseball the object is to go home! And to be safe!—I hope I'll be safe at home!

4. Critics often see the violence, homophobia, and misogyny of football as naturalizing militarism and hegemonic masculinity in people's everyday lives. Burstyn (1999); Curry (1991); Foley (1990); Messner (2002); Trujillo (1995).

5. *Sports Illustrated* was the last great project of Henry Luce, founder of *Time, Fortune, Life,* and *McClure.*

6. The demographic composition of *SI*'s audience is an empirical question beyond the scope of this book.

7. "US Football: In Maps and Diagrams" (1954, 4).

8. Despite the claim to objective, scientific precision in the text, creating maps always includes a degree of subjective decision making in order to create clarity and a desired effect. For instance, the Missouri Valley Conference (D) does not indicate that Bradley College, in Peoria, Illinois, is a member of the conference. Very likely, the authors of the map did not want to create an overly elaborate shaded area to represent the conference since that may have been confusing. Regardless, an inaccuracy made for a cleaner, clearer appearance.

9. This is not to overlook the obvious fact that one is a human and the other a nonhuman technology.

10. Although the position of women is beyond the concerns of this chapter, we should note that the dominant, authorial position of a woman, even a successful professional athlete, in this article is unique in football coverage. Figure 6.4, which shows Patty Berg standing over the boys on *her* football team, gives Berg the appearance of a field marshal—in fact, Berg served as a lieutenant in the Marines during the Second World War. The domineering position of Berg in the photo and article might strike some as consistent with 1950s anxiety around "momism." However, rather than emasculating the men, as Philip Wylie argued in *Generation of Vipers,* Berg's *female masculinity* is crucial to fortifying the manhood of the successful men. Berg would go on to become one of the all-time great golfers in U.S. history and one of the founders of the LPGA. Biographies on Berg tend to describe her as a "tom-boy," her participation in the 50th Street Tigers, and the details of her golf career, but they never mention relationships to men other than her father. The lack of reference to a significant man in her life is unusual in sport reporting on female athletes, which suggests Berg's possible sexual difference is also contained in the reporting. Nevertheless, Berg's sexual ambiguity provides the article with the voice of a childhood female friend who describes the formative years in highly emphatic language about competitiveness and success. We can also see the growing political importance placed on white women's athletics in the early Cold War that was triggered by the success of female Soviet athletes in the Olympics. See Oriard (2001); "Patty Berg: 1918–2006" (2011); Roberts (2007); Wade (2001); Woolum (1998); Wylie (1942/1955).

## 7. CONCLUSION

1. The first line in this passage came from a letter that Church's uncle sent him to congratulate him on earning his varsity letter. Church used his uncle's words as a starting point for his speech at the dinner. See "Soundtrack—What Football Means" (1954).

2. Clifford Geertz attended graduate school at Harvard in the mid-1950s. I have no knowledge of whether or not he ever attended a football game at Harvard or elsewhere.

3. Recent historiography does not locate the origin of "football" in Greece or follow a linear model of diffusion that links the past with an inevitable future. See Gillmeister (1997); Penz (1991); Smith (1988); Watterson (2000).

4. Kurt Edward Kemper argues that Chester LaRoche saw football as central to the U.S. Cold War mission and attempted to discredit critics of college football. Kemper (2009, 27–28).

5. Talcott Parsons's widely read translation of Weber's term *stahlhartes Gehause* as an "iron cage" rather than a "steel-hard casing" is seen as an attempt to soften Weber's pessimistic vision of Western capitalism. See Gorski (2003a).

6. Determining the boundary between external regulation and individual liberty is a socially and historically specific question that can ultimately never be fully resolved, and probably should not be. Berlin (1999, 157).

7. The term "small war" can be confusing since it refers not to the scale of fighting but to a war of any scale where regular troops face irregular forces typically engaged in some form of guerilla warfare. The term "small war" emerged to describe the regular U.S. interventions in Latin America during the nineteenth century (known as the "Banana Wars") and in other parts of the world such as the Philippines. Critics, such as Major General Smedley D. Butler, view small wars as colonial operations where U.S. forces are deployed in service of capital accumulation. See Schlosser (2010); Butler (1935).

## APPENDIX

1. See https://archive.org/details/opensource_movies.

# REFERENCES

Aaron, Daniel. 1979. Review of *From Ritual to Record: The Nature of Modern Sports* by Allen Guttmann. *Journal of American Studies* 13 (1):129–130.

A.A.U. Opens Drive for 1956 Olympics. 1953. *New York Times*, November 28, 20.

Adams, David Wallace. 1995. *Education for Extinction: American Indians and the Boarding School Experience, 1875–1928.* Lawrence: University Press of Kansas.

Aden, Roger C., and Christina L. Reynolds. 1993. Lost and Found in America: The Function of Place Metaphor in *Sports Illustrated. Southern Communication Journal* 59 (1):1–14.

Alba, Richard, and Victor Nee. 1997. Rethinking Assimilation Theory for a New Era of Immigration. *International Migration Review* 31 (4):826–874.

Allen, Robert C., ed. 1992. *Channels of Discourse Reassembled: Television and Contemporary Criticism.* Chapel Hill: University of North Carolina Press.

Allison, Lincoln. 1994. The Olympic Movement and the End of the Cold War. *World Affairs* 157 (2):92–97.

———. 1998. Sport and Civil Society. *Political Studies* 46 (4):709–727.

Altman, Lawrence, and Todd S. Purdum. 2002. In J.F.K. File, Hidden Illness, Pain and Pills. *New York Times*, November 17, 1, 26.

America's Youth: Fit or Unfit? 1960. *Senior Scholastic*, April 27, 12–13.

Anderson, Benedict. 1991. *Imagined Communities: Reflections on the Origins and Spread of Nationalism.* New York: Verso.

Andrews, David L. 2002. Coming to Terms with Cultural Studies. *Journal of Sport & Social Issues* 26 (1):110–117.

Andrews, David L., and Ben Carrington, eds. In press. *Blackwell Companion to Sport.* Blackwell Companions in Cultural Studies. Oxford: Wiley-Blackwell.

Andrews, David L., and Michael D. Giardina. 2008. Sport Without Guarantees: Toward a Cultural Studies That Matters. *Cultural Studies <=> Critical Methodologies* 8 (4):395–422.

Antonio, Robert J., and Alessandro Bonanno. 2000. A New Global Capitalism? From "Americanism and Fordism" to "Americanization-Globalization." *American Studies* 41 (2/3):33–77.

Are We Becoming Soft? 1955. *Newsweek*, September 26, 35–36.

Arens, William. 1976. Professional Football: An American Symbol and Ritual. In *The American Dimension: Cultural Myths and Social Realities,* edited by W. Arens and S. P. Montague. Port Washington, NY: Alfred.

Azzarito, Laura, Petra Munro, and Melinda Solmon. 2004. Unsettling the Body: The Institutionalization of Physical Activity at the Turn of the 20th Century. *Quest* 56 (4):377–396.

Baade, Robert A., and Richard F. Dye. 1990. The Impact of Stadium and Professional Sports on Metropolitan Area Development. *Growth and Change* 21 (2):1–14.

Baade, Robert A., and Allen R. Sanderson. 1997. The Employment Effects of Teams and Sports Facilities. In *Sports, Jobs, and Taxes: The Economic Impact of Sports Teams and Stadiums,* edited by R. G. Noll and A. Zimbalist. Washington, DC: Brookings Institution.

Bacevich, Andrew J. 2005. *The New American Militarism: How Americans Are Seduced by War.* New York: Oxford University Press.

Baim, Dean V. 1994. *The Sports Stadium as a Municipal Investment.* Westport, CT: Greenwood.

Bale, John. 1994. *Landscapes of Modern Sport.* London: Leicester University Press.

Ban on Video Discussed: Justice Department Talks to NCAA Men on Football. 1951. *New York Times*, April 13, 35.

Barclay, Dorothy. 1958. Fitness Test, a Preview. *New York Times Magazine*, July 6, 25.

Barnett, Steven. 1990. *Games and Sets: The Changing Face of Sport on Television.* London: BFI.

Barthes, Roland. 1972. *Mythologies.* Translated by A. Lavers. New York: Noonday Press.

————. 1989. The Reality Effect. In *The Rustle of Language.* Berkeley: University of California Press.

Bass, Amy. 2004. *Not the Triumph but the Struggle: 1968 Olympics and the Making of the Black Athlete.* Minneapolis: University of Minnesota Press.

Baudrillard, Jean. 1995. *The Gulf War Did Not Happen.* Translated by P. Patton. Bloomington: Indiana University Press.

Beamish, Rob, and Ian Ritchie. 2005. The Specter of Steroids: Nazi Propaganda, Cold War Anxiety, and Patriarchal Paternalism. *International Journal of the History of Sport* 22 (5):777–795.

Bennett, Tony. 1992. Putting Policy into Cultural Studies. In *Cultural Studies*, edited by L. Grossberg, C. Nelson, and P. A. Treichler. New York: Routledge.

————. 1995. *The Birth of the Museum: History, Theory, and Politics.* London: Routledge.

Berg, Patty, and Seth Kantor. 1954. I Taught Bud Wilkinson to Play Football. *Sports Illustrated*, November 8, 26–29.

Berlant, Lauren. 1997. *The Queen of America Goes to Washington City: Essays on Sex and Citizenship.* Durham, NC: Duke University Press.

Berlin, Isaiah. 1999. Two Concepts of Liberty. In *Arguments for Freedom*, edited by N. Warburton. Milton Keyes, UK: Open University.

Bhabha, Homi K. 1991. DissemiNation: Time, Narrative, and the Margins of the Modern Nation. In *Nations and Narration*, edited by H. K. Bhabha. London: Routledge.

Bialasiewicz, Luiza, David Campbell, Stuart Elden, Stephen Graham, Alex Jeffrey, and Alison J. Williams. 2007. Performing Security: The Imaginative Geographies of Current US Strategy. *Political Geography* 26 (4):405–422.

Bicycle Makers Rolling Up Record Sales as Adults Discover New Way to Keep Fit. 1965. *Wall Street Journal*, October 7, 32.

Binder, Amy. 1993. Constructing Racial Rhetoric: Media Depictions of Harm in Heavy Metal and Rap Music. *American Sociological Review* 58:753–767.

Binder Johnson, Hildegard. 1948. Football as Seen—An American Vignette. *American-German Review*, October, 19–21.

Biskind, Peter. 2000. *Seeing Is Believing: How Hollywood Taught Us to Stop Worrying and Love the Fifties.* New York: Owl Books. Original edition 1983.

Black, Ralph W. 1954. Olympic Funds. *Los Angeles Times*, December 7, A4.

Blauner, Bob. 2009. *Resisting McCarthyism: To Sign or Not to Sign California's Loyalty Oath.* Stanford, CA: Stanford University Press.

Blunk, Frank M. 1956. U.S. Olympians of Past Hope for Triumph of Amateur Spirit. *New York Times*, August 12, 163.

Bob Kennedy Rests after 50-Mile Hike. 1963. *Los Angeles Times*, February 11, 23.

Boddy, William. 1993. *Fifties Television: The Industry and Its Critics.* Urbana: University of Illinois Press.

Bodner, Allen. 1997. *When Boxing Was a Jewish Sport.* Westport, CT: Praeger.

Bonacich, Edna. 1972. A Theory of Ethnic Antagonism: The Split Labor Market. *American Sociological Review* 37 (5):547–559.

———. 1976. Advanced Capitalism and Black/White Race Relations in the United States: A Split Labor Market Interpretation. *American Sociological Review* 41 (1):34–51.

Boon, Kevin. 2005. Heroes, Metanarratives, and the Paradox of Masculinity in Contemporary Western Culture. *Journal of Men's Studies* 13 (3):301–312.

Bordwell, David, Janet Staiger, and Kristin Thompson. 1985. *The Classical Hollywood Cinema: Film Style and Mode of Production to 1960*. New York: Columbia University Press.

Borstelmann, Thomas. 2001. *The Cold War and the Color Line: American Race Relations in the Global Arena*. Cambridge, MA: Harvard University Press.

Bosses Lack Physical Stamina to Cope with Strains of the Job. 1956. *Business Week*, June 23, 66.

Bourdieu, Pierre. 1977. *Outline of a Theory of Practice*. New York: Cambridge University Press.

———. 1986. *Distinctions: A Social Critique of the Judgment of Taste Richard Nice*. Translated by R. Nice. Cambridge, MA: Harvard University Press.

———. 1991. *Language and Symbolic Power*. Translated by G. Raymond and M. Adamson. Edited by J. B. Thompson. Cambridge, MA: Harvard University Press.

Boyer, Paul. 1994. *By the Bomb's Early Light: American Thought and Culture at the Dawn of the Atomic Age*. Chapel Hill: University of North Carolina Press.

Boyle, Robert H. 1955. The Report That Shocked the President. *Sports Illustrated*, August 15, 30–33, 72–73.

———. 1963. *Sport: Mirror of American Life*. Boston: Little, Brown.

Brands, H. W. 1993. *The Devil We Knew: America and the Cold War*. New York: Oxford University Press.

Bratich, Jack Z., Jeremy Packer, and Cameron McCarthy, eds. 2003. *Foucault, Cultural Studies, and Governmentality*. Albany: State University of New York Press.

Brealy, Ken. 1995. Mapping Them "Out": Euro-Canadian Cartography and the Appropriation of the Nuxalk and Ts'ilhqot'in First Nations Territory, 1793–1916. *Canadian Geographer* 39 (2):140–156.

Breines, Paul. 1990. *Tough Jews: Political Fantasies and the Moral Dilemma of American Jewry*. New York: Basic Books.

Bretz, Rudy. 1953. *Techniques of Television Production*. New York: McGraw-Hill.

Briordy, William J. 1953. A.A.U. Launches Drive for $500,000 to Maintain U.S. Olympic Supremacy. *New York Times*, January 27, 29.

Brod, Harry. 1990. Pornography and the Alienation of Male Sexuality. In *Men, Masculinities, and Social Theory*, edited by J. Hearn and D. Morgan. London: Unwin Hyman.

Brodkin, Karen. 1998. *How Jews Became White Folks and What That Says about Race in America*. New Brunswick, NJ: Rutgers University Press.

Brohm, Jean-Marie. 1978. *Sport: A Prison of Measured Time*. London: Ink Links.

Buchanan, Lamont. 1952. *The Story of Football in Text and Pictures*. New York: Vanguard Press.

Buchwald, Art. 1963. "Amis de Pierre" Pursue U.S. Way. *Los Angeles Times*, February 26, D3.

———. 1964. Hike Planned as Memorial to Kennedy. *Los Angeles Times*, November 15, CS5.

Burnell, Max R. 1956. How Much and What Kind of Physical Exercise Should a Business Man Take? For His Job? *Vital Speeches of the Day*, April 15, 406–408.

Burstyn, Varda. 1999. *The Rites of Men: Manhood, Politics and the Culture of Sport*. Toronto: University of Toronto Press.

Bush, George H. W. 1991. Remarks to the American Legislative Exchange Council, March 1, 1991. American Presidency Project. Accessed March 12, 2012, http://www.presidency.ucsb.edu/ws/index.php?pid=19351—axzz10jqoUDDe.

Bushnell, Asa. 1953. Why Football on TV Is Limited. *Look*, October 20, 106.

Butler, Smedley D. 1935. *War Is a Racket*. New York: Round Table Press.

Butterworth, Michael L., and Stormi D. Moskal. 2009. American Football, Flags, and "Fun": The Bell Helicopter Armed Forces Bowl and the Rhetorical Production of Militarism. *Communication, Culture & Critique* 2:411–433.

Cagen, Joanna, and Neil deMause. 1998. *Field of Schemes: How the Great Stadium Swindle Turns Public Money into Private Profits*. Monroe, ME: Common Courage Press.

Campbell, Alec. 2010. The Sociopolitical Origins of the American Legion. *Theory and Society* 39 (1):1–24.

Canham, Don. 1954. Russia Will Win the 1956 Olympics. *Sports Illustrated*, October 25, 11–12, 60–65.

Capraro, Rocco L. 2000. Why College Men Drink: Alcohol, Adventure, and the Paradox of Masculinity. In *Men's Lives*, 7th ed., edited by M. S. Kimmel and M. A. Messner. New York: Pearson.

Card, David, and Gordon B. Dahl. 2010. Family Violence and Football: The Effect of Unexpected Emotional Cues on Violent Behavior. Discussion Paper Series,. IZA, Bonn, Germany.

Carlin, George. 1975. Baseball-Football. In *An Evening with Wally Londo, Featuring Bill Slaszo*. Los Angeles: Little David Records.

Carrington, Ben. 2010. *Race, Sport, and Politics: The Sporting Black Diaspora*. Thousand Oaks, CA: Sage.

Carter, Bob. 2005. Wilkinson Created Sooners Dynasty. ESPN Classic. Accessed September 11, 2004, http://espn.go.com/classic/biography/s/Wilkinson_Bud.html

Carter, Ian. 2008. Positive and Negative Liberty. In *Stanford Encyclopedia of Philosophy*. Accessed February 28, 2012, http://plato.stanford.edu/archives/spr2012/entries/liberty -positive-negative/.

Catsis, John R. 1996. *Sports Broadcasting*. Chicago: Nelson-Hall.

Chardy, Alfonso. 1986. Reagan Warns of a "Second Cuba" Meets Nicaraguan Rebel Leaders, Presses Congress on Aid. *The Inquirer*, March 4.

Clarke, Alan. 1993. Civic Ideology in the Public Domain: Victorian Ideology in the "Lifestyle Crisis" of the 1990s. In *Sport in Social Development: Traditions, Transitions, and Transformations*, edited by A. G. Ingham and J. W. Loy. Champaign, IL: Human Kinetics.

Clayton, Ben, and John Harris. 2004. Footballers' Wives: The Role of the Soccer Player's Partner in the Construction of Idealized Masculinity. *Soccer & Society* 5 (3):317–335.

Coates, Dennis, and Brad R. Humphreys. 2003. The Effect of Professional Sports on Earnings and Employment in the Services and Retail Sectors in US Cities. *Regional Science and Urban Economics* 33:175–198.

Coates, Paul. 1963. Hooray for Pierre Salinger—Fuehrer of Fat Freedom Fighters. *Los Angeles Times*, February 15, A6.

Cohane, Tim. 1951. *The Yale Football Story*. New York: Putnam.

Cohen, Lizabeth. 2003. *A Consumer's Republic: The Politics of Mass Consumption in Postwar America*. New York: Knopf.

Cohen, Scott. 1983. Certain USIA Overseas Activities: A Staff Report. In *Committee on Foreign Relations*, edited by U.S. Senate. Washington, DC: Government Printing Office.

Cole, C. L. 1994. Resisting the Canon: Feminist Cultural Studies, Sport, and Technologies of the Body. In *Women, Sport, and Culture*, edited by S. Birrell and C. L. Cole. Champaign, IL: Human Kinetics.

Coleman, James S. 1965. *Adolescents and the School*. New York: Basic Books.

College Football: Has It Really Gone "Pro"? 1956. *U.S. News & World Report*, October 26, 56–58.

College Football Limiting TV Again. 1952. *New York Times,* June 3, 40.

College Journalists Get in Shape for 50-Mile Memorial Hike Friday. 1964. *Los Angeles Times,* February 27, G1.

Condor, R., and D. F. Anderson. 1984. Longitudinal Analysis of Coverage Accorded Black and White Athletes in Feature Articles of *Sports Illustrated* (1960–1980). *Journal of Sport Behavior* 7 (1):39–43.

Conklin, William R. 1959. Olympic Group Seeks Pennies and Dollars. *New York Times,* January 6, 37.

———. 1961. 4 Tired Collegians End 237-Mile Fitness Hike. *New York Times,* March 31, 29.

Corber, Robert J. 1997. *Homosexuality in Cold War America: Resistance and the Crisis of Masculinity, New Americanists.* Durham, NC: Duke University Press.

Costigliola, Frank. 1997. "Unceasing Pressure for Penetration": Gender, Pathology, and Emotion in George Keenan's Formation of the Cold War. *Journal of American History* 83 (4):1309–1333.

Covert, Cathrine. 1984. We May Hear Too Much: American Sensibility at the Response to Radio, 1919–1924. In *Mass Media between the Wars: Perceptions of Cultural Tensions,* edited by C. Covert and J. D. Stevens. Syracuse, NY: Syracuse University Press.

Crawford, Russell E. 2004. Consensus All-American: Sport and the Promotion of the American Way of Life during the Cold War, 1946–1965. PhD diss., University of Nebraska–Lincoln.

Crosset, Todd, and Lisa Masteralexis. 2008. The Changing Collective Definition of Collegiate Sport and the Potential Demise of Title IX Protections. *Journal of College and University Law* 34 (3):671–694.

Cruikshank, Barbara. 1999. *The Will to Empower: Democratic Citizens and Other Subjects.* Ithaca, NY: Cornell University Press.

Cuordileone, Kyle A. 2000. Politics in an Age of Anxiety: Cold War Political Culture and the Crisis of American Masculinity. *Journal of American History* 87 (2):515–545.

Curry, Timothy Jon. 1991. Fraternal Bonding in the Locker Room: A Profeminist Analysis of Talk about Competition and Women. *Sociology of Sport Journal* 8 (2):119–135.

———. 2000. Booze and Bar Fights: A Journey into the Dark Side of College Athletics. In *Masculinities, Gender Relations, and Sport: Research on Men and Masculinities,* edited by J. McKay, M. A. Messner, and D. Sabo. Thousand Oaks, CA: Sage.

Custers, Peter. 2010. Military Keynesianism Today: An Innovative Discourse. *Race & Class* 51 (4):79–94.

Cypher, James M. 2007. From Military Keynesianism to Global-Neoliberal Militarism. *Monthly Review* 59 (June). Accessed December 2, 2010, http://monthlyreview.org/2007/06/01/from-military-keynesianism-to-global-neoliberal-militarism.

Daly, Arthur. 1951. Blackout at Penn. *New York Times,* June 15, 30.

Danzig, Allison. 1956. *The History of American Football: Its Great Teams, Players, and Coaches.* Englewood Cliffs, NJ: Prentice Hall.

Davis, Belinda. 1996. Reconsidering Habermas, Gender, and the Public Sphere: The Case of Wilhelmine Germany. In *Society, Culture, and the State in Germany, 1870–1930,* edited by G. Eley. Ann Arbor: University of Michigan Press.

Davis, Laurel R. 1993. Critical Analysis of the Popular Media and the Concept of Ideal Subject Position: *Sports Illustrated* as Case Study. *Quest* 45 (2):165–181.

———. 1997. *The Swim Suit Issue and Sport Hegemonic Masculinity in Sports Illustrated.* Albany: State University of New York Press.

Dean, Robert D. 1998. Masculinity as Ideology: John F. Kennedy and the Domestic Politics of Foreign Policy. *Diplomatic History* 22 (1):29–62.

Deleuze, Gilles, and Felix Guattari. 1977. *Anti-Oedipus: Capitalism and Schizophrenia*. Translated by R. Hurley, M. Seem, and H. R. Lane. New York: Viking.

Demas, Lane. 2010. *Integrating the Gridiron: Black Civil Rights and American College Football*. New Brunswick, NJ: Rutgers University Press.

Deutsche, Rosalyn. 1995. Surprising Geography. *Annals of the Association of American Geographers* 85 (1):168–175.

DiMaggio, Paul. 1983. Cultural Policy Studies: What They Are and Why We Need Them. *Journal of Arts Management and Law* 13 (1):241–248.

Domer, Thomas M. 1976. Sport in Cold War America, 1953–1963: The Diplomatic and Political Use of Sport in the Eisenhower and Kennedy Administration. PhD diss., Marquette University.

Doyle, Andrew. 1996. Bear Bryant: Symbol for an Embattled South. *Colby Quarterly* 2 (1):72–86.

Drezner, Paul. 1963. Tour by Bicycle. *New York Times*, May 26, 388.

Dudziak, Mary L. 2000. *Cold War Civil Rights: Race and the Image of American Democracy*. Princeton, NJ: Princeton University Press.

Dundes, Alan. 1978. Into the Endzone for a Touchdown: A Psychoanalytic Consideration of American Football. *Western Folklore* 37:75–88.

Dunning, Eric. 1972. The Development of Modern Football. In *Sport: Readings from a Sociological Perspective*, edited by E. Dunning. Toronto: University of Toronto Press.

———. 1975. Industrialization and the Incipient Modernization of Football: A Study in Historical Sociology. *Stadion: Journal of the History of Sport and Physical Education* 1 (1):101–139.

———. 2004. "Figuring" Modern Sport: Autobiographical and Historical Reflections on Sport, Violence, and Civilization. Chester Centre for Research into Sport and Society.

Duquesne Drops Sport. 1951. *New York Times*, January 21, 7.

Durkheim, Emile. 1961. *Moral Education: A Study in the Theory and Application of the Sociology of Education*. Translated by E. K. Wilson and H. Schnurer. New York: Free Press of Glencoe.

———. 1997. *The Division of Labor in Society*. Translated by W. D. Halls. New York: Free Press. Original edition 1933.

———. 2001. *The Elementary Forms of Religious Life*. Translated by C. Cosman. New York: Oxford University Press. Original edition 1915.

Dworkin, Shari, and Faye Wachs. 2009. *Body Panic: Gender, Health, and the Selling of Fitness*. New York: New York University Press.

Dyke, Henry Van. 1901. Introduction. In *Athletics at Princeton: A History*, edited by F. Presbrey and J. H. Moffatt. New York: Frank Presbrey.

Eastman, Max. 1961. Let's Close the Muscle Gap. *Reader's Digest*, November, 122–125.

Eckstein, Rick, and Kevin Delaney. 2002. New Sports Stadiums, Community Self-Esteem, and Community Collective Conscience. *Journal of Sport & Social Issues* 26 (3):236–248.

Edwards, Harry. 1969. *The Revolt of the Black Athlete*. New York: Free Press.

Eichberg, Henning. 1998. *Body Cultures: Essays on Sport, Space, and Identity*. Edited by J. Bale and C. Philo. London: Routledge.

Eisenhower, Dwight D. 1961. Farewell Address to the American People. Eisenhower Presidential Library and Museum. Accessed March 8, 2007, http://www.eisenhower.archives.gov/research/online_documents/farewell_address/Reading_Copy.pdf.

Eitzen, D. Stanley. 1999. *Fair and Foul: Beyond the Myths and Paradoxes of Sport*. Lanham, MD: Rowman & Littlefield.

Elias, Norbert, and Eric Dunning. 1986a. Folk Football in Medieval and Early Modern Britain. In *Quest for Excitement: Sport and Leisure in the Civilizing Process*, edited by N. Elias and E. Dunning. Oxford: Basil Blackwell.

————, eds. 1986b. *Quest for Excitement: Sport and Leisure in the Civilizing Process.* Oxford: Basil Blackwell.

Executive Tensions Aren't All Jitters; They Can Wreck Health Too, Says Doctors. 1956. *Business Week*, December 8, 183.

Fair, Laura. 2001. *Pastimes and Politics: Culture, Community, and Identity in Post-Abolition Urban Zanzibar, 1890–1945.* Athens: Ohio University Press.

Falcous, Mark, and Michael L. Silk. 2005. Manufacturing Consent: Mediated Sporting Spectacle and the Cultural Politics of the "War on Terror." *International Journal of Media and Cultural Politics* 1 (1):59–65.

Featherstone, Mike. 1987. Lifestyle and Consumer Culture. *Theory, Culture & Society* 4 (1):55–87.

Fensterwald, Bernard, Jr. 1958a. The Anatomy of American "Isolationism" and Expansionism. Part I. *Journal of Conflict Resolution* 2 (2):111–139.

————. 1958b. The Anatomy of American "Isolationism" and Expansionism. Part II. *Journal of Conflict Resolution* 2 (4):280–309.

Fink, Janet S., and Linda Jean Kensicki. 2002. An Imperceptible Difference: Visual and Textual Constructions of Femininity in *Sports Illustrated* and *Sports Illustrated for Women*. *Mass Communication & Society* 5 (3):317–339.

Finley, Laura L., and Peter S. Finley. 2007. They're Just as Sadistic as Any Group of Boys! A Content Analysis of News Coverage of Sport-Related Hazing Incidents in High Schools. *Journal of Criminal Justice and Popular Culture* 14 (2):197–219.

Fitness Footnotes. 1959. *Sports Illustrated*, May 4, 41.

Foley, Douglas. 1990. The Great American Football Ritual: Reproducing Race, Class, and Gender Inequality. *Sociology of Sport Journal* 7:111–134.

Football and Strategy. 1950. *Freeman*, October 30, 71.

Football and Video. 1950. *Newsweek*, November 20, 60–61.

Football Ethics Scrutinized. 1951. *Christian Century*, December 12, 1428.

Football Excesses to be Investigated. 1951. *Christian Century*, November 28, 1365.

Football Heretic. 1951. *Time*, June 18, 69.

Football TV Plan Aides All Colleges. 1951. *New York Times*, April 29, S7.

Fordham Drops Sport Because of Financial Loses. 1954. *New York Times*, December 16, 57.

Foster, Robert J. 1999. The Commercial Construction of "New Nations." *Journal of Material Culture* 4 (3):263–282.

Foucault, Michel. 1979. *Discipline and Punish: The Birth of the Prison.* Translated by A. Sheridan. New York: Vintage.

————. 1984. Nietzsche, Genealogy, History. In *The Foucault Reader*, edited by P. Rabinow. New York: Pantheon.

————. 1988a. The Political Technology of Individuals. In *Technologies of the Self: A Seminar with Michel Foucault*, edited by L. H. Martin, H. Gutman, and P. H. Hutton. Amherst: University of Massachusetts Press.

————. 1988b. Technologies of the Self. In *Technologies of the Self: A Seminar with Michel Foucault*, edited by L. H. Martin, H. Gutman, and P. H. Hutton. Amherst: University of Massachusetts Press.

————. 1991. Governmentality. In *The Foucault Effect: Studies in Governmentality with Two Lectures by and an Interview with Michel Foucault*, edited by G. Burchell, C. Gordon, and P. Miller. Chicago: University of Chicago Press.

Fox, Christy. 1963. A Fitness Walk in the Smog. *Los Angeles Times*, March 1, C3.

Frankenburg, Ruth. 1993. *White Women, Race Matters: The Social Construction of Whiteness.* Minneapolis: University of Minnesota Press.

Fraser, Nancy, and Linda Gordon. 1998. Contract versus Charity: Why Is There No Social Citizenship in the United States? In *The Citizenship Debates: A Reader*, edited by G. Shafir. Minneapolis: University of Minnesota Press.

Fried, Richard M. 1998. *The Russians Are Coming, the Russians Are Coming: Pageantry and Patriotism in Cold War America*. New York: Oxford University Press.

Friedan, Betty. 1963. *The Feminine Mystique*. New York: Dell Books.

Friedman, Andrea. 2005. The Smearing of Joe McCarthy: The Lavender Scare, Gossip, and Cold War Politics. *American Quarterly* 57 (4):1105–1130.

Friedman, Michael T., David L. Andrews, and Michael L. Silk. 2004. Sport and the Facade of Redevelopment in the Postindustrial City. *Sociology of Sport Journal* 21 (2):119–139.

Fromm, Erich. 1959. Freedom in the Work Situation. In *Labor in a Free Society*, edited by M. Harrington and P. Jacobs. Berkeley: University of California Press.

———. 1994. *Escape from Freedom*. New York: Owl Books. Original edition 1941.

Gaddis, John Lewis. 1982. *Strategies of Containment: A Critical Appraisal of Postwar American National Security Policy*. New York: Oxford University Press.

Galbraith, John Kenneth. 1958. *The Affluent Society*. New York: New American Library.

Gazell, James A. 1973. Arthur H. Vandenberg, Internationalism, and the United Nations. *Political Science Quarterly* 88 (3):375–394.

Geertz, Clifford. 1973. Deep Play: Notes on the Balinese Cockfight. In *The Interpretation of Culture*. New York: Basic Books.

Gems, Gerald R. 2000. *For Pride, Profit, and Patriarchy: Football and the Incorporation of American Cultural Values*. Lanham, MD: Scarecrow Press.

Georgetown Drops Sport. 1951. *New York Times*, March 28, 37.

Gerrie, Jim. 2003. Was Foucault a Philosopher of Technology? *Techné: Research in Philosophy and Technology* 7 (2):14–26.

Gerstle, Gary. 1995. Race and the Myth of the Liberal Consensus. *Journal of American History* 82 (2):579–586.

Geva, Dorith. 2006. To Father or to Fight? Mass Conscription and the Politics of Masculine Obligation, France, 1913–1940, and the United States, 1917–1945. PhD diss., New York University.

Geyer, Michael. 1989. The Militarization of Europe, 1914–1945. In *The Militarization of the Western World*, edited by J. R. Gillis. New Brunswick, NJ: Rutgers University Press.

Giardina, Michael. 2003. "Bending It Like Beckham" in the Global Popular: Stylish Hybridity, Performativity, and the Politics of Representation. *Journal of Sport & Social Issues* 27 (1):65–82.

Gilbert, James Burkhart. 1986. *A Cycle of Outrage: America's Reaction to the Juvenile Delinquent in the 1950s*. New York: Oxford University Press.

———. 2005. *Men in the Middle: Searching for Masculinity in the 1950s*. Chicago: University of Chicago Press.

Gillmeister, Heiner. 1997. *Tennis: A Cultural History*. New York: New York University Press.

Glass, Z. R. 1955. How Good Is Your Bread Winner's Diet? *Parents Magazine*, February, 86.

Glassner, Barry. 1999. *The Culture of Fear: Why Americans Are Afraid of the Wrong Things*. New York: Basic Books.

Glenn, Evelyn Nakano. 2002. *Unequal Freedom: How Race and Gender Shaped American Citizenship and Labor*. Cambridge, MA: Harvard University Press.

Goldman, Eric F. 1960. *The Crucial Decade—And After: America, 1945–1960*. New York: Vintage.

Gordon, S. 1962. LA Sierra High Shows How American Kids Can Get Physically Tough. *Look*, January 30, 49–52.

Gorski, Philip S. 2003a. Book Reviews: The Protestant Ethic and the Spirit of Capitalism. *Social Forces* 82 (2):833–839.

———. 2003b. *The Disciplinary Revolution: Calvinism and the Rise of the State in Early Modern Europe.* Chicago: University of Chicago Press.

Gould, Jack. 1951. Rah, Rah Team! College Football Enters Television Era. *New York Times*, September 16, X13.

———. 1953. Football on Video. *New York Times*, November 15, X11.

———. 1961. TV: "Flabby American." *New York Times*, May 31, 67.

Graham, Otto. 1954. Football Is Getting Too Vicious. *Sports Illustrated*, October 11, 26, 50–52.

Gregory, Derek. 1994. *Geographical Imaginations.* Cambridge, MA: Blackwell.

———. 1995. Between the Book and the Lamp: Imaginative Geographies of Egypt, 1849–50. *Transactions of the Institute of British Geographers* 20 (1):29–57.

Griffith, Thomas. 1995. *Harry & Teddy: The Turbulent Friendship of the Press Lord Henry R. Luce and His Favorite Reporter, Theodore H. White.* New York: Random House.

Griswold, Robert L. 1993. *Fatherhood in America: A Cultural History.* New York: Basic Books.

———. 1998. The "Flabby American," the Body, and the Cold War. In *A Shared Experience: Men, Women, and the History of Gender*, edited by L. McCall and D. Yacovone. New York: New York University Press.

Gruneau, Richard. 1999. *Class, Sports, and Social Development.* Champaign, IL: Human Kinetics. Original edition 1983.

Guttmann, Allen. 1978. *From Ritual to Record: The Nature of Modern Sports.* New York: Columbia University Press.

———. 1998. The Appeal of Violent Sports. In *Why We Watch: The Attractions of Violent Entertainment*, edited by J. H. Goldstein. New York: Oxford University Press.

Hall, Robert. 1955. TV Money May Wreck College Athletics. *Sports Illustrated*, January 10, 26, 52–53.

Hall, Stuart. 1986. The Problem of Ideology-Marxism without Guarantees. *Journal of Communication Inquiry* 10 (2):28–44.

Harbrecht, Thomas, and C. Robert Barnett. 1979. College Football during World War II, 1941–1945. *The Physical Educator* 36 (1):31–35.

Harley, J. B. 1989. Deconstructing the Map. *Cartographica* 26 (2):1–20.

Hartmann, Douglas. 2003. *Race, Culture, and the Revolt of the Black Athlete: The 1968 Olympic Protests and Their Aftermath.* Chicago: University of Chicago Press.

Harvey, David. 1990. *The Condition of Postmodernity: An Enquiry into the Origins of Cultural Change.* Cambridge, MA: Blackwell.

———. 2003. *The New Imperialism.* Oxford: Oxford University Press.

Hazard, Patrick D. 1979. Review of *From Ritual to Record: The Nature of Modern Sports* by Allen Guttmann. *Annals of the American Academy of Political and Social Science* 441:220–221.

Healthy Bosses. 1956. *Business Week*, January 7, 72–73.

Hebdige, Dick. 2002. *Subculture: The Meaning of Style.* New York: Taylor & Francis.

Heffelfinger, William W. "Pudge," and John McCallum. 1954. *This Was Football.* New York: A. S. Barnes.

Henricks, Thomas S. 1980. Review of *From Ritual to Record: The Nature of Modern Sports* by Allen Guttmann. *American Journal of Sociology* 85 (5):1294–1296.

Hershey, Major General Lewis B. 1946. We Must Improve Our Youth. *New York Times*, February 10, 10, 54.

Hickman, Herman. 1954. Football: The Solid South. *Sports Illustrated*, October 4, 60–65.

Hill, Mike. 1997. *Whiteness: A Critical Reader.* New York: New York University Press.

Hirschman, Charles. 1983. America's Melting Pot Reconsidered. *Annual Review of Sociology* 9:397–423.

Hoch, Paul. 1972. *Rip Off, the Big Game: The Exploitation of Sports by the Power Elite*. Garden City, NY: Doubleday Anchor.

Hoffleit, H. B. 1963. Traveling on Foot, He Feels Like a Heel. *Los Angeles Times*, April 19, A6.

Holloway, Julian, and James Kneale. 2000. Mikhail Bakhtin: Dialogics of Space. In *Thinking Space: Critical Geographies*, edited by M. Crang and N. Thrift. New York: Routledge.

Horne, Gerald. 1999. Race from Power: U.S. Foreign Policy and the General Crisis of "White Supremacy." *Diplomatic History* 23 (3):437–461.

Horowitz, Elliott. 2002. "They Fought Because They Were Fighters and They Fought Because They Were Jews": Violence and the Construction of Modern Jewish Identity. In *Jews and Violence: Images, Ideologies, Realities*, edited by P. Y. Medding. New York: Oxford University Press.

Houlihan, Barrie. 2001. Citizenship, Civil Society and the Sport and Recreation Professions. *Managing Leisure* 6 (1):1–14.

How Executives Relax. 1956. *Time*, January 23, 84.

How to Live with Job Pressure. 1965. *Nation's Business*, September, 38–39, 85–87.

Hunsicker, P. 1959. How Fit Are Our Youth? *National Education Association Journal*, March, 26–27.

Hunt, Thomas M. 2006. American Sport Policy and the Cultural Cold War: The Lyndon B. Johnson Presidential Years. *Journal of Sport History* 33 (3):273–297.

Hutchins, Robert M. 1954. College Football Is an Infernal Nuisance. *Sports Illustrated*, October 18, 34–36, 82.

Hutchison, Ralph C. 1952. Football: Symbolic of College Unity. *Christian Century*, April 6, 461-3.

Huyssen, Andreas. 1986. *After the Great Divide: Modernism, Mass Culture, Postmodernism*. Bloomington: Indiana University Press.

Ignatiev, Noel. 1996. *How the Irish Became White*. New York: Routledge.

Ingham, Alan G. 1997. Toward a Department of Physical Cultural Studies and an End to Tribal Warfare. In *Critical Postmodernism in Human Movement, Physical Education, and Sport*, edited by J.-M. Fernandez-Balboa. Albany: State University of New York Press.

Ingham, Alan G., Jeremy W. Howell, and Todd S. Schilperoort. 1987. Professional Sport and Community: A Review and Exegesis. *Exercise and Sport Science Review* 15:427–465.

Ingham, Alan G., and John Loy. 1974. Structure of Ludic Action. *International Review of Sport Sociology* 9 (1):23–62.

Isaac, Larry W., and Kevin T. Leicht. 1999. Regimes of Power and the Power of Analytic Regimes: Explaining U.S. Military Procurement Keynesianism as Historical Process. *Historical Methods* 30 (1):28–45.

Isaacs, Arnold R. 1997. *Vietnam Shadows: The War, Its Ghosts, and Its Legacy*. Baltimore: Johns Hopkins University Press.

Is American Youth Physically Fit? 1957. *U.S. News & World Report*, August 2, 66–77.

Jackson, Allen. 1951. Too Much Football. *Atlantic Monthly*, July/December, 27–33.

James, Dennis. 1973. *Radical Software* 2. http://www.radicalsoftware.org/volume2nr2/pdf/VOLUME2NR2_art03.pdf.

James, Sidney L. 1994. *Press Pass: The Journalist's Tale*. Laguna Hills, CA: Aegean Park Press.

James of the Telewaves. 1948. *Newsweek*, April 26, 56–57.

Jameson, Fredric. 1986. Third-World Literature in the Era of Multinational Capitalism. *Social Text* 15:65–88.

Jansen, Sue Curry, and Don Sabo. 1994. The Sport/War Metaphor: Hegemonic Masculinity, the Persian Gulf War, and the New World Order. *Sociology of Sport Journal* 11 (1):1–17.

Jay, Kathryn. 2004. *More Than Just a Game: Sports in American Life since 1945*. Columbia Histories of Modern American Life. New York: Columbia University Press.

Jessop, Bob. 1990. Putting States in Their Place: Once More on Capitalist States and Capitalist Society. In *State Theory: Putting the Capitalist State in Its Place*. University Park: Pennsylvania State University Press.

Jewkes, Yvonne. 2005. Men Behind Bars: "Doing" Masculinity as an Adaptation to Imprisonment. *Men and Masculinities* 8 (1):44–63.

Jhally, Sut. 1984. The Spectacle of Accumulation: Material and Cultural Factors in the Evolution of the Sports/Media Complex. *Insurgent Sociologist* 12:41–57.

Johansen, Herbert. 1949. Best Seat in the Ball Park. *Popular Science*, August, 105–108.

Johnson, Chalmers A. 2007. Republic or Empire: A National Intelligence Estimate on the United States. *Harper's*. Accessed December 2, 2010, http://www.harpers.org/archive/2007/01/0081346.

———. 2008. Why the US Has Really Gone Broke: The Economic Disaster That Is Military Keynesianism. *Le Monde diplomatique*, February. Accessed December 2, 2010, http://mondediplo.com/2008/02/05military.

Johnson, David K. 2004. *The Lavender Scare: The Cold War Persecution of Gays and Lesbians in the Federal Government*. Chicago: University of Chicago Press.

Jordan, Ellen, and Angela Cowan. 1995. Warrior Narratives in the Kindergarten Classroom Renegotiating the Social Contract? *Gender and Society* 9 (6):727–743.

June 28 Deadline Set on College TV Plans. 1951. *New York Times*, June 9, 23.

Katznelson, Ira. 2005. *When Affirmative Action Was White: An Untold History of Racial Inequality in Twentieth-Century America*. New York: Norton.

Kaufman, Michael. 1999. Men, Feminism, and Men's Contradictory Experiences of Power. In *Men and Power*, edited by J. A. Kuypers. Halifax: Fernwood Books.

Kazal, Russell A. 1995. Revisiting Assimilation: The Rise, Fall, and Reappraisal of a Concept in American Ethnic History. *American Historical Review* 100 (2):437–471.

Kemper, Kurt Edward. 2009. *College Football and American Culture in the Cold War Era*. Urbana: University of Illinois Press.

Kennan, George F. 1950. *American Diplomacy: 1900–1950*. New York: Mentor Books.

Kennedy, John F. 1960. The Soft American. *Sports Illustrated*, December 26, 14–17.

———. 1961. Address in New York City at the National Football Foundation and Hall of Fame Banquet, December 5. American Presidency Project. Accessed March 31, 2010, http://www.presidency.ucsb.edu/ws/?pid=8473.

———. 1962. The Vigor We Need. *Sports Illustrated*, July 16, 12–15.

Kimmel, Michael S. 1990. Baseball and the Reconstitution of American Masculinity, 1880–1920. In *Sport, Men, and the Gender Order: Critical Feminist Perspectives*, edited by M. A. Messner and D. F. Sabo. Champaign, IL: Human Kinetics.

———. 1994. Masculinity as Homophobia: Fear, Shame, and Silence in the Construction of Gender Identity. In *Theorizing Masculinity*, edited by H. Brod and M. Kaufman. Thousand Oaks, CA: Sage.

———. 2012. *Manhood in America: A Cultural History*. 3rd ed. New York: Oxford University Press.

King, C. Richard, and Charles Fruehling Springwood. 2001. *Beyond the Cheers: Race as Spectacle in College Sports*. Albany: State University of New York Press.

King, Samantha J. 2003. Doing Good by Running Well: Breast Cancer, the Race for the Cure, and New Technologies of Ethical Citizenship. In *Foucault, Cultural Studies, and Governmentality*, edited by J. Z. Bratich, J. Packer, and C. McCarthy. Albany: State University of New York Press.

———. 2008. Offensive Lines: Sport-State Synergy in an Era of Perpetual War. *Cultural Studies <=> Critical Methodologies* 8 (4):527–539.

Kirk, David. 1997. Schooling Bodies in New Times: The Reform of School Physical Education in High Modernity. In *Critical Postmodernism in Human Movement, Physical Education, and Sport*, edited by J.-M. Fernández-Balboa. Albany: State University of New York Press.

———. 1998. *Schooling Bodies: School Practice and Public Discourse, 1880–1950.* London: Leicester University Press.

Klare, Michael T. 1989. East-West versus North-South: Dominant and Subordinate Themes in U.S. Military Strategy since 1945. In *The Militarization of the Western World*, edited by J. R. Gillis. New Brunswick, NJ: Rutgers University Press.

Klein, Christina. 2003. *Cold War Orientalism: Asia in the Middlebrow Imagination, 1945–1961.* Berkeley: University of California Press.

Kobler, John. 1968. *Luce: His Time, Life, and Fortune.* Garden City, NY: Doubleday.

Kolko, Gabriel. 1963. *The Triumph of Conservatism: A Reinterpretation of American History, 1900–1916.* New York: Free Press of Glencoe.

Kraus, Hans, and Wilhelm Raab. 1961. *Hypokinetic Disease: Diseases Produced by Lack of Exercise.* Springfield, IL: Charles C. Thomas.

Krause, Kent M. 1998. From Americanism to Athleticism: A History of the American Legion Junior Baseball Program. PhD diss., University of Nebraska–Lincoln.

Kristol, Irving. 1958. *The Affluent Society*, by John Kenneth Galbraith. *Commentary*, August, 176–178.

Kugelmass, Jack, ed. 2007. *Jews, Sports, and the Rites of Citizenship.* Champaign: University of Illinois Press.

Kusz, Kyle W. 2007. From NASCAR Nation to Pat Tillman: Notes on Sport and the Politics of White Cultural Nationalism in Post-9/11 America. *Journal of Sport & Social Issues* 31 (1):77–88.

Lanegran, David L. 1994. Hildegard L. Binder Johnson. *Journal of Geography* 93:107–108.

Langman, Lauren. 2003. Culture, Identity, and Hegemony: The Body in a Global Age. *Current Sociology* 51 (3/4):223–247.

Lardner, John. 1955. Sports on TV—A Critical Survey. *New York Times*, December 25, SM10–11, 27.

Larson, Jordan L. 1955. Athletics and Good Citizenship. *Journal of Educational Sociology* 28 (6):257–259.

Lawrence, Paul R. 1987. *Unsportsmanlike Conduct: The National Collegiate Athletic Association and the Rise of Collegiate Football.* New York: Praeger.

Lawson, Hal A., and Alan G. Ingham. 1980. Conflicting Ideologies Concerning the University and Intercollegiate Athletics: Harper and Hutchins at Chicago, 1892–1940. *Journal of Sport History* 7 (3):37–67.

Lears, T. J. Jackson. 1983. From Salvation to Self-Realization: Advertising and the Therapeutic Roots of the Consumer Culture, 1880–1930. *Advertising & Society Review* 1 (1). Accessed November 25, 2008, http://muse.jhu.edu/journals/asr/v001/1.11ears.html.

Leath, Virginia M., and Angela Lumpkin. 1992. An Analysis of Sportswomen on the Covers and in the Feature Articles of *Women's Sports and Fitness Magazine, 1975–1989. Journal of Sport & Social Issues* 16 (2):121–126.

Lederman, Douglas. 1988. Do Winning Teams Spur Contributions? Scholars and Fund Raisers Are Skeptical. *Chronicle of Higher Education*, January 13, A1, 32.

———. 1993. Draft Report by Business Officers' Group Says Colleges Must Rein in Sports Budgets. *Chronicle of Higher Education*, July 21, A27–28.

Lee, Mabel. 1983. *A History of Physical Education and Sports in the USA.* New York: John Wiley.

Lees, Hannah. 1956. Our Men Are Killing Themselves. *Saturday Evening Post*, January 28, 25, 111, 114.

Lefebvre, Henri. 1991. *The Production of Space*. Translated by D. Nicholson-Smith. Oxford: Blackwell.

Legis to Force Okla Univ to Telecast Games Shelved by Okla Sen after Big 7 Threatens Boycott. 1951. *New York Times*, March 20, 39.

Lemke, Thomas. 2001. "The Birth of Bio-Politics": Michel Foucault's Lecture at the Collège de France on Neo-Liberal Governmentality. *Economy and Society* 30 (2):190–207.

———. 2002. Foucault, Governmentality, and Critique. *Rethinking Marxism* 14 (3):49–64.

Levine, Peter. 1997. "Oy Such a Fighter!" Boxing and the American Jewish Experience. In *The New American Sport History: Recent Approaches and Perspectives*, edited by S. W. Pope. Urbana: University of Illinois Press.

Levinson, Fred. 1954. Cartoon: Player on Stretcher. *Sports Illustrated*, October 11, 51.

Levy, Karen D., and James E. Bryant. 1993. A Content Analysis of Copy and Advertisement Photographs in *Sports Illustrated* and *Sport*: A Measure of Discrimination. *The Physical Educator* 50 (3):114–119.

Lewis, Guy. 1970. The Beginning of Organized Collegiate Sport. *American Quarterly* 22 (2):222–229.

Lewis, Justin, and Toby Miller. 2003. *Critical Cultural Policy Studies: A Reader*. Malden, MA: Blackwell.

*Life* Goes to a Football Broadcast. 1946. *Life*, October 14, 130.

Lipshutz, Ronnie D. 2001. *Cold War Fantasies: Film, Fiction, and Foreign Policy*. Lanham, MD: Rowman & Littlefield.

Lipsitz, George. 1998. *The Possessive Investment in Whiteness: How White People Profit from Identity Politics*. Philadelphia: Temple University Press.

Locke, John. 1980. *Second Treatise of Government*. Edited by C. B. Macpherson. Indianapolis: Hackett. Original edition 1690.

Lohman, Sid. 1951. News of TV & Radio: New Video Concert Shows: Football—Other Items. *New York Times*, July 29, X9.

Loy, John. 1995. The Dark Side of Agon: Fratriarchies, Performative Masculinities, Sport Involvement, and the Phenomenon of Gang Rape. In *International Sociology of Sport Contemporary Issues: Festschrift in Honor of Günther Luschen*, edited by K. H. Bette and A. Rutten. Stuttgart: Verlag Stephanie Naglschmid.

Luce, Henry. 1969a. The American Century. In *The Ideas of Henry Luce*, edited by J. K. Jessup. New York: Atheneum. Original edition 1941.

———. 1969b. Journalism and Responsibility. In *The Ideas of Henry Luce*, edited by J. K. Jessup. New York: Atheneum. Original edition 1953.

———. 1969c. Objectivity. In *The Ideas of Henry Luce*, edited by J. K. Jessup. New York: Atheneum. Original edition 1952.

Lumpkin, Angela, and Linda D. Williams. 1991. An Analysis of *Sports Illustrated* Feature Articles, 1954–1987. *Sociology of Sport Journal* 8 (1):16–32.

MacCambridge, Michael. 1997. *The Franchise: A History of Sports Illustrated Magazine*. New York: Hyperion.

Malec, Michael A. 1993. Patriotic Symbols in Intercollegiate Sports during the Gulf War: A Research Note. *Sociology of Sport Journal* 10 (1):98–106.

Mandell, Richard D. 1979. Review of *From Ritual to Record: The Nature of Modern Sports* by Allen Guttmann. *Journal of American History* 66 (2):358–359.

Mangan, J. A. 1986. *The Games Ethic and Imperialism: Aspects of the Diffusion of an Ideal*. New York: Viking Penguin.

Marathon Madness. 1963. *Los Angeles Times*, March 21, I5.

Marathon Walks Defy State Law. 1963. *Los Angeles Times*, February 28, G1.

Markula, Pirkko, and Richard Pringle. 2006. *Foucault, Sport, and Exercise: Power, Knowledge, and Transforming the Self.* London: Routledge.

Markusen, Ann, Peter Hall, Scott Campbell, and Sabina Deitrick. 1991. *The Rise of the Gunbelt: The Military Remapping of Industrial America.* New York: Oxford University Press.

Marshall, George O. 1958. Epic Motifs in Modern Football. *Tennessee Folklore Society Bulletin* 24 (4):123–128.

Martin, Christopher R., and Jimmie L. Reeves. 2001. The Whole World Isn't Watching (But We Thought They Were): The Super Bowl and U.S. Solipsism. In *Sport and Memory in North America*, edited by S. G. Wieting. Portland, OR: Frank Cass.

Marvin, Carolyn. 1988. Annihilating Space, Time, and Difference. In *When Old Technologies Were New*. New York: Oxford University Press.

Marx, Karl. 1977. From Volume One of *Capital*. In *Karl Marx: Selected Writings*, edited by D. McLellan. New York: Oxford University Press.

———. 1978a. Economic and Philosophic Manuscripts of 1844. In *Marx-Engels Reader*, 2nd ed., edited by R. C. Tucker. New York: Norton.

———. 1978b. The Eighteenth Brumaire of Louis Bonaparte. In *Marx-Engels Reader*, 2nd ed., edited by R. C. Tucker. New York: Norton.

Massa, Mark Stephen. 1999. *Catholics and American Culture: Fulton Sheen, Dorothy Day, and the Notre Dame Football Team*. New York: Crossroad.

Massaro, John. 2003. Press Box Propaganda? The Cold War and *Sports Illustrated*, 1956. *Journal of American Culture* 26 (3):361–370.

May, Elaine Tyler. 1999. *Homeward Bound: American Families in the Cold War Era.* New York: Basic Books.

Mayer, Jean. 1955. Muscular State of the Union. *New York Times Magazine*, November 6, 17.

McArthur, Benjamin. 1975. The Chicago Playground Movement: A Neglected Feature of Social Justice. *Social Service Review* 49 (3):376–395.

McAuley, Ed. 1947. Clubs Seek Answers to Solve Television Problems. *The Sporting News*, July 2, 11.

McCarthy, Anna. 1995. "The Front Row Is Reserved for Scotch Drinkers": Early Television's Tavern Audience. *Cinema Journal* 34 (4):31–48.

———. 2001. *Ambient Television: Visual Culture and Public Space.* Durham, NC: Duke University Press.

McClintock, Anne. 1991. No Longer a Future in Heaven: Women and Nationalism in South Africa. *Transition* 51:104–123.

McDonald, Mary G., and Susan Birrell. 1999. Reading Sport Critically: A Methodology for Interrogating Power. *Sociology of Sport Journal* 16 (4):283–300.

McGee, Lemuel C. 1957. Suicidal Cult of Manliness. *Today's Health*, January, 28–30.

McGovern, John T. 1954. We'll Lose the Next Olympics. . . . *Los Angeles Times*, May 16, K7, K16.

McInnes, Colin. 2002. *Spectator-Sport War: The West and Contemporary Conflict.* Boulder, CO: Lynne Rienner.

McLorg, Penelope A., and Diane E. Taub. 1987. Anorexia Nervosa and Bulimia: The Development of Deviant Identities. *Deviant Behavior* 8 (2):179–189.

McMahan, Harry Wayne. 1957. *Television Production: The Creative Techniques and Language of TV Today.* New York: Hastings House.

Meehan, Eileen R. 1990. Why We Don't Count: The Commodity Audience. In *Logics of Television: Essays in Cultural Criticism*, edited by P. Mellencamp. Bloomington: Indiana University Press.

Meggyesy, Dave. 1971. *Out of Their League.* New York: Paperback Library.

Men Are Sicklier Hospital Figures Show. 1955. *Science News Letter*, March 19, 183.

Mennell, James. 1989. The Service Football Program of World War I: Its Impact on the Popularity of the Game. *Journal of Sport History* 16 (3):248–260.

Messenger, Christian. 1981. Review of *From Ritual to Record: The Nature of Modern Sports* by Allen Guttmann; *Rites of Fall: High School Football in Texas* by Geoff Winningham, Al Reinert, Don Meredith. *Winterthur Portfolio* 16 (2/3):246–249.

Messner, Michael A. 1992. *Power at Play: Sports and the Problem of Masculinity*. Boston: Beacon.

———. 2002. *Taking the Field: Women, Men, and Sports*. Minneapolis: University of Minnesota Press.

Messner, Michael A., Michele Dunbar, and Darnell Hunt. 2000. The Televised Sports Manhood Formula. *Journal of Sport & Social Issues* 24 (4):380–394.

Messner, Michael A., and Jeffrey Montez de Oca. 2005. The Male Consumer as Loser: Beer and Liquor Ads in Mega Sports Media Events. *Signs: Journal of Women in Culture and Society* 30 (3):1879–1910.

Messner, Michael A., and Mark A. Stevens. 2002. Scoring Without Consent: Confronting Male Athletes Violence against Women. In *Paradoxes of Youth and Sport*, edited by M. Gatz, M. A. Messner, and S. J. Ball-Rokeach. Albany: State University of New York Press.

Metzger, L. Paul. 1971. American Sociology and Black Assimilation: Conflicting Perspectives. *American Journal of Sociology* 76 (4):627–647.

Miller, Andrew C. 2010. The American Dream Goes to College: The Cinematic Student Athletes of College Football. *Journal of Popular Culture* 43 (6):1222–1241.

Miller, Kathleen E. 2009. Sport-Related Identities and the "Toxic Jock." *Journal of Sport Behavior* 32 (1):69–92.

Miller, Kathleen E., Merrill J. Melnick, Michael P. Farrell, Donald F. Sabo, and Grace M. Barnes. 2006. Jocks, Gender, Binge Drinking, and Adolescent Violence. *Journal of Interpersonal Violence* 21 (1):105–120.

Miller, Toby. 1993. *The Well-Tempered Self: Citizenship, Culture, and the Postmodern Subject*. Baltimore: Johns Hopkins University Press.

———. 1998. *Technologies of Truth: Cultural Citizenship and the Popular Media*. Minneapolis: University of Minnesota Press.

———. 2001. *Sportsex*. Philadelphia: Temple University Press.

———. 2007. *Cultural Citizenship: Cosmopolitanism, Consumerism, and Television in a Neoliberal Age*. Philadelphia: Temple University Press.

———. 2008. *Makeover Nation: The United States of Reinvention*. Columbus: Ohio State University Press.

Miller, Toby, and Marie Claire Leger. 2003. A Very Childish Moral Panic: Ritalin. *Journal of Medical Humanities* 24 (1/2):9–33.

Miller, Toby, and George Yúdice. 2002. *Cultural Policy*. Thousand Oaks, CA: Sage.

Mills, C. Wright. 1951. *White Collar: The American Middle Classes*. New York: Oxford University Press.

———. 1956. *The Power Elite*. New York: Oxford University Press.

Monmonier, Mark. 1991. *How to Lie with Maps*. Chicago: University of Chicago Press.

Montague, Susan P., and Robert Morais. 1976. Football Games and Rock Concerts: The Ritual Enactments of American Success Models. In *The American Dimension: Cultural Myths and Social Realities*, edited by W. Arens and S. P. Montague. Port Washington, NY: Alfred.

Montez de Oca, Jeffrey. 2007. The "Muscle Gap": Physical Education and US Fears of a Depleted Masculinity, 1954–1963. In *East Plays West: Sport and the Cold War*, edited by S. Wagg and D. Andrews. London: Routledge.

———. 2013. Sport as Social Institution: Football Films and the American Dream. In *Cinematic Sociology: Social Life in Film*, edited by J.-A. Sutherland and K. Feltey. Thousand Oaks, CA: Pine Forge Press.

Morford, W. Robert, and Martha J. McIntosh. 1993. Sport and the Victorian Gentleman. In *Sport in Social Development: Traditions, Transitions, and Transformations*, edited by A. G. Ingham and J. W. Loy. Champaign, IL: Human Kinetics.

Morse, Arthur. 1954. How Fit Are Our Kids? *Sports Illustrated*, September 20, 43–44.

Morse, Margaret. 1983. Sport on Television: Replay and Display. In *Regarding Television: Critical Approaches—An Anthology*, edited by E. Ann Kaplan. Washington, DC: United Publications of America.

Mrozek, Donald J. 1995. The Cult and Ritual of Toughness in Cold War America. In *Sport in America: From Wicked Amusement to National Obsession*, edited by D. K. Wiggins. Champaign, IL: Human Kinetics.

Munn, Clarence L. 1954. Thumbs Down on the One Platoon. *Sports Illustrated*, November 29, 35–36.

Murphy, John M. 2004. The Language of the Liberal Consensus: John F. Kennedy, Technical Reason, and the "New Economics" at Yale University. *Quarterly Journal of Speech* 90 (2):133–162.

Murray, James. 1956. The Greatest Show on Earth. *Sports Illustrated*, November 26, 14–17, 60–61.

Nadel, Alan. 1995. *Containment Culture: American Narratives, Postmodernism, and the Atomic Age*. Durham, NC: Duke University Press.

National Collegiate Athletic Association. 1953. Report of the 1952 N.C.A.A. Television Committee to the Forty-Seventh Annual Convention of the National Collegiate Athletic Association. Washington, DC: National Collegiate Athletic Association.

———. 1954. Report of the 1953 N.C.A.A. Television Committee to the Forty-Eighth Annual Convention of the National Collegiate Athletic Association. Cincinnati: National Collegiate Athletic Association.

———. 1955. Report of the 1954 N.C.A.A. Television Committee to the Forty-Ninth Annual Convention of the National Collegiate Athletic Association. New York: National Collegiate Athletic Association.

———. 1956. Report of the 1955 N.C.A.A. Television Committee to the Fiftieth Annual Convention of the National Collegiate Athletic Association. Los Angeles: National Collegiate Athletic Association.

———. 1957. Report of the 1956 N.C.A.A. Television Committee to the Fifty-First Annual Convention of the National Collegiate Athletic Association. St. Louis: National Collegiate Athletic Association.

———. 1959. Report of the 1958 N.C.A.A. Television Committee to the Fifty-Third Annual Convention of the National Collegiate Athletic Association. Cincinnati: National Collegiate Athletic Association.

———. 1961. Report of the 1960 N.C.A.A. Television Committee to the Fifty-Fifth Annual Convention of the National Collegiate Athletic Association. Pittsburgh: National Collegiate Athletic Association.

———. 1962. Report of the 1961 N.C.A.A. Television Committee to the Fifty-Sixth Annual Convention of the National Collegiate Athletic Association. Chicago: National Collegiate Athletic Association.

———. 1963. Report of the 1962 N.C.A.A. Television Committee to the Fifty-Seventh Annual Convention of the National Collegiate Athletic Association. Los Angeles: National Collegiate Athletic Association.

———. 1965. Report of the 1964 N.C.A.A. Television Committee to the Fifty-Ninth Annual Convention of the National Collegiate Athletic Association. Chicago: National Collegiate Athletic Association.

*National Collegiate Athletic Association v. Board of Regents of the University of Oklahoma*, 468 U.S. 85 (1984).

NCAA Ban on Live Telecasting Studied by Justice Dept Anti-Trust Div. 1951. *New York Times*, April 3, 35.

NCAA Committee Recommends Football Video on Limited Basis. 1951. *New York Times*, April 12, 47.

N.C.A.A. Study Attacked. 1952. *New York Times*, May 17, 27.

Nehls, Christopher Courtney. 2007. "A Grand and Glorious Feeling": The American Legion and American Nationalism between the World Wars. PhD diss., University of Virginia.

Neils, Patricia. 1990. *China Images in the Life and Times of Henry Luce*. Savage, MD: Rowman & Littlefield.

Neilson, Brian J. 1995. Baseball. In *The Theater of Sport*, edited by K. B. Raitz. Baltimore: Johns Hopkins University Press.

A New Lease on Fitness. 1959. *Sports Illustrated*, January 26, 25.

Newman, Joshua I. 2007. Army of Whiteness? Colonel Reb and the Sporting South's Cultural and Corporate Symbolic. *Journal of Sport & Social Issues* 31 (4):315–339.

Newman, Joshua I., and Michael D. Giardina. 2010. Neoliberalism's Last Lap? NASCAR Nation and the Cultural Politics of Sport. *American Behavioral Scientist* 53 (10):1511–1529.

Next to Sideline Seat. 1947. *The Sporting News*, December 17, 2.

Niagara Drops Sport for Duration of National Emergency. 1951. *New York Times*, March 7, 45.

Nietzsche, Friedrich. 1956. *The Birth of Tragedy*. Translated by F. Golfing. New York: Anchor Doubleday. Original edition 1870–1871.

1959 National Youth Fitness Week. 1959. *Sports Illustrated*, May 4, 39–53.

Nitze, Paul. 1993. NSC 68. In *American Cold War Strategy: Interpreting NSC 68*, edited by E. R. May. Boston: Bedford.

Nixon Issues Health Test Challenge. 1960. *Los Angeles Times*, November 5, 5.

Norwood, Stephen H. 2009. "American Jewish Muscle": Forging a New Masculinity in the Streets and in the Ring, 1890–1940. *Modern Judaism* 29 (2):167–193.

Oberlander, Susan, and Douglas Lederman. 1988. Big-Time College Sports: The Seductions and Frustrations of NCAA's Division I. *Chronicle of Higher Education*, May 11, A32–34.

O'Hanlon, Timothy. 1980. Interscholastic Athletics, 1900–1940: Shaping Citizens for Unequal Roles in the Modern Industrial State. *Educational Theory* 30 (2):89–103.

O'Meara, Carroll. 1955. *Television Program Production*. New York: Ronald Press.

Omi, Michael, and Howard Winant. 1994. *Racial Formations in the United States*. New York: Routledge.

One Saturday Football Telecast for Each Area Set by NCAA. 1951. *New York Times*, April 19, 42.

Oriard, Michael. 1993. *Reading Football: How the Popular Press Created and American Spectacle*. Chapel Hill: University of North Carolina Press.

———. 2001. *King Football: Sport & Spectacle in the Golden Age of Radio & Newsreels, Movies & Magazines, the Weekly & the Daily Press*. Chapel Hill: University of North Carolina Press.

———. 2009. *Bowled Over: Big-Time College Football from the Sixties to the BCS Era*. Chapel Hill: University of North Carolina Press.

Packard, Vance. 1957. *The Hidden Persuaders*. New York: D. McKay.

Patty Berg: 1918–2006. 2011. LPGA. Accessed July 27, 2011, http://www.lpga.com/content_1
.aspx?pid=8002&mid=2.

Paxton, Harry T., and Charles Bud Wilkinson. 1952. How to Watch Football. *Saturday Evening Post*, November 1, 19.

Pelissero, John P., Beth M. Henschen, and Edward I. Sidlow. 1991. Urban Regimes, Sports Stadiums, and the Politics of Economic Agendas in Chicago. *Policy Study Review* 10 (2–3):117–129.

Penz, Otto. 1991. Ballgames of the North American Indians and in Late Medieval Europe. *Journal of Sport & Social Issues* 15 (1):43–58.

Perlmutter, Emanuel. 1962. National Olympics Urged by Ribicoff. *New York Times*, August 26, 45.

Perrine, Toni A. 1998. *Film and the Nuclear Age: Representing Cultural Anxiety*. New York: Garland.

Peterson, Robert W. 1997. *Pigskin: The Early Years of Pro Football*. New York: Oxford University Press.

Pew Research Center. 2011. The Military-Civilian Gap: War and Sacrifice in the Post-9/11 Era. *Pew Social & Demographic Trends*. Washington, DC: Pew Research Center.

Phillips, William. 1969. A Season in the Stands. *Commentary* 48 (1):65–69.

Phillips-Fein, Kim. 2007. "If Business and the Country Will Be Run Right": The Business Challenge to the Liberal Consensus, 1945–1964. *International Labor and Working-Class History* 72 (1):192–215.

Pietrykowski, Bruce. 1995. Fordism at Ford: Spatial Decentering and Labor Segmentation at the Ford Motor Company, 1920–1950. *Economic Geography* 71 (4):383–401.

Pleck, Joseph H. 1983. Men's Power with Women, Other Men, and Society: A Men's Movement Analysis. In *Feminist Frontiers: Rethinking Sex, Gender, and Society*, edited by L. Richardson and V. Taylor. Reading, MA: Addison-Wesley.

Plummer, Brenda Gayle. 1996. "Below the Level of Men": African Americans, Race, and the History of U.S. Foreign Relations. *Diplomatic History* 20 (4):639–650.

Pope, Stephen W. 1995. An Army of Athletes: Playing Fields, Battlefields, and the American Military Sporting Experience, 1890–1920. *Journal of Military History* 59 (3):435–456.

Popkewitz, Thomas S. 2000. *Educational Knowledge: Changing Relationships between the State, Civil Society, and the Educational Community*. Frontiers in Education. Albany: State University of New York Press.

Powers, Marcus, and Andrew Crampton. 2005. Reel Geopolitics: Cinemato-graphing Political Space. *Geopolitics* 10 (2):193–205.

Powers-Beck, Jeffrey. 2001. "Chief": The American Indian Integration of Baseball, 1897–1945. *American Indian Quarterly* 25 (4):508–538.

President's Council on Physical Fitness. 1961. *Youth Physical Fitness: Suggested Elements of a School-Centered Program*. Washington, DC: Government Printing Office.

Pronger, Brian. 1999. Outta My Endzone: Sport and the Territorial Anus. *Journal of Sport & Social Issues* 23:373–389.

Prudden, Bonnie. 1956. *Is Your Child Really Fit?* New York: Harper.

Rader, Benjamin G. 1984. *In Its Own Image: How TV Transformed Sports*. New York: Free Press.

Radway, Janice A. 1991. *Reading the Romance: Women, Patriarchy, and Popular Literature*. Chapel Hill: University of North Carolina Press.

Reagan, Ronald. 1980. Peace: Restoring the Margin of Safety. *Archives of the Ronald Reagan Presidential Library*, August 18. Accessed March 3, 2012, http://www.reagan.utexas.edu/archives/reference/8.18.80.html.

Real, Michael R. 1979. The Super Bowl: Mythic Spectacle. In *Television: The Critical View*, 2nd ed., edited by H. Newcomb. New York: Oxford University Press.

Reimann, Paul A. 2004. The G.I. Bill and Collegiate Football Recruiting after World War II. *International Sports Journal* 8 (2):126–133.

Remy, John. 1990. Patriarchy and Fratriarchy as Forms of Androcracy. In *Men, Masculinities, and Social Theory*, edited by J. Hearn and D. Morgan. London: Unwin Hyman.

Riesman, David, and Reuel Denney. 1951. Football in America: A Study in Cultural Diffusion. *American Quarterly* 3 (4):309–325.

Riesman, David, with Nathan Glazer and Reuel Denney. 1950. *The Lonely Crowd: A Study of the Changing American Character*. Garden City, NY: Doubleday Anchor.

Riess, Steven A. 1997. Sports and the American Jew: An Introduction. In *Sports and the American Jew*, edited by S. A. Riess. Syracuse, NY: Syracuse University Press.

Rigauer, Bero. 1981. *Sport and Work*. New York: Columbia University Press.

Rinehart, Robert E. 1998. *Players All: Performances in Contemporary Sports*. Bloomington: Indiana University Press.

Roberts, Kate. 2007. *Minnesota 150: The People, Places, and Things That Shape Our State*. St. Paul: Minnesota Historical Society.

Roediger, David R. 1991. *The Wages of Whiteness: Race and the Making of the American Working Class*. London: Verso.

———. 2000. *Towards the Abolition of Whiteness: Essays on Race, Politics, and Working Class History*. London: Verso.

———. 2006. *Working toward Whiteness: How America's Immigrants Became White: The Strange Journey from Ellis Island to the Suburbs*. New York: Basic Books.

Rondeau, Charles. 1964. Physical Fitness of Americans Demonstrated in Olympic Finals. *Los Angeles Times*, September 22, A4.

Rooney, John F., Jr., and Audrey B. Davidson. 1995. Football. In *The Theater of Sports*, edited by K. B. Raitz. Baltimore: Johns Hopkins University Press.

Roosevelt, Theodore. 1899. The Strenuous Life. History Tools. Accessed March 31, 2004, http://www.historytools.org/sources/strenuous.html.

———. 1909. Address at the Harvard Union, Harvard University, February 23, 1907. In *Addresses and Papers*, edited by W. F. Johnson. New York: Unit Book.

Rose, Nikolas, Pat O'Malley, and Mariana Valverde. 2006. Governmentality. *Annual Review of Law and Social Science* 2:83–104.

Roskin, Michael. 1974. From Pearl Harbor to Vietnam: Shifting Generational Paradigms and Foreign Policy. *Political Science Quarterly* 89 (3):563–588.

Rusk, Howard A. 1947. Concrete Standards Lacking for Physically Fit Persons. *New York Times*, November 2, 24.

———. 1963. Science: Physically Fit—But for What? *New York Times*, March 1, 8.

Ryskind, Morrie. 1963. Hiker Out of Step. *Los Angeles Times*, February 16, B1.

Sabo, Donald F. 1994. Pigskin, Patriarchy, and Pain. In *Sex, Violence, and Power in Sport: Rethinking Masculinity*, edited by M. A. Messner and D. F. Sabo. Freedom, CA: Crossing Press.

———. 1998. Women's Athletics and the Elimination of Men's Sports Programs. *Journal of Sport & Social Issues* 22 (1):27–31.

———. 2001. Pigskin, Patriarchy, and Pain. In *Race, Class, and Gender in the United States: An Integrated Study*, edited by P. S. Rothenberg. New York: W. H. Freeman.

Sabo, Donald F., Philip M. Gray, and Linda A. Moore. 2000. Domestic Violence and Televised Athletic Events: "It's a Man Thing." In *Masculinities, Gender Relations, and Sport*, edited by J. McKay, M. A. Messner, and D. Sabo. Thousand Oaks, CA: Sage.

Said, Edward W. 1978. *Orientalism*. New York: Vintage.

Salmon, Marylynn. 2000. The Limits of Independence: 1760–1800. In *No Small Courage: A History of Women in the United States*, edited by D.N.F. Cott. New York: Oxford University Press.

Salwen, Michael B., and Natalie Wood. 1994. Depictions of Female Athletes on *Sports Illustrated* Covers, 1957–1989. *Journal of Sport Behavior* 17 (2):98–108.

Sammons, Jeffrey T. 1990. *Beyond the Ring: The Role of Boxing in American Society*. Urbana: University of Illinois Press.

Sandomir, Richard. 2009. NBC Still Likes Its Notre Dame Strategy. *New York Times*, December 11, B15.

Saudek, Robert. 1950. Radio: Air Wave of the Future. *Time*, January 30, 66.

Schlesinger, Arthur, Jr. 1949. *The Vital Center: The Politics of Freedom*. Boston: Houghton Mifflin.

Schlosser, Nicholas J. 2010. The Marine Corps' Small Wars Manual: An Old Solution to a New Challenge? *Fortitudine: Bulletin of the Marine Corps Historical Program* 35 (1):4–9.

Seidman, Steven. 1998. *Contested Knowledge: Social Theory in the Postmodern Era*. 2nd ed. Malden, MA: Blackwell.

Shaw, Gary. 1972. *Meat on the Hoof*. New York: Dell.

Sheehan, Joseph M. 1957. Performance of American Gymnasts in the Olympic Games Pleases Coach. *New York Times*, January 9, 36.

Sherry, Michael S. 1995. *In the Shadow of War: The United States since the 1930s*. New Haven: Yale University Press.

Shirts, Mathew. 1988. Socrates, Corinthians, and Questions of Democracy and Citizenship. In *Sport and Society in Latin America: Diffusion, Dependency, and the Rise of Mass Culture*, edited by J. Arbena. New York: Greenwood.

Shogan, Debra. 2002. Disciplinary Technologies of Sport Performance. In *Sport Technology: History, Philosophy and Policy*, edited by A. Miah and S. B. Eassom. New York: Elsevier.

Shohat, Ella, and Robert Stam. 1994. *Unthinking Eurocentrism: Multiculturalism and the Media*. New York: Routledge.

Shores, Kindad A., Kristi Montandon, Michael Hunt, and Tufan Adiguzel. 2005. A Critical Analysis of the Portrayal of Female Professional Athletes in *Sports Illustrated* 1963–2003. *Research Quarterly for Exercise and Sport* 76 (1):A-110.

Siegel, Ed. 1993. TV Testosterone: War in Iraq and Football. *Boston Globe*, January 18, 3.

Siegfried, John J., and Molly Gardner Burba. 2003. The College Football Association: Television Broadcast Cartel. Working Paper No. 03-W20, Vanderbilt University, Nashville, TN.

Silk, Michael L., and David L. Andrews. 2011. Toward a Physical Cultural Studies. *Sociology of Sport Journal* 28 (1):4–35.

Silk, Michael L., and Mark Falcous. 2005. One Day in September/A Week in February: Mobilizing American (Sporting) Nationalisms. *Sociology of Sport Journal* 22 (4):447–471.

Silva, Edward T. 1978. Before Radical Rejection: A Comment on Block's "Beyond Corporate Liberalism." *Social Problems* 25 (3):345–349.

Sklar, Martin J. 1988. *The Corporate Reconstruction of American Capitalism, 1890–1916*. New York: Cambridge University Press.

Slotkin, Richard. 1992. *Gunfighter Nation: The Myth of the Frontier in Twentieth-Century America*. New York: Atheneum.

Smith, Adam. 2003. *The Wealth of Nations*. New York: Bantam. Original edition 1776.

Smith, Andrew F. 2002. *Peanuts: The Illustrious History of the Goober Pea*. Urbana: University of Illinois Press.

Smith, Jack. 1961. His New Frontier: San Juan Hill. *Los Angeles Times*, February 17, A1.

———. 1963. Hiking Plan Puts U.S. on Its Feet. *Los Angeles Times*, February 15, A5.

Smith, Jason M., and Alan G. Ingham. 2003. On the Waterfront: Retrospectives on the Relationship between Sport and Communities. *Sociology of Sport Journal* 20 (3):252–274.

Smith, Ronald A. 1988. *Sports and Freedom: The Rise of Big-Time College Athletics*. New York: Oxford University Press.

———. 2001. *Play-by-Play: Radio, Television, and Big-Time College Sport*. Baltimore: Johns Hopkins University Press.

Smuckler, Ralph H. 1953. The Region of Isolation. *American Political Science Review* 47 (2):386–401.

Snider, Arthur J. 1957. Don't Exercise Just to Prove Manliness, Says MD. *Science Digest*, May, 49–50.

Social Justice for Football Labor! 1951. *Christian Century*, October 24, 12–13.

Soundtrack—Sound and Fury. 1954. *Sports Illustrated*, November 1, 27.

Soundtrack—What Football Means. 1954. *Sports Illustrated*, October 25, 14.

Sowder, William T. 1954. Fragile Male. *Today's Health*, July, 13.

Spencer-Wood, Suzanne M. 1994. Turn of the Century Women's Organizations, Urban Design, and the Origin of the American Playground Movement. *Landscape Journal* 13 (2):124–137.

Sperber, Murray. 2000. *Beer and Circus: How Big-Time College Sports Is Crippling Undergraduate Education*. New York: Henry Holt.

Spigel, Lynn. 1992. *Make Room for TV: Television and the Family Ideal in Postwar America*. Chicago: University of Chicago Press.

Sport Dropped by Adelphia for Lack of Student Interest. 1954. *New York Times*, January 30, 11.

St. Mary's Drops Sport for Duration of National Emergency. 1951. *New York Times*, January 6, 11.

Stare, F. J. 1953. How to Keep Your Husband Alive. *McCall's*, October, 80.

Stasheff, Edward, and Rudy Bretz. 1962. *The Television Program: Its Direction and Production*. New York: Hill & Wang.

Staurowsky, Ellen J. 1998. Critiquing the Language of the Gender Equity Debate. *Journal of Sport & Social Issues* 22 (1):7–27.

Stern, Bill. 1951. Exploding the Myth about "Too Much Talk" In TV Sports. *Variety*, January 3, 105.

Stoddard, Theodore Lothrop. 1920. *The Rising Tide of Color against White World-Supremacy*. New York: C. Scribner's Sons.

Stoddart, Brian. 1988. Sport, Cultural Imperialism, and Colonial Response in the British Empire. *Comparative Studies in Society and History* 30 (4):649–673.

Stormann, Wayne F. 1991. The Ideology of the American Urban Parks and Recreation Movement: Past and Future. *Leisure Sciences* 13 (2):137–151.

Stull, Dorothy. 1956. Conference at Annapolis: First Blow for Fitness. *Sports Illustrated*, July 2, 22–24.

Sturken, Marita. 2007. *Tourists of History: Memory, Kitsch, and Consumerism from Oklahoma City to Ground Zero*. Durham, NC: Duke University Press.

Substitute for Hike. 1963. *Los Angeles Times*, May 13, B8.

Swanberg, W. A. 1972. *Luce and His Empire*. New York: Scribner.

Swidler, Ann. 1986. Culture in Action: Symbols and Strategies. *American Sociological Review* 51:273–286.

———. 2001. *Talk of Love: How Culture Matters*. Chicago: University of Chicago Press.

Swyngedouw, Erik. 2004. Globalisation or "Glocalisation"? Networks, Territories, and Rescaling. *Cambridge Review of International Affairs* 17 (1):25–48.

TeCube, Leroy. 1999. *Year in Nam: A Native American Soldier's Story*. Lincoln: University of Nebraska Press.

Theberge, Nancy. 1981. A Critique of Critiques: Radical and Feminist Writings on Sport. *Social Forces* 60 (2):341–353.

———. 1985. Toward a Feminist Alternative to Sport as a Male Preserve. *Quest* 37 (2):193–202.

Thomas, Damion Lamar. 2002. "The Good Negroes": African-American Athletes and the Cultural Cold War, 1945–1968. PhD diss., University of California, Los Angeles.

———. 2012. *Globetrotting: African American Athletes and Cold War Politics.* Champaign: University of Illinois Press.

Thomas, Robert McG., Jr. 1997. Dennis James, 79, TV Game Show Host and Announcer, Dies. *New York Times,* June 6. Accessed December 27, 2011, http://www.nytimes .com/1997/06/06/arts/dennis-james-79-tv-game-show-host-and-announcer-dies .html?pagewanted=all&src=pm.

Thompson, Mark. 2011. An Army Apart: The Widening Military-Civilian Gap. *Time,* November 10. Accessed January 17, 2012, http://battleland.blogs.time.com/2011/11/10/ an-army-apart-the-widening-military-civilian-gap/.

3 on Cross-Vermont Hike. 1964. *New York Times,* March 26, 13.

3-Year U. of P. Feud with NCAA Ends; TV Back. 1954. *Variety,* July 28, 30.

Tolchin, Martin. 1962. President's Fitness Plan Spurs School Programs. *New York Times,* December 12, 14.

Touchdowns at Any Price! Discard of Sanity Code. 1951. *Christian Century,* January 31, 136–137.

Trujillo, Nick. 1993. Interpreting (the Work and the Talk of) Baseball: Perspectives on Ballpark Culture. *Western Journal of Communication* 56 (4):350–371.

———. 1995. Machines, Missiles, and Men: Images of the Male Body on ABC's *Monday Night Football. Sociology of Sport Journal* 12:403–423.

Trujillo, Nick, and Bob Krizek. 1994. Emotionality in the Stands and in the Field: Expressing Self through Baseball. *Journal of Sport & Social Issues.* 18 (4):303–325.

*United States v. National Football League et al.,* 116 F. Supp 319 (E.D. PA 1953).

UP May Be Excluded from Ohio Regatta—Inter-Collegiate Rowing Association Undecided. 1951. *New York Times,* June 13, 39.

U.S. Football: In Maps and Diagrams. 1954. *Sports Illustrated,* November 15, 4–5.

von Eschen, Penny M. 1996. Changing Cold War Habits: African Americans, Race, and Foreign Policy. *Diplomatic History* 20 (4):627–638.

———. 1997. *Race against Empire: Black Americans and Anticolonialism, 1937–1957.* Ithaca, NY: Cornell University Press.

Waddell, Brian. 1999. Corporate Influence and World War II: Resolving the New Deal Political Stalemate. *Journal of Policy History* 11 (3). Accessed December 30, 2011, http://muse .jhu.edu/journals/journal_of_policy_history/v011/11.3waddell.html.

———. 2001. Limiting National Interventionism in the United States: The Warfare-Welfare State as Restrictive Governance Paradigm. *Capital & Class* 25 (2):109–139.

Wade, Don. 2001. *Talking on Tour: The Best Anecdotes from Golf's Master Storyteller.* New York: McGraw-Hill.

Wagg, Stephen, and David Andrews, eds. 2006. *East Plays West: Sport and the Cold War.* London: Routledge.

Walker, Martin. 1994. *The Cold War: A History.* New York: Henry Holt.

Walton, Jennifer L. 2004. Moral Masculinity: The Culture of Foreign Relations during the Kennedy Administration. PhD diss., Ohio State University.

Warner, Michael. 1993. The Mass Public and the Mass Subject. In *The Phantom Public Sphere,* edited by B. Robbins. Minneapolis: University of Minnesota Press.

Watterson, John S. 2000. *College Football: History-Spectacle-Controversy.* Baltimore: Johns Hopkins University Press.

Weales, Gerald. 1959. Ritual in Georgia. *Southern Folklore Quarterly* 21 (1):104–109.

Weber, Max. 1947. *The Theory of Social and Economic Organization*. New York: Free Press.

———. 1958a. Bureaucracy. In *From Max Weber: Essays in Sociology*, edited by H. H. Gerth and C. W. Mills. New York: Oxford University Press.

———. 1958b. Class, Status, Party. In *From Max Weber: Essays in Sociology*, edited by H. H. Gerth and C. W. Mills. New York: Oxford University Press.

———. 2002. *The Protestant Ethic and the Spirit of Capitalism*. 3rd Roxbury ed. Translated by S. Kalberg. Los Angeles: Roxbury.

Wehrle, Edmund F. 2003. Welfare and Warfare: American Organized Labor Approaches the Military-Industrial Complex, 1949–1964. *Armed Forces & Society* 29 (4):525–546.

Weidman, Jerome. 1954. At Home—Where to Park? *Sports Illustrated*, November 29, 49–51.

Weinstein, James. 1968. *The Corporate Ideal in the Liberal State: 1900–1918*. Boston: Beacon.

Weistart, John. 1998. Title IX and Intercollegiate Sports: Equal Opportunity? *Brookings Review* 16 (4):39–44.

Welch, Paula D. 1996. *History of American Physical Education and Sport*. Springfield, IL: Charles C. Thomas.

Westad, Odd Arne. 2007. *The Global Cold War: Third World Interventions and the Making of Our Times*. New York: Cambridge University Press.

Westby, David L., and Allen Sack. 1976. The Commercialization and Functional Rationalization of College Football: Its Origins. *Journal of Higher Education* 47 (6):625–647.

Western Conf Bans "Live" TV of All '50 Games. 1950. *New York Times*, April 17, 1.

Weston, Arthur. 1962. *The Making of American Physical Education*. New York: Appleton-Century-Crofts.

Weyand, Alexander M. 1955. *The Saga of American Football*. New York: Macmillan.

Whannel, Garry. 1993. No Room for Uncertainty: Gridiron Masculinity in *North Dallas Forty*. In *You Tarzan: Masculinity, Movies, Men*. New York: St. Martin's.

What Price Football? 1950. *Time*, January 23, 45–46.

White, Hayden. 1978. *Tropics of Discourse: Essays in Cultural Criticism*. Baltimore: Johns Hopkins University Press.

Whitfield, Stephan J. 1991. *The Culture of the Cold War*. Baltimore: Johns Hopkins University Press.

Whitson, David. 1998. Circuits of Promotion: Media, Marketing and the Globalization of Sport. In *MediaSport*, edited by L. A. Wenner. London: Routledge.

Whyte, William H. 1956. *The Organization Man*. Garden City, NY: Doubleday Anchor.

Wilkinson, Charles Bud. 1961. How Does Your Child Rate in Fitness? *Parents Magazine*, October, 78–91, 144–149.

———. 1962. Physical Fitness and Community Recreation: A Pattern for Action. *Recreation*, September, 343–344.

———. 2004. Infoplease—Pearson Education. Accessed September 11, 2004, http://www.infoplease.com/ce6/people/A0852277.html.

Williams, William Appleman. 1962. *The Tragedy of American Diplomacy*. Rev. and enl. ed. New York: Dell.

Wismer, Harry. 1947. Greatest Contribution to Television Supplied so Far through Sports. *Variety*, January 8, 119.

Wolf, Al. 1964. Physical Fitness Programs Claims "Massive Support." *Los Angeles Times*, March 13, B1.

Woods, C. 1998. The Socio-Spatial Construction of the Mississippi Delta. In *Development Arrested: Race, Power, and the Blues in the Mississippi Delta*. New York: Verso.

Woolum, Janet. 1998. *Outstanding Women Athletes: Who They Are and How They Influenced Sports in America*. 2nd ed. Phoenix, AZ: Orynx Press.

Wylie, Philip. 1955. *Generation of Vipers*. New York: Pocket Books. Original edition 1942.

Yúdice, George. 2003. *The Expediency of Culture: Uses of Culture in the Global Era, Post-Contemporary Interventions*. Durham, NC: Duke University Press.

Zeigler, Mark. 2008. Commentary: A No-Win Situation. *Union Tribune*, December 28.

Zimbalist, Andrew. 1999. *Unpaid Professionals: Commercialism and Conflict in Big-Time College Sports*. Princeton, NJ: Princeton University Press.

# INDEX

AAU, *see* Amateur Athletic Union

ABC, *see* American Broadcating Company

Acheson, Dean, 111

advertisers, 14, 59, 84, 90, 98, 102, 103, 110, 112. *See also* sponsors

*Affluent Society, The* (Galbraith), 32

allegory, 116, 117; Cold War, 115; national, 112, 114, 115, 116, 117, 123; of spectator sport, 59; of suburban life, 108; of the South, 104

alumni, 7, 8, 75, 85

Amateur Athletic Union (AAU), 40, 56

American Broadcasting Company (ABC), 65, 79, 88, 90, 92

American Century, 5

American exceptionalism, 117

*American-German Review*, 17, 19

Americanization, 2, 27, 30, 117, 129

*American Physical Education Review*, 129

American way of life, 14, 20, 25, 26–27, 30, 33, 37, 52, 58, 59–62, 64, 71, 82, 87, 89, 112, 116, 118, 129

American (un)exceptionalism, 49, 51, 136n11

anxiety, 5, 11, 14, 39, 52, 54, 62, 123; Cold War, 42, 54, 62, 74, 80, 81, 89, 91, 97; technological, 80–81; about white male bodies, 11, 13, 33, 51, 140n10

Army (United States Military Academy), 12, 16, 128, 138n15

Army-Navy football game, 65, 88, 138n15

assimilation, 2, 27, 30, 112, 131, 134n12. *See also* Americanization; integration; national incorporation

attendance (in stadiums), 10, 73, 79, 83, 87, 90, 91

authority, 7, 62, 63, 70, 87, 88

Barclay, Dorothy, 50

Barthes, Roland, 68

baseball, 5, 6, 18, 31, 96, 97, 98, 139n5; American Legion, 6; Little League, 40, 46, 56; professional, 52, 96; televised, 57, 59, 65–66, 67, 69

Bell Helicopter Armed Forces Bowl, 128

Berg, Patty, 100, 103, 107–110, 112, 140n10

Bhabha, Homi K., 87, 104

Big Seven Conference, 80

Big Ten Conference, 8, 80, 90

Billing, L. H., 100

Binder Johnson, Hildegard, 17–20, 113, 116

*Blackboard Jungle* (film), 54

Blair, Tony, 3

Bonacich, Edna, 134n10

Bonaparte, Napoleon, 11

*Boston Globe*, 126

Bourdieu, Pierre, 49, 61

Boyer, Paul, 138n13

Boyle, Robert, 117

Boy Scouts of America, 40, 46, 47, 56

Boys' Club, 47

Bretz, Rudy, 66–68, 71

Britain, 10, 49, 50, 115, 117, 139n1

British boarding/public schools, 49, 51, 133n8

British Empire, 48

broadcasters, 57, 58, 65–69, 136n6

broadcasting, 64, 72, 73, 79, 91, 138n12, 139n21; baseball, 57; cartel, 6, 14, 74, 78, 82, 88–92; college football, 14, 16, 31, 56, 61, 63, 67, 68, 69, 71, 74, 79, 80, 81, 83, 84, 86, 88, 91, 131, 133n2, 136n4; commercial, 3, 58–59, 65, 71, 72, 79; controlled, 74–75, 79, 84, 88–90; history, ix; manuals, 31, 67, 132, 136n6; market, 14, 74, 91, 138n14; model, 14, 59, 72, 79, 80, 90; pedagogical, 14; professional football, 3, 90, 126, 139n21; radio, 11, 59, 65, 72, 76, 85, 136n2; ratings, 88; regulations (*see* regulation: broadcasting);

War on Terror, Global, ix, 3–5, 15, 115, 123, 127, 128
Watterson, John Sayle, 8–10, 76
Waynesburg College, 73, 137n8
Weales, Gerald, 18
*Wealth of Nations, The* (Adam Smith), 118
Weber, Max, 61, 118–120, 141n5
Weidman, Jerome, 29–30
West Point, *see* Army
Western Conference, *see* Big Ten
Westinghouse Electronic Corp., 64, 138n16
*What You Should Know About Biological Warfare* (educational film), 26
Wheaties Sports Federation, 40, 46
*White Collar* (Mills), 33
white supremacy, and whiteness, 27–28, 48–54, 93, 109, 134n12
Whyte, William H., 33, 55, 62

*Wild One, The* (film), 54
Wilkinson, Charles "Bud," 43, 46, 54, 80, 100, 107, 110, 135n4
Wilson, Meredith, 135n7
Wismer, Harry, 65
World War I, *see* First World War
World War II, *see* Second World War
Wylie, Philip, 140n10

Yale University, 7, 8, 77, 115
Yankees, New York (baseball), ix
Young Men's Christian Association (YMCA), 40, 46, 47
"Youth Fitness Song, The" (Wilson), 48, 135n7

Zimbalist, Andrew, 77, 92
zoom lens, 67–68

# ABOUT THE AUTHOR

JEFFREY MONTEZ DE OCA is an assistant professor of sociology at the University of Colorado, Colorado Springs, where he teaches courses on sport, sociological theory, inequalities, identities, and popular culture.